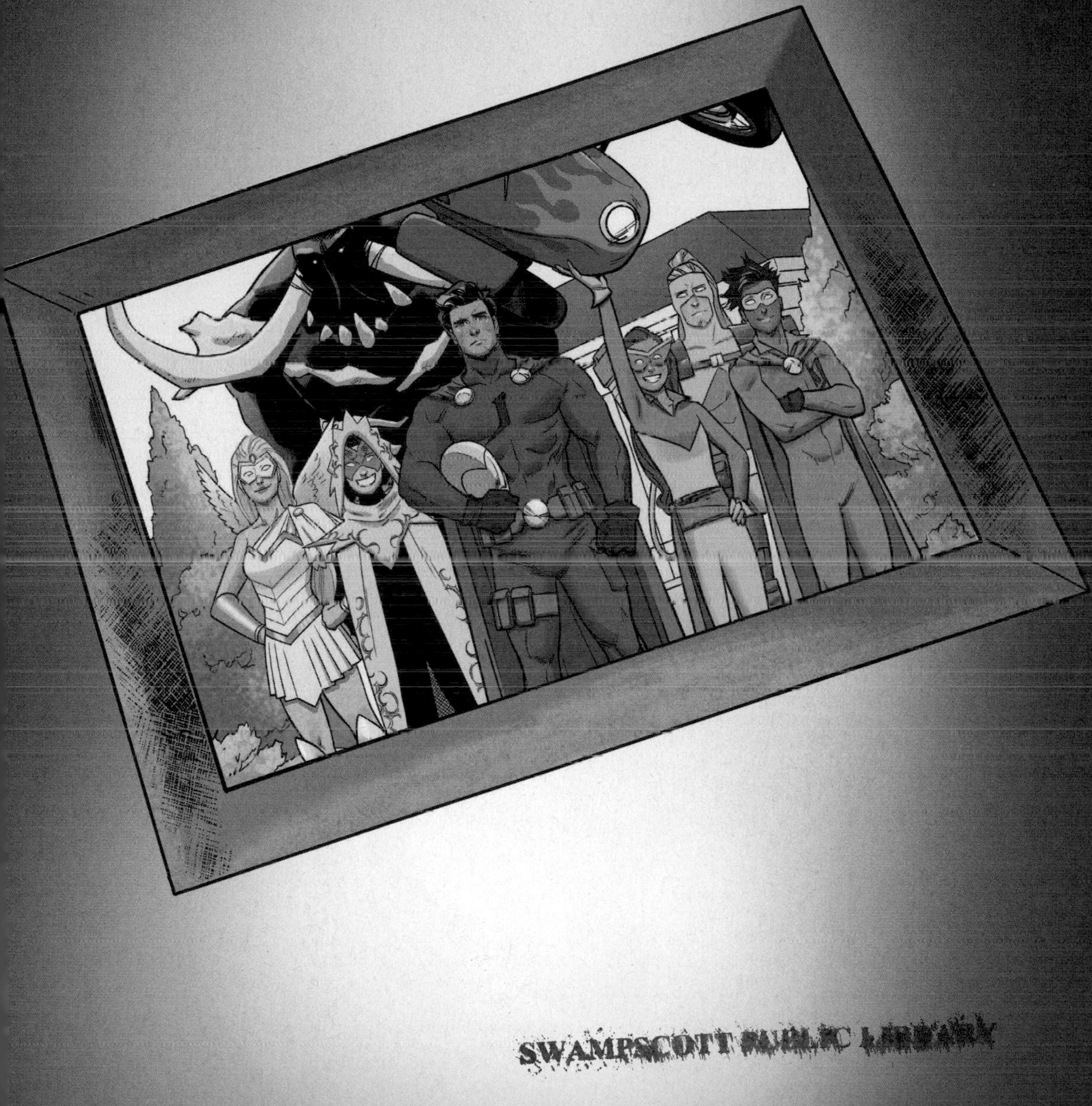

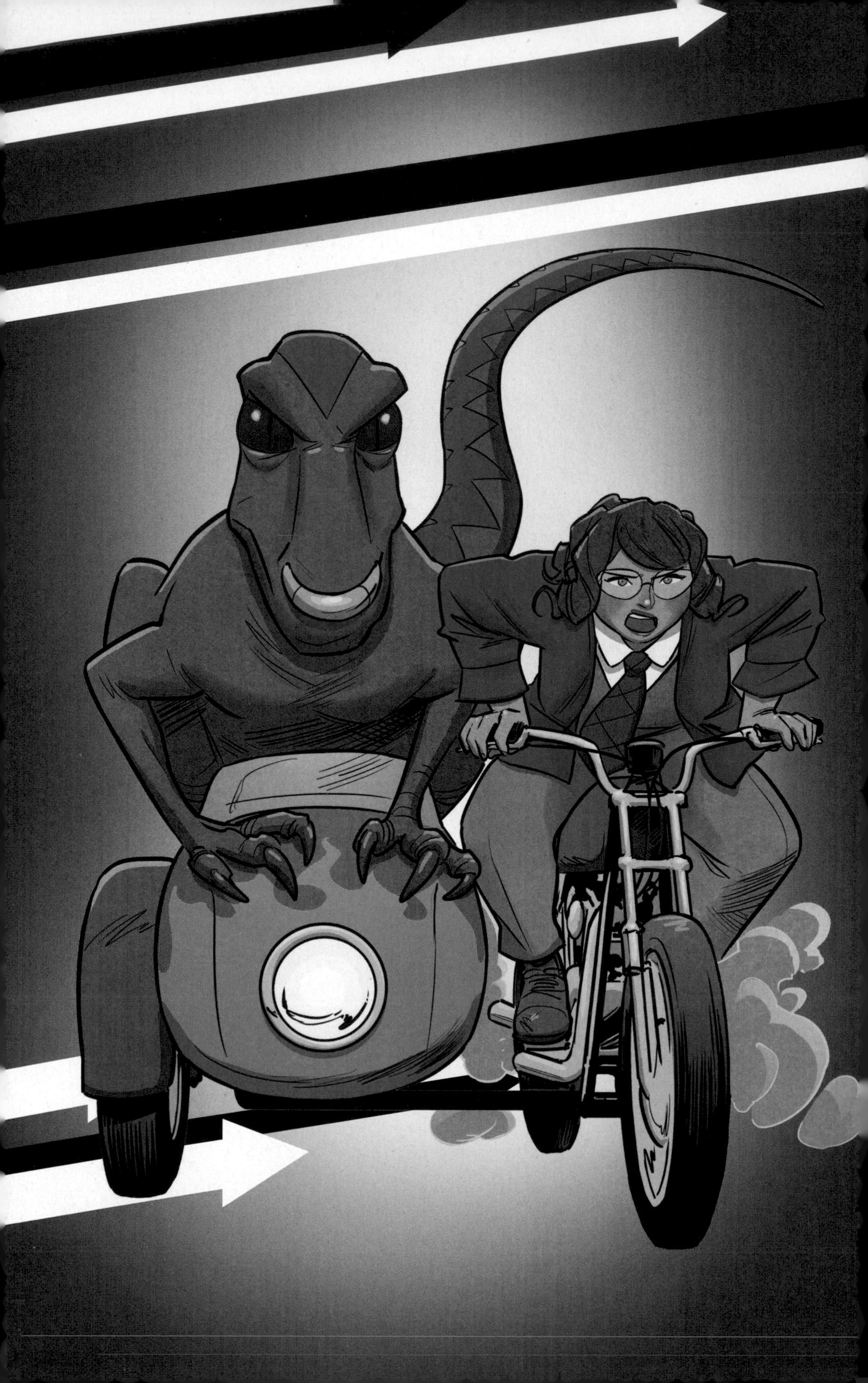

RUNAWAYS

CANON FODDER

WRITER **RAINBOW ROWELL**

ARTISTS **ANDRÉS GENOLET** (#25-26, #28-31)

& **KRIS ANKA** (#27)

WITH **WALDEN WONG** (ADDITIONAL INKS, #27)

COLOR ARTISTS

FEDERICO BLEE (#25) & **DEE CUNNIFFE** (#26-31),

WITH **MATTHEW WILSON** (#25) & **JIM CAMPBELL** (#27)

LETTERER **VC's JOE CARAMAGNA**

COVER ART **KRIS ANKA**

ASSISTANT EDITOR **KATHLEEN WISNESKI**

EDITOR **NICK LOWE**

RUNAWAYS CREATED BY **BRIAN K. VAUGHAN** & **ADRIAN ALPHONA**

COLLECTION EDITOR **JENNIFER GRÜNWALD** | ASSISTANT MANAGING EDITOR **MAIA LOY** | ASSISTANT MANAGING EDITOR **LISA MONTALBANO**

EDITOR, SPECIALAL PROJECTS **MARK D. BEAZLEY** | VP PRODUCTION & SPECIAL PROJECTS **JEFF YOUNGQUIST** | BOOK DESIGNER **JAY BOWEN**

SVP PRINT, SALES & MARKETING **DAVID GABRIEL** | EDITOR IN CHIEF **C.B. CEBULSKI**

RUNAWAYS BY RAINBOW ROWELL VOL. 5: CANON FODDER. Contains material originally published in magazine form as RUNAWAYS (2017) #25-31. First printing 2020. ISBN 978-1-302-92028-9. Published by MARVEL WORLDWIDE, INC., a subsidiary of MARVEL ENTERTAINMENT, LLC. OFFICE OF PUBLICATION: 1290 Avenue of the Americas, New York, NY 10104. **Printed in the U.S.A.** KEVIN FEIGE, Chief Creative Officer; DAN BUCKLEY, President, Marvel Entertainment; JOHN NEE, Publisher; JOE QUESADA, EVP & Creative Director; TOM BREVOORT, SVP of Publishing; DAVID BOGART, Associate Publisher & SVP of Talent Affairs; Publishing & Partnership; DAVID GABRIEL, VP of Print & Digital Publishing; JEFF YOUNGQUIST, VP of Production & Special Projects; DAN CARR, Executive Director of Publishing Technology; ALEX MORALES, Director of Publishing Operations; DAN EDINGTON, Managing Editor; SUSAN CRESPI, Production Manager; STAN LEE, Chairman Emeritus. For information regarding advertising in Marvel Comics or on Marvel.com, please contact Vit DeBellis, Custom Solutions & Integrated Advertising Manager, at vdebellis@marvel.com. For Marvel subscription inquiries, please call 888-511-5480. **Manufactured between 7/22/2020 and 8/18/2020 by FRY COMMUNICATIONS, MECHANICSBURG, PA, USA.**

10 9 8 7 6 5 4 3 2 1

PREVIOUSLY

LIVING WITH THE RUNAWAYS IN THE HOSTEL, KAROLINA AT LAST HAD LOVE, FAMILY AND SECURITY, BUT SHE'D LOST A SENSE OF PURPOSE. SO SHE'S TRIED SOME LIGHT SUPER-HEROICS, AND LAST NIGHT ASKED NICO TO JOIN HER. MEANWHILE, MAINTAINING THAT SECURITY KAROLINA HAS BEEN ENJOYING IS JUST ABOUT THE LAST THING CHASE HAS GOING FOR HIM, AS HIS HOPE OF SOMEDAY REUNITING WITH GERT GROWS FAINTER AS SHE GROWS CLOSER TO VICTOR. AND WITH NO NUTRITIVE SUBSTITUTE FOR HUMAN SOULS FORTHCOMING, YOUNG OLD GOD GIB IS STARVING. SOMETHING IS ABOUT TO BREAK.

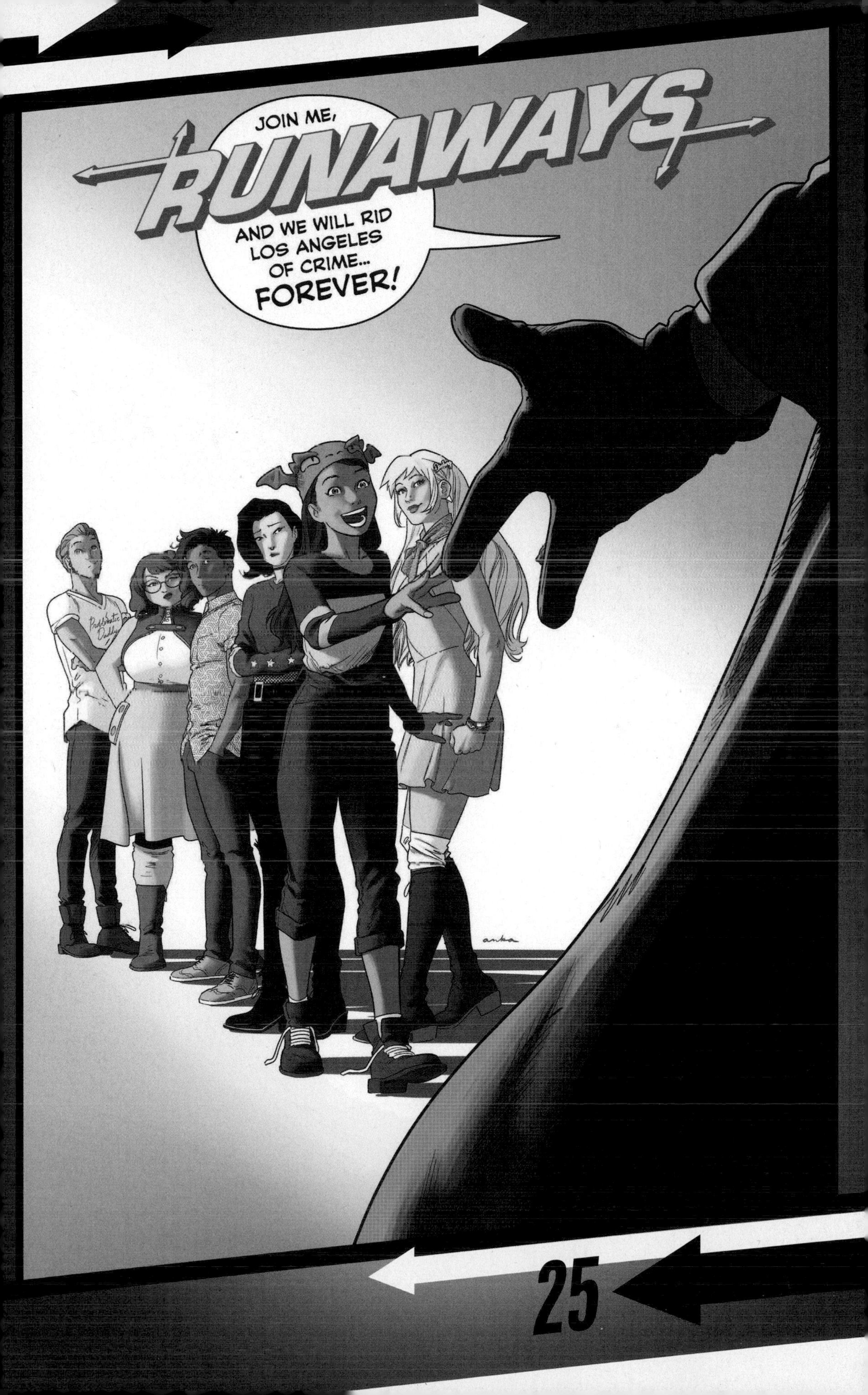
RUNAWAYS
JOIN ME,
AND WE WILL RID LOS ANGELES OF CRIME... FOREVER!
25

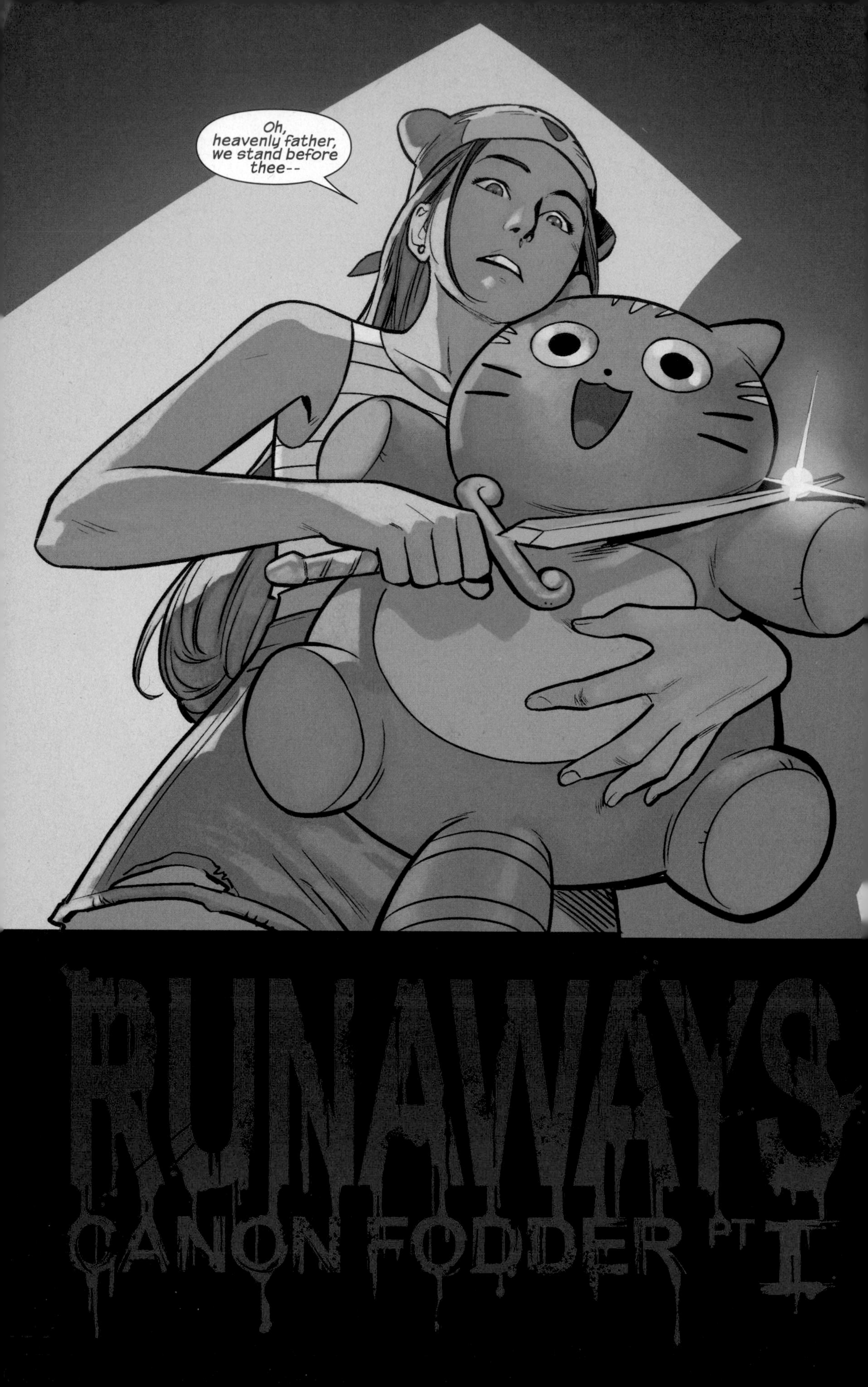
Oh, heavenly father, we stand before thee--
RUNAWAYS
CANON FODDER PT I

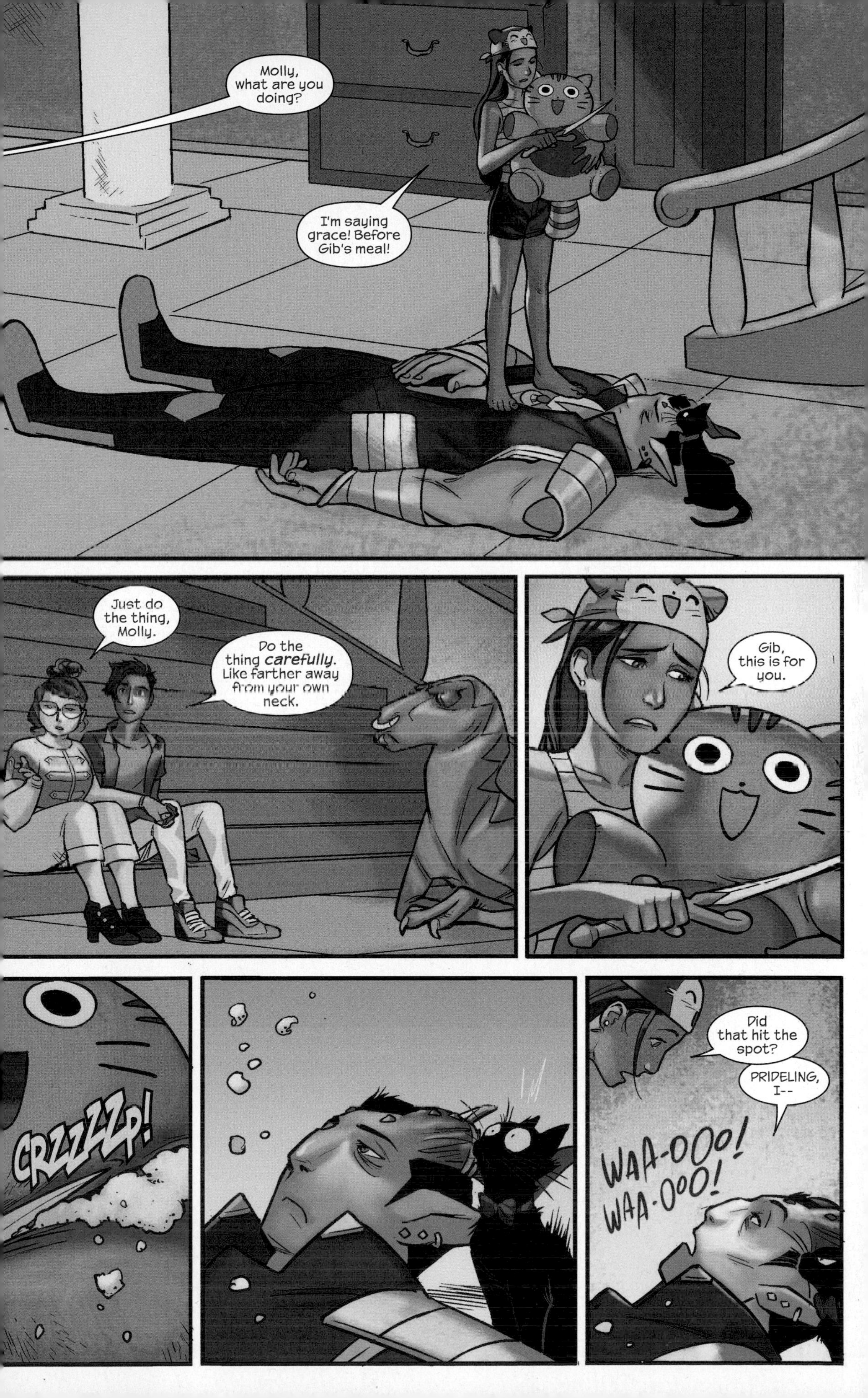
Molly, what are you doing?
I'm saying grace! Before Gib's meal!
Just do the thing, Molly.
Do the thing *carefully*. Like farther away from your own neck.
Gib, this is for you.
CRZZZZP!
Did that hit the spot?
PRIDELING, I--
WAA-OOO! WAA-OOO!

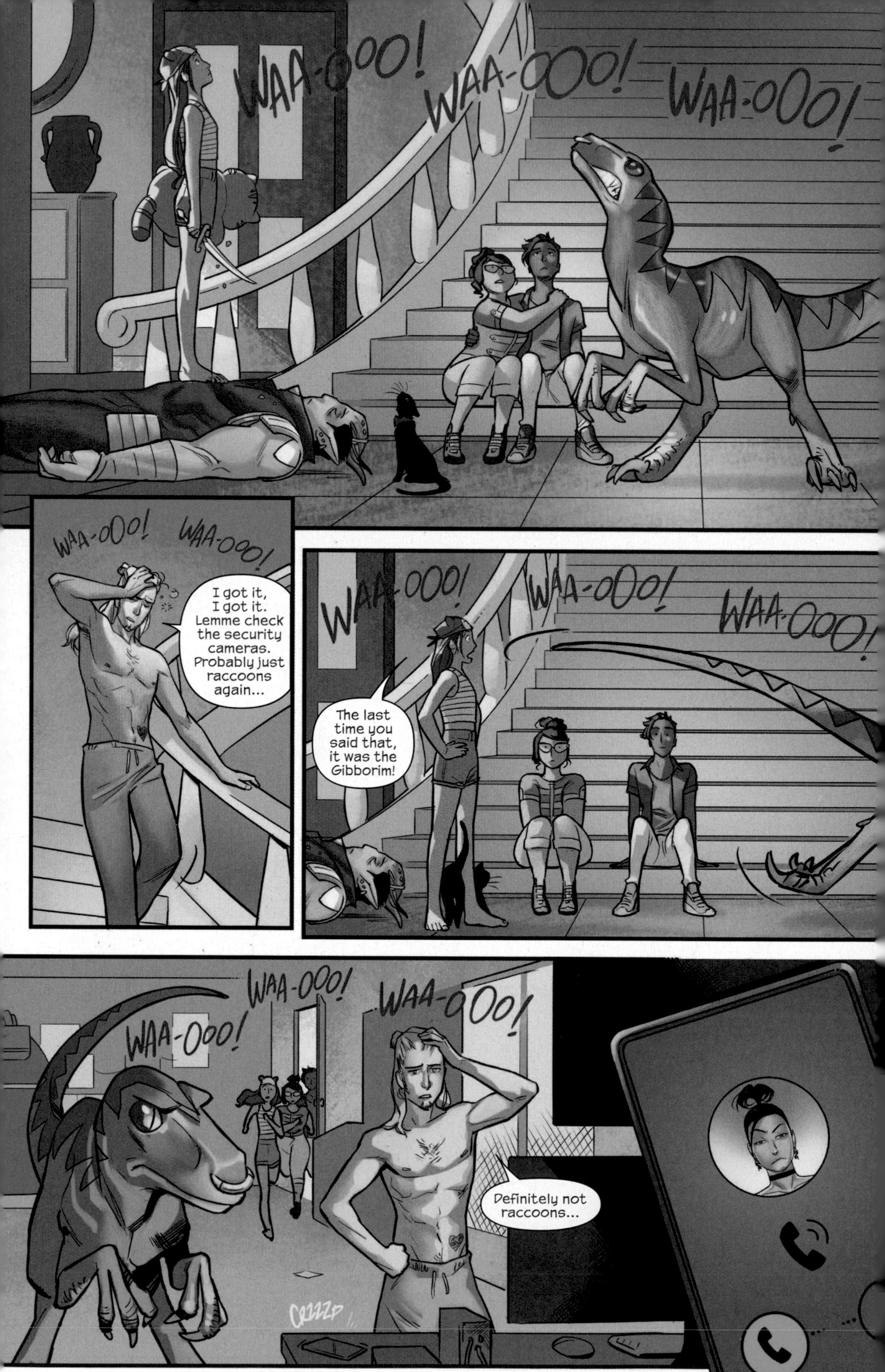
WAA-OOO!
WAA-OOO!
WAA-OOO!
WAA-OOO!
WAA-OOO!
I got it, I got it. Lemme check the security cameras. Probably just raccoons again...
WAA-OOO!
WAA-OOO!
WAA-OOO!
The last time you said that, it was the Gibborim!
WAA-OOO!
WAA-OOO!
WAA-OOO!
Definitely not raccoons...

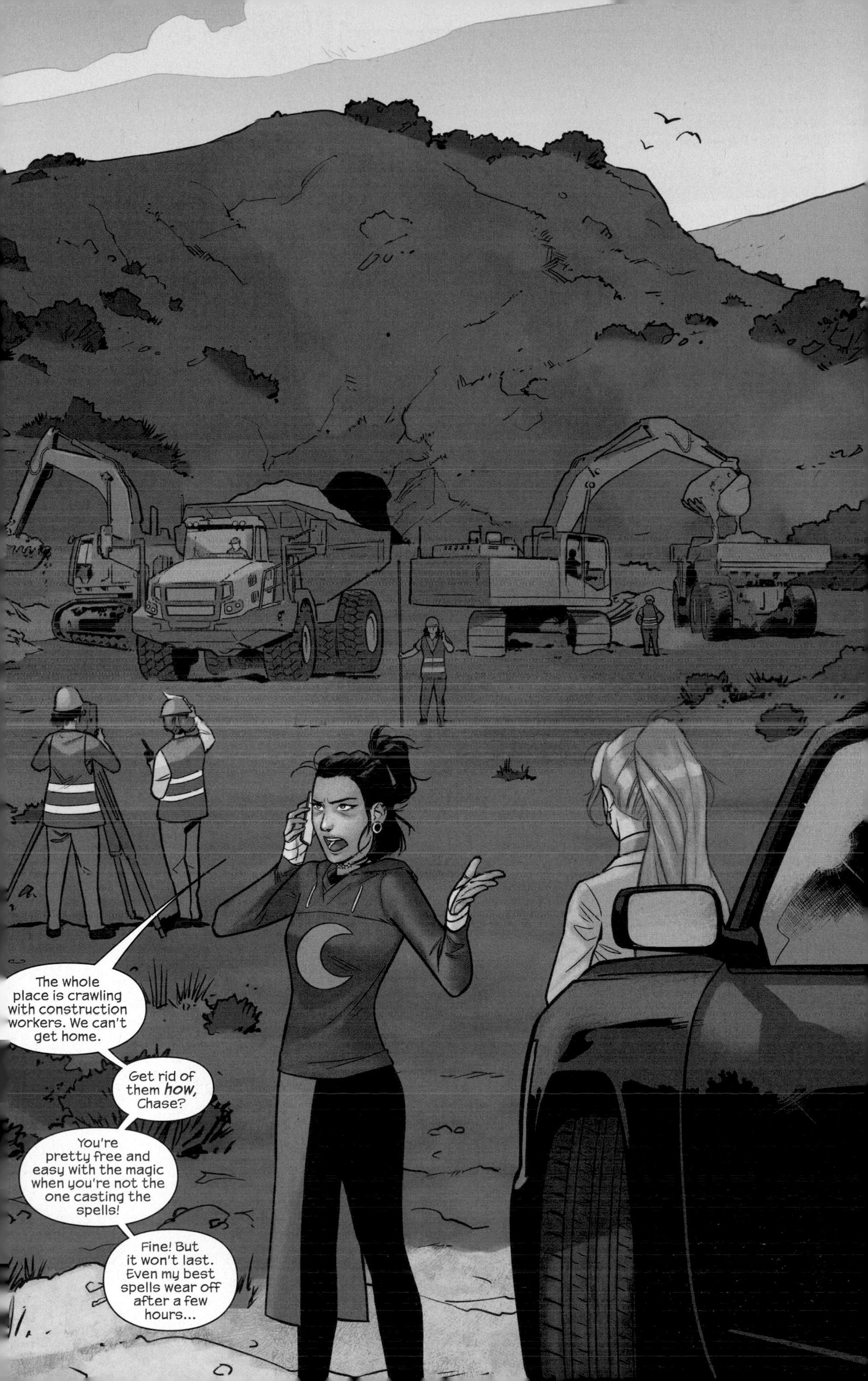
The whole place is crawling with construction workers. We can't get home.
Get rid of them *how,* Chase?
You're pretty free and easy with the magic when you're not the one casting the spells!
Fine! But it won't last. Even my best spells wear off after a few hours...

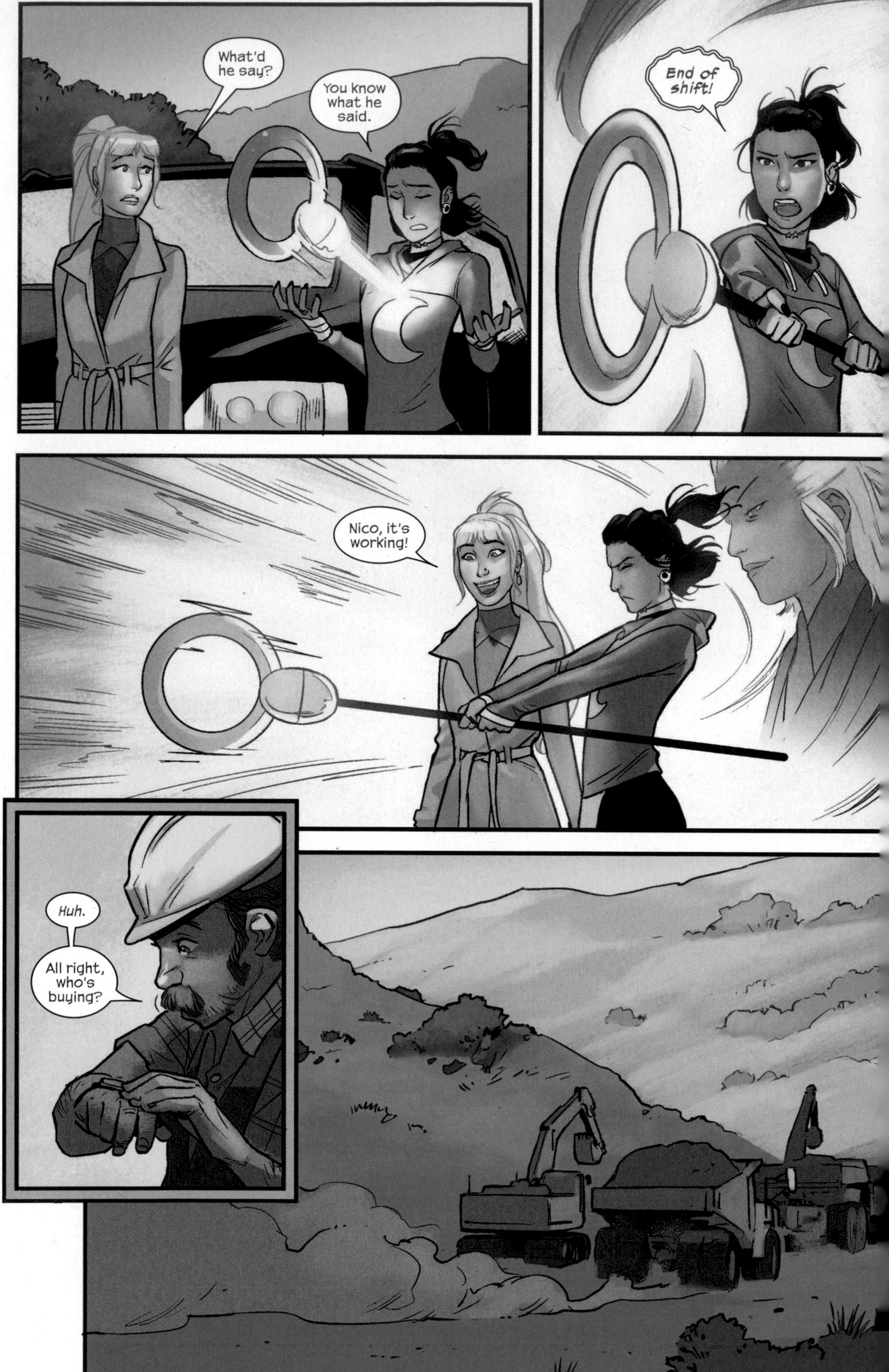
What'd he say?
You know what he said.
End of shift!
Nico, it's working!
Huh.
All right, who's buying?

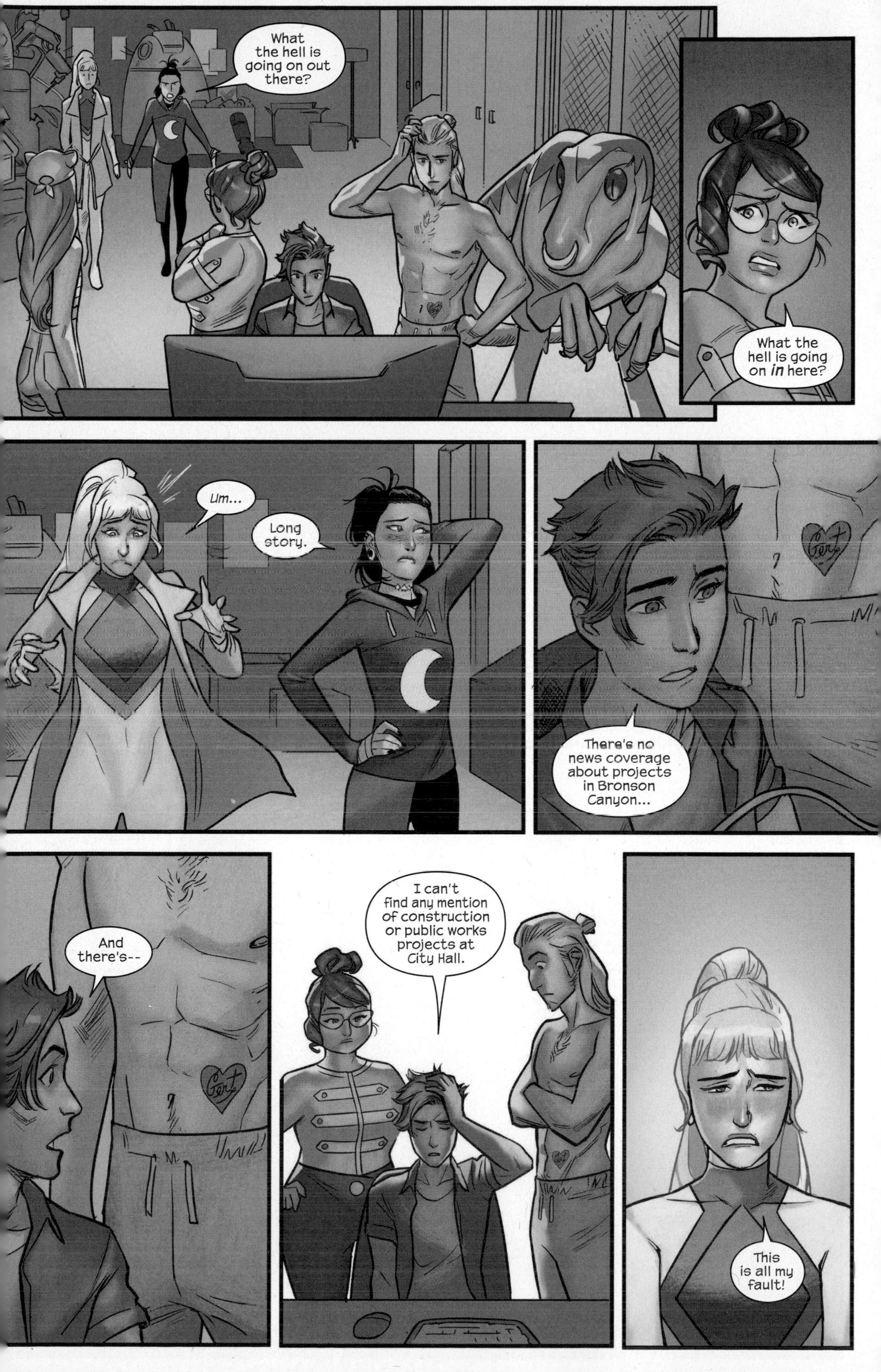
What the hell is going on out there?
What the hell is going on *in* here?
Um...
Long story.
There's no news coverage about projects in Bronson Canyon...
And there's--
I can't find any mention of construction or public works projects at City Hall.
This is all my fault!

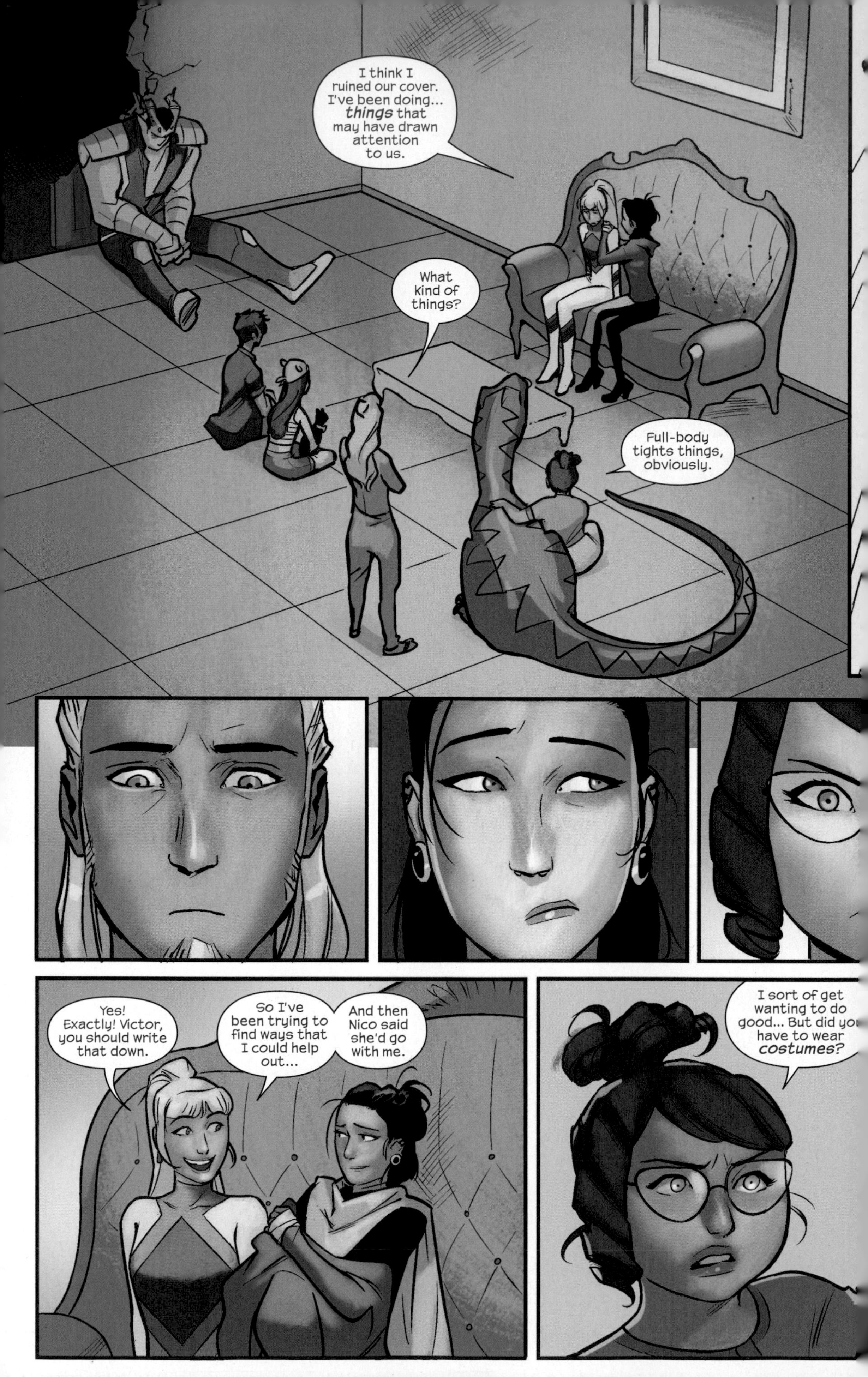
I think I ruined our cover. I've been doing... *things* that may have drawn attention to us.
What kind of things?
Full-body tights things, obviously.
Yes! Exactly! Victor, you should write that down.
So I've been trying to find ways that I could help out...
And then Nico said she'd go with me.
I sort of get wanting to do good... But did you have to wear *costumes?*

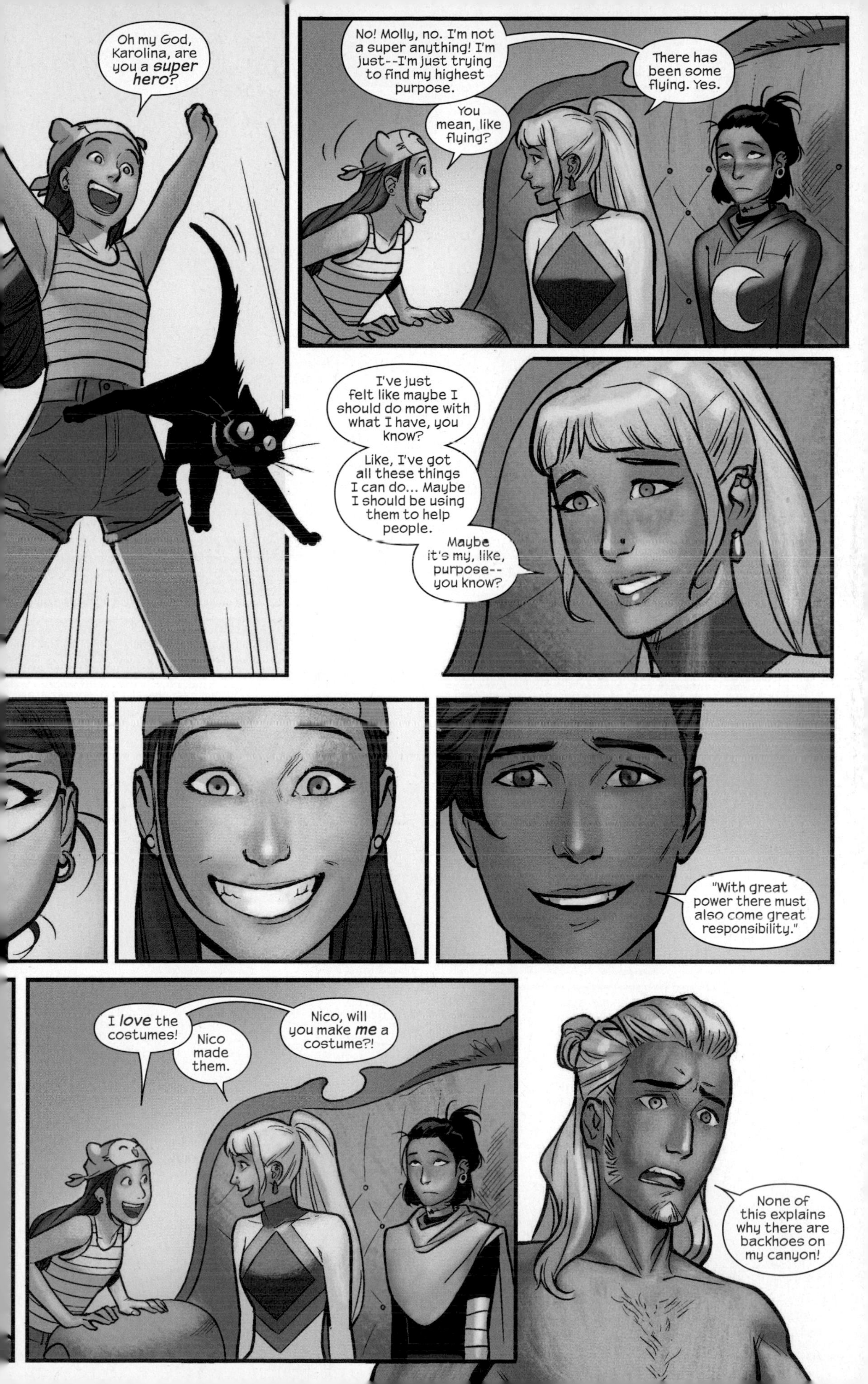

Oh my God, Karolina, are you a *super hero*?
No! Molly, no. I'm not a super anything! I'm just--I'm just trying to find my highest purpose.
You mean, like flying?
There has been some flying. Yes.
I've just felt like maybe I should do more with what I have, you know?
Like, I've got all these things I can do... Maybe I should be using them to help people.
Maybe it's my, like, purpose--you know?
"With great power there must also come great responsibility."
I *love* the costumes!
Nico made them.
Nico, will you make *me* a costume?!
None of this explains why there are backhoes on my canyon!

I'm sorry, Chase, I thought I was being stealthy!

You were *not* being stealthy.

I *was*. I wore a mask! And I bought a black car, even though black cars always look dirty.

I can't help it that everybody in Los Angeles has a cell phone with a video camera!

I don't have a cell phone...

Hold up, somebody got video of the Hostel?!

No! I mean, I don't think so...

But there are videos of-- of me. And, like, hashtags, I guess.

Doc Justice says I'm all over Reddit...

You met Doc Justice?!

Who's Doc Justice? Is he somebody from my dead years?

I think he's a professional wrestler.

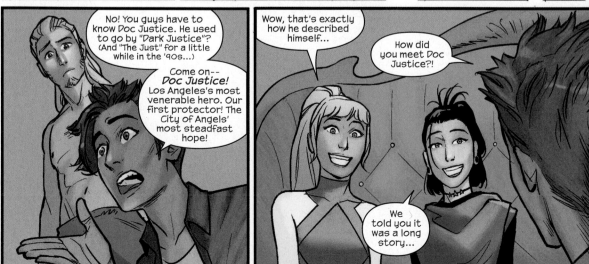

No! You guys have to know Doc Justice. He used to go by "Dark Justice"? (And "The Just" for a little while in the '90s...)

Come on-- *Doc Justice!* Los Angeles's most venerable hero. Our first protector! The City of Angels' most steadfast hope!

Wow, that's exactly how he described himself...

How did you meet Doc Justice?!

We told you it was a long story...

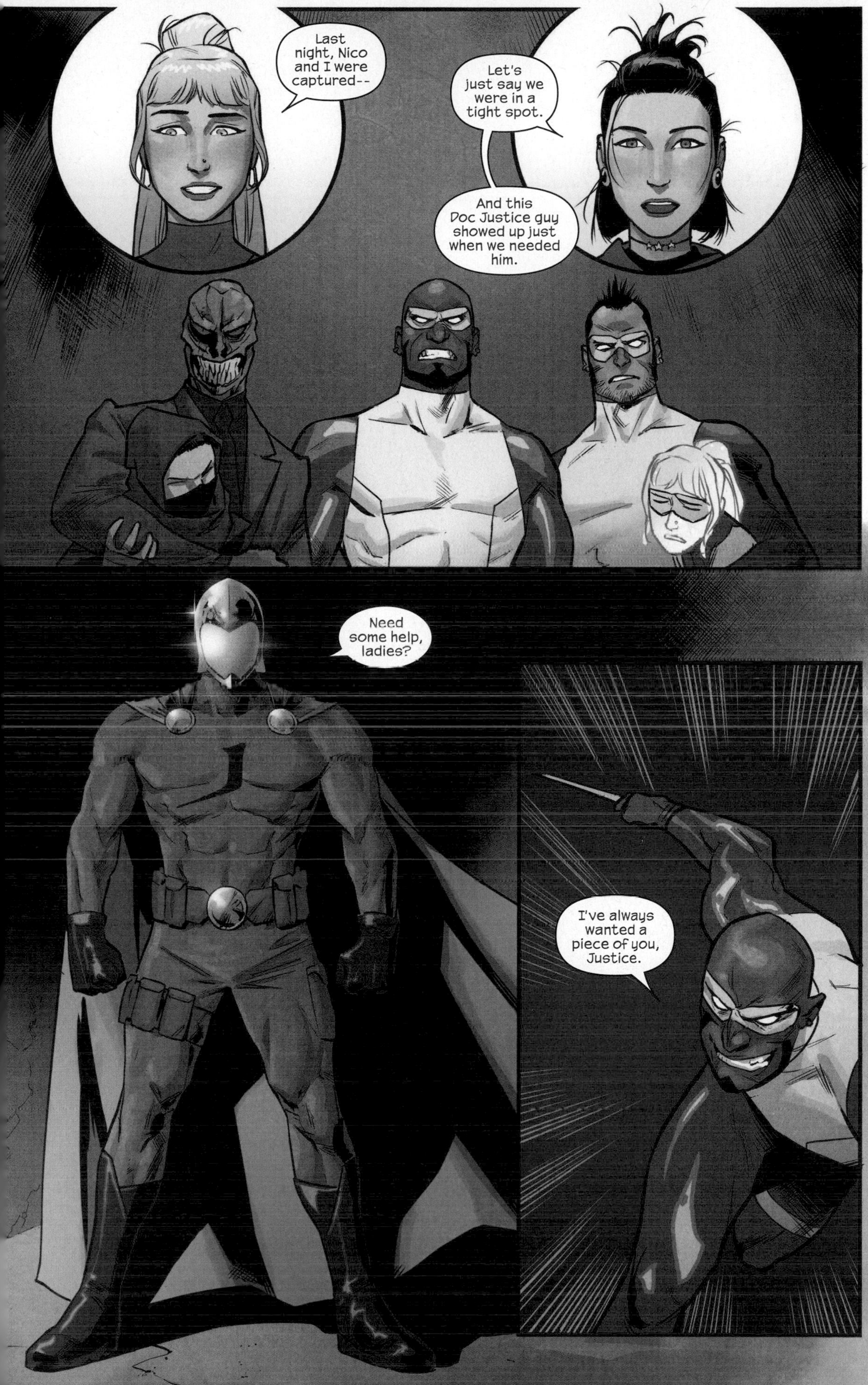
Last night, Nico and I were captured--
Let's just say we were in a tight spot.
And this Doc Justice guy showed up just when we needed him.
Need some help, ladies?
I've always wanted a piece of you, Justice.

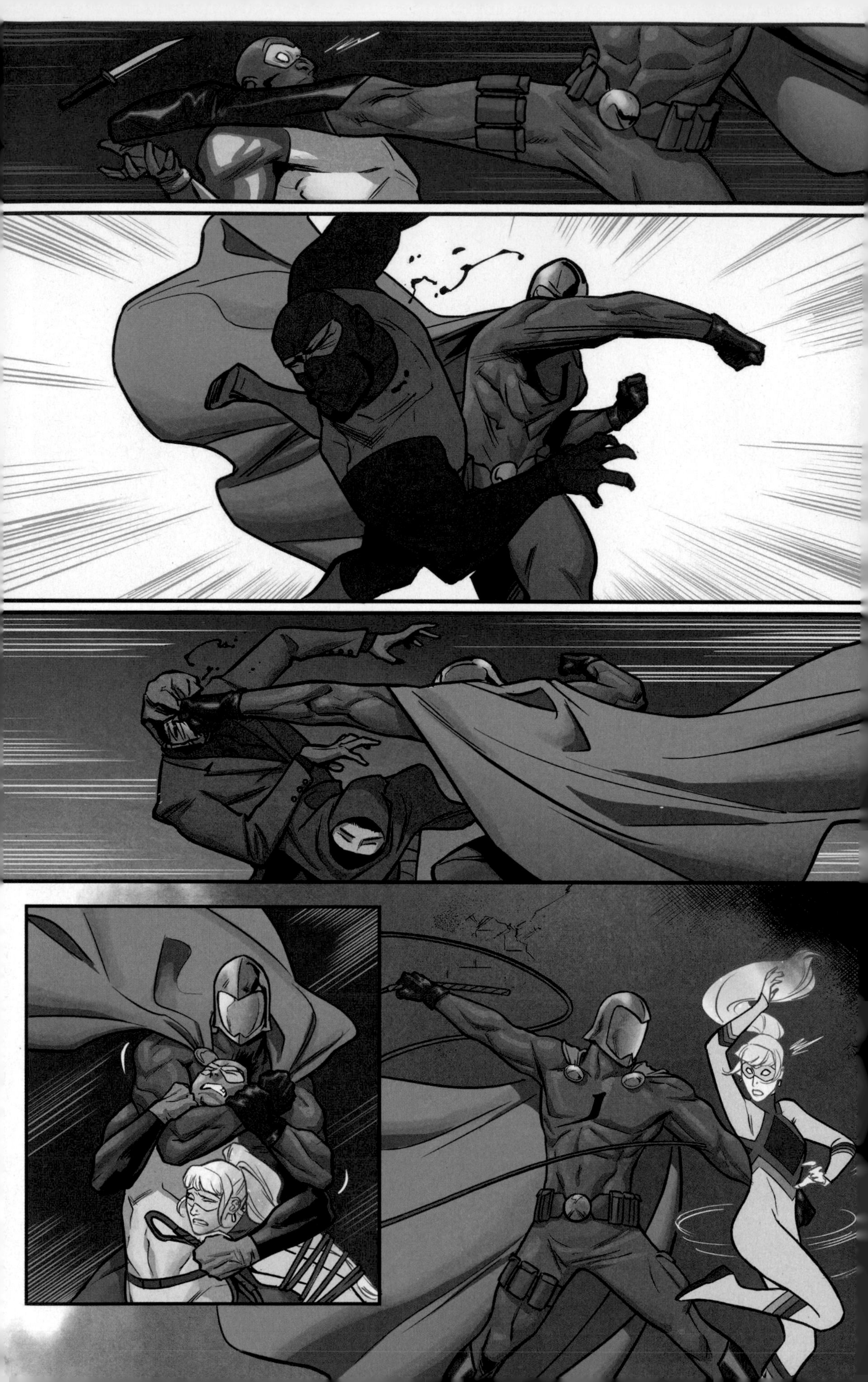

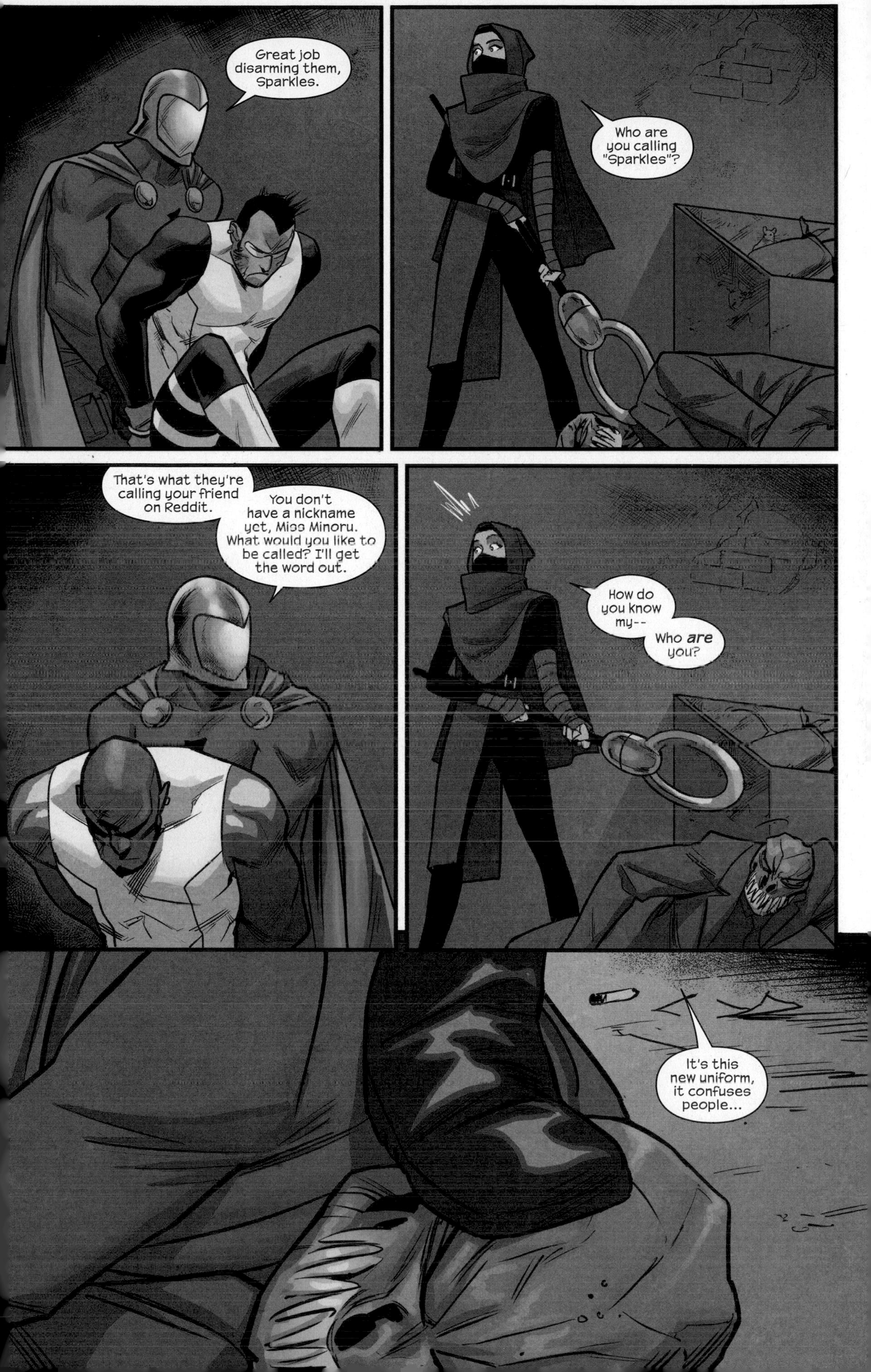
Great job disarming them, Sparkles.
Who are you calling "Sparkles"?
That's what they're calling your friend on Reddit.
You don't have a nickname yet, Miss Minoru. What would you like to be called? I'll get the word out.
How do you know my--
Who *are* you?
It's this new uniform, it confuses people...

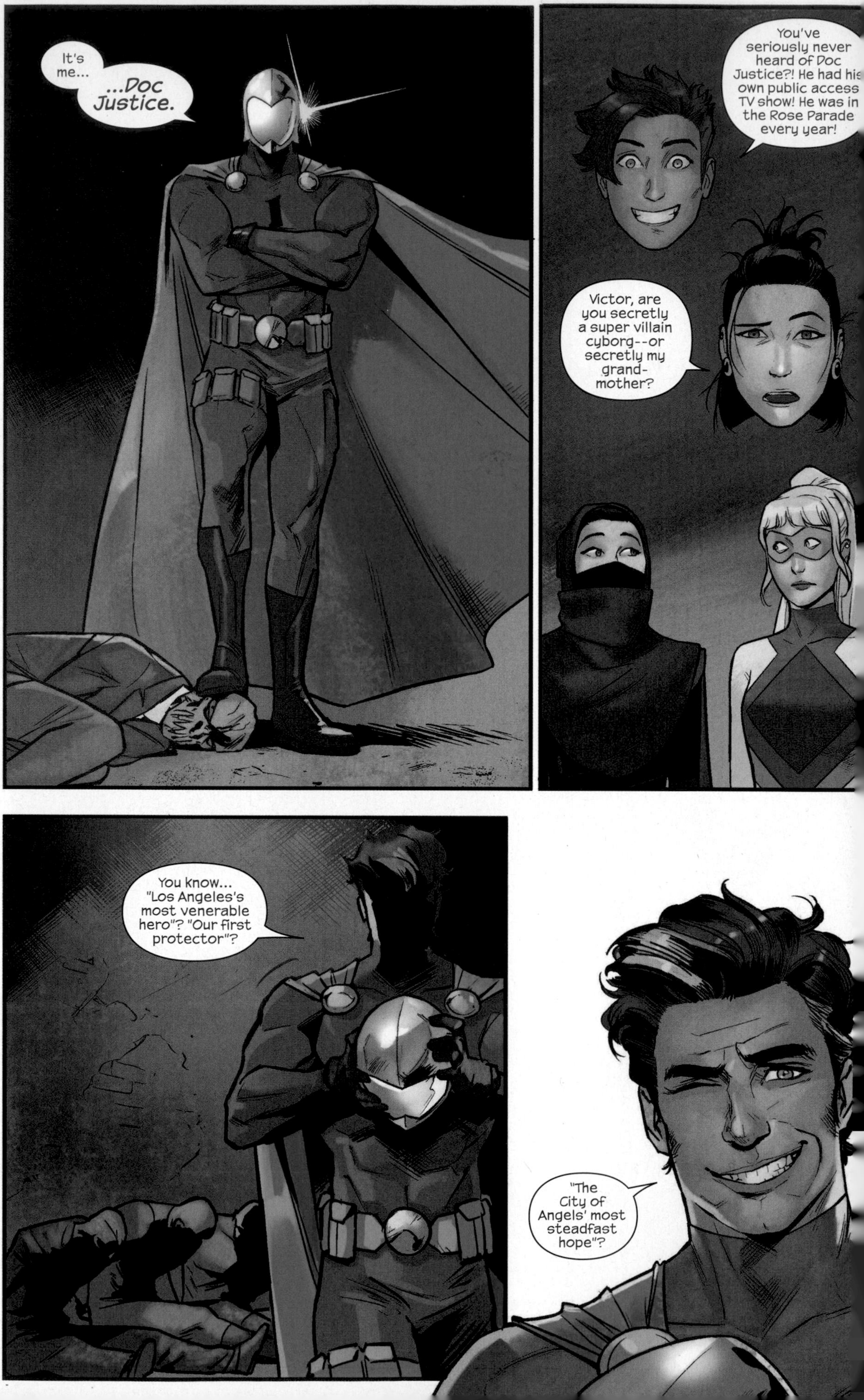
It's me...
...Doc Justice.
You've seriously never heard of Doc Justice?! He had his own public access TV show! He was in the Rose Parade every year!
Victor, are you secretly a super villain cyborg--or secretly my grand-mother?
You know... "Los Angeles's most venerable hero"? "Our first protector"?
"The City of Angels' most steadfast hope"?

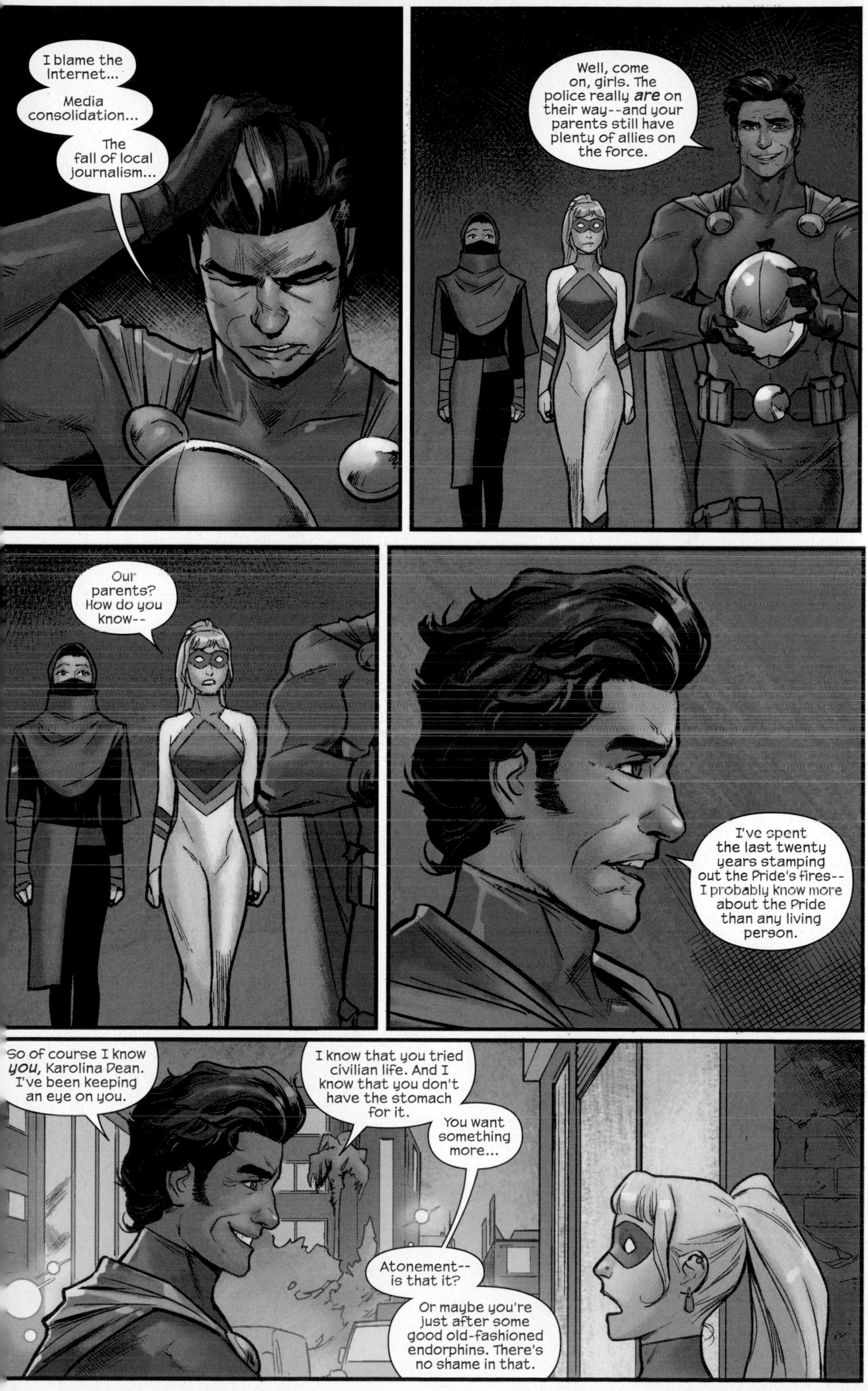
I blame the Internet...
Media consolidation...
The fall of local journalism...
Well, come on, girls. The police really *are* on their way--and your parents still have plenty of allies on the force.
Our parents? How do you know--
I've spent the last twenty years stamping out the Pride's fires-- I probably know more about the Pride than any living person.
So of course I know *you,* Karolina Dean. I've been keeping an eye on you.
I know that you tried civilian life. And I know that you don't have the stomach for it.
You want something more...
Atonement-- is that it?
Or maybe you're just after some good old-fashioned endorphins. There's no shame in that.

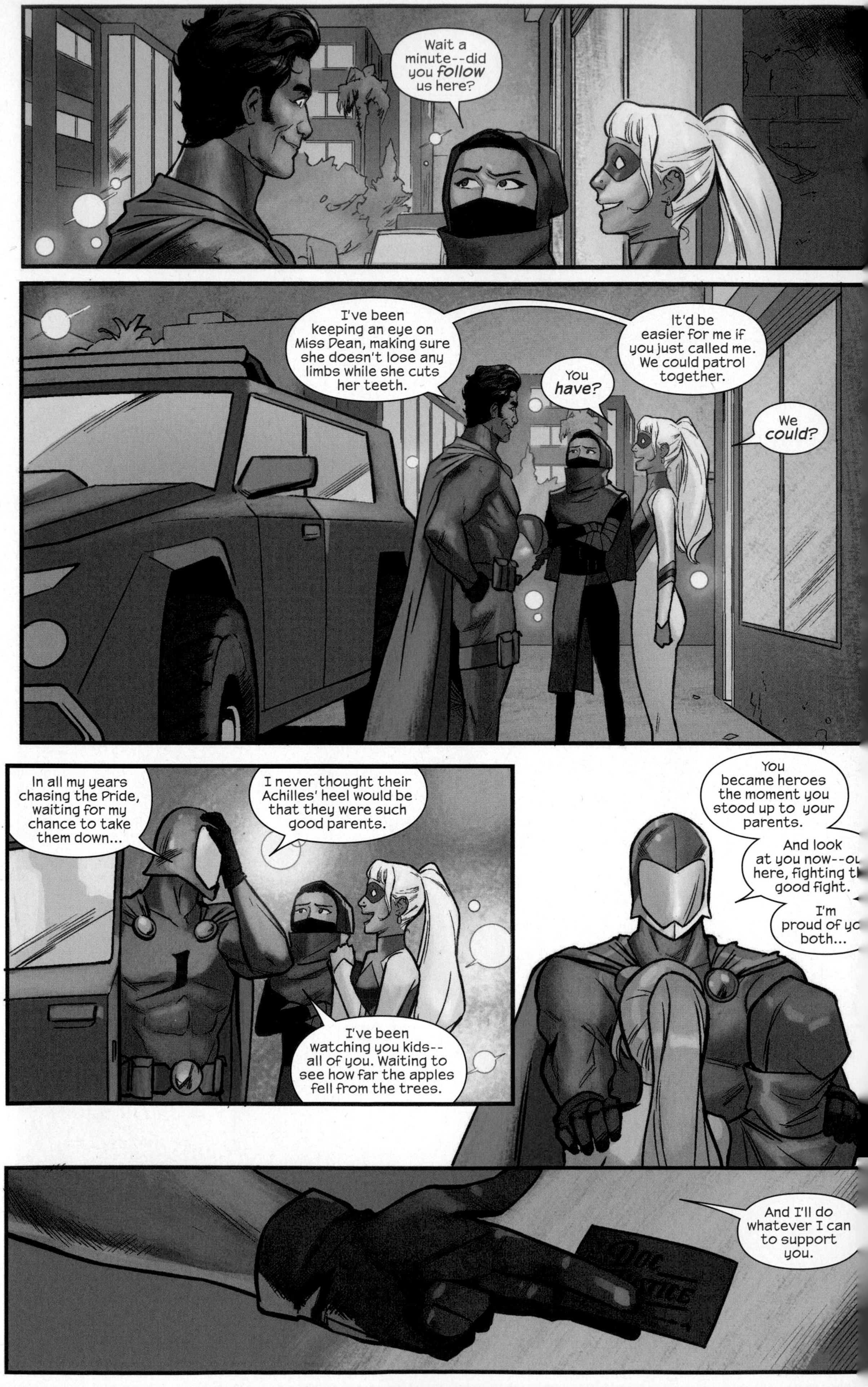
Wait a minute--did you *follow* us here?
I've been keeping an eye on Miss Dean, making sure she doesn't lose any limbs while she cuts her teeth.
You *have?*
It'd be easier for me if you just called me. We could patrol together.
We *could?*
In all my years chasing the Pride, waiting for my chance to take them down...
I never thought their Achilles' heel would be that they were such good parents.
I've been watching you kids--all of you. Waiting to see how far the apples fell from the trees.
You became heroes the moment you stood up to your parents.
And look at you now--ou here, fighting th good fight.
I'm proud of yo both...
And I'll do whatever I can to support you.

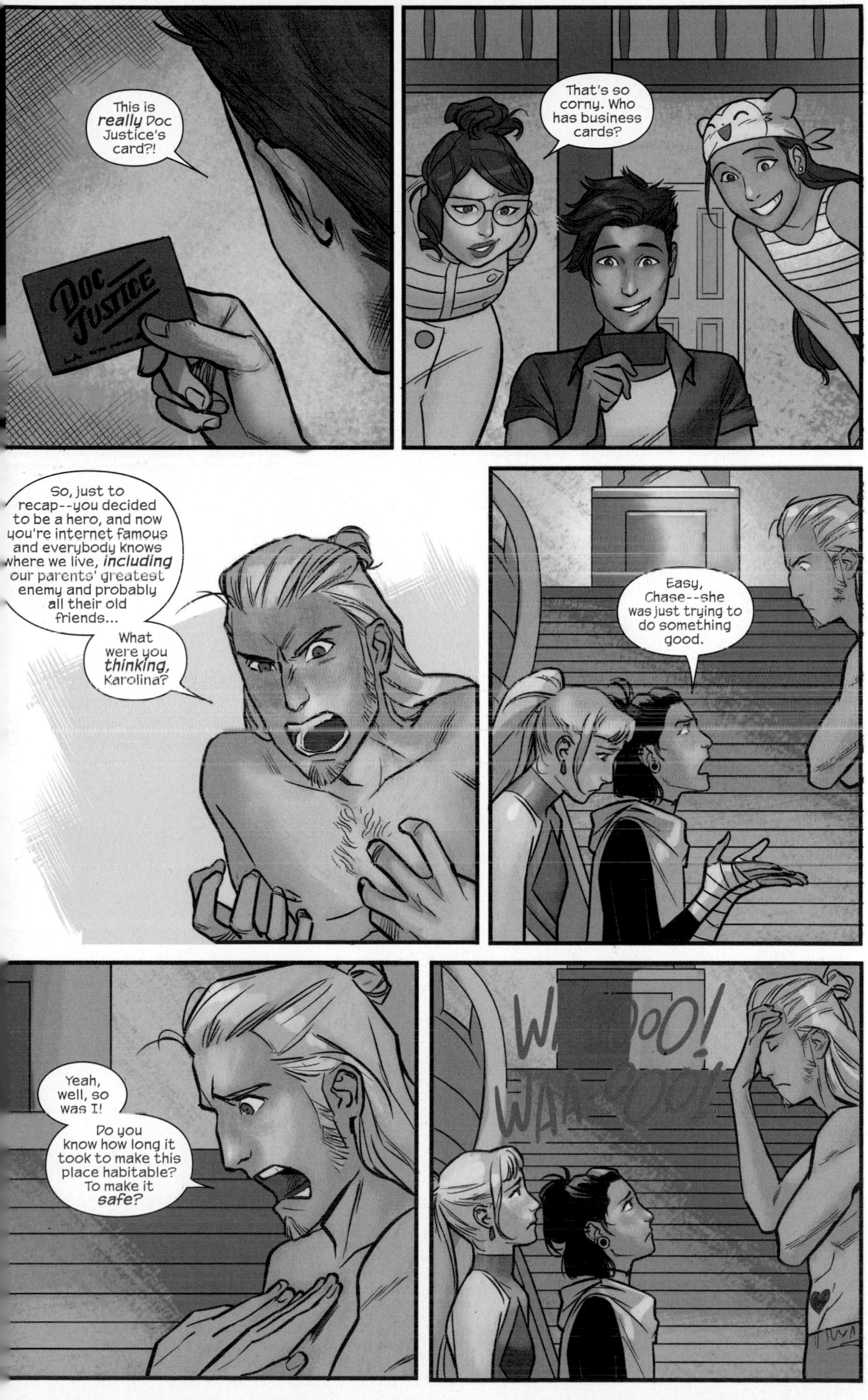
This is *really* Doc Justice's card?!
DOC JUSTICE
That's so corny. Who has business cards?
So, just to recap--you decided to be a hero, and now you're internet famous and everybody knows where we live, *including* our parents' greatest enemy and probably all their old friends...
What were you *thinking,* Karolina?
Easy, Chase--she was just trying to do something good.
Yeah, well, so was I!
Do you know how long it took to make this place habitable? To make it *safe?*

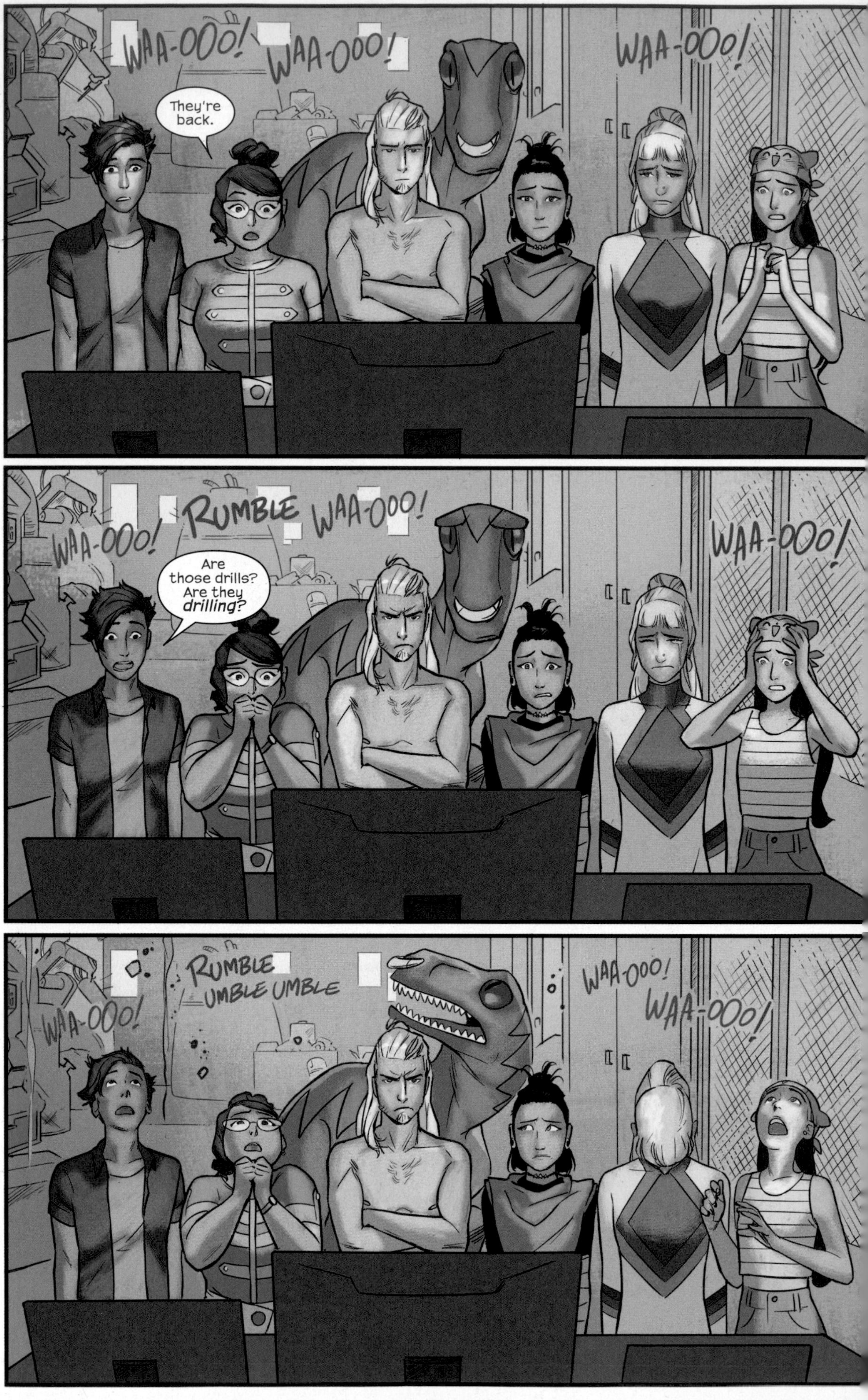
WAA-OOO!
WAA-OOO!
WAA-OOO!
They're back.
RUMBLE
WAA-OOO!
WAA-OOO!
WAA-OOO!
Are those drills? Are they *drilling?*
RUMBLE
UMBLE UMBLE
WAA-OOO!
WAA-OOO!
WAA-OOO!

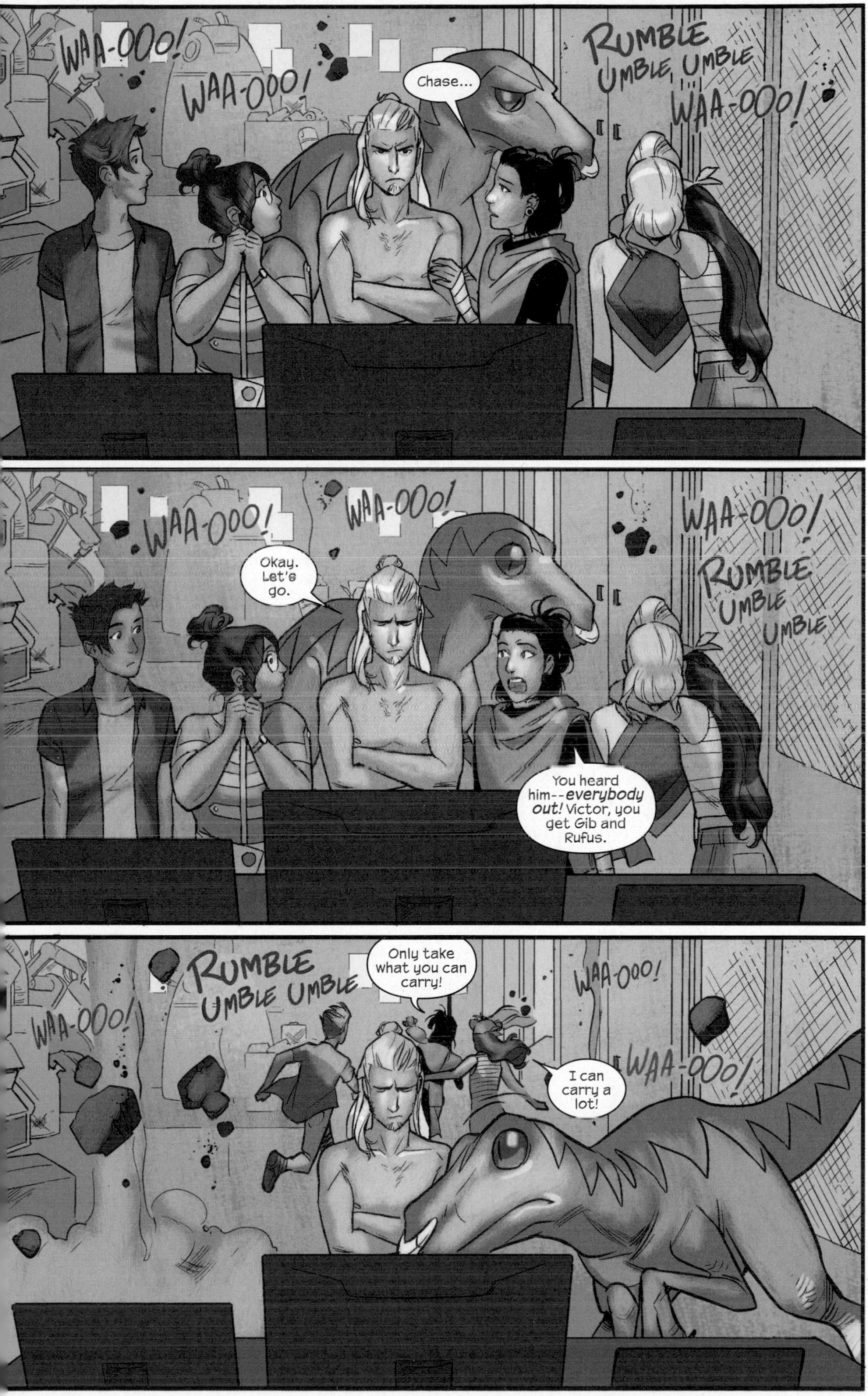
WAA-OOO!
WAA-OOO!
Chase...
RUMBLE
UMBLE UMBLE
WAA-OOO!
WAA-OOO!
WAA-OOO!
WAA-OOO!
Okay. Let's go.
RUMBLE
UMBLE
UMBLE
You heard him--*everybody out!* Victor, you get Gib and Rufus.
RUMBLE
UMBLE UMBLE
Only take what you can carry!
WAA-OOO!
WAA-OOO!
WAA-OOO!
I can carry a lot!

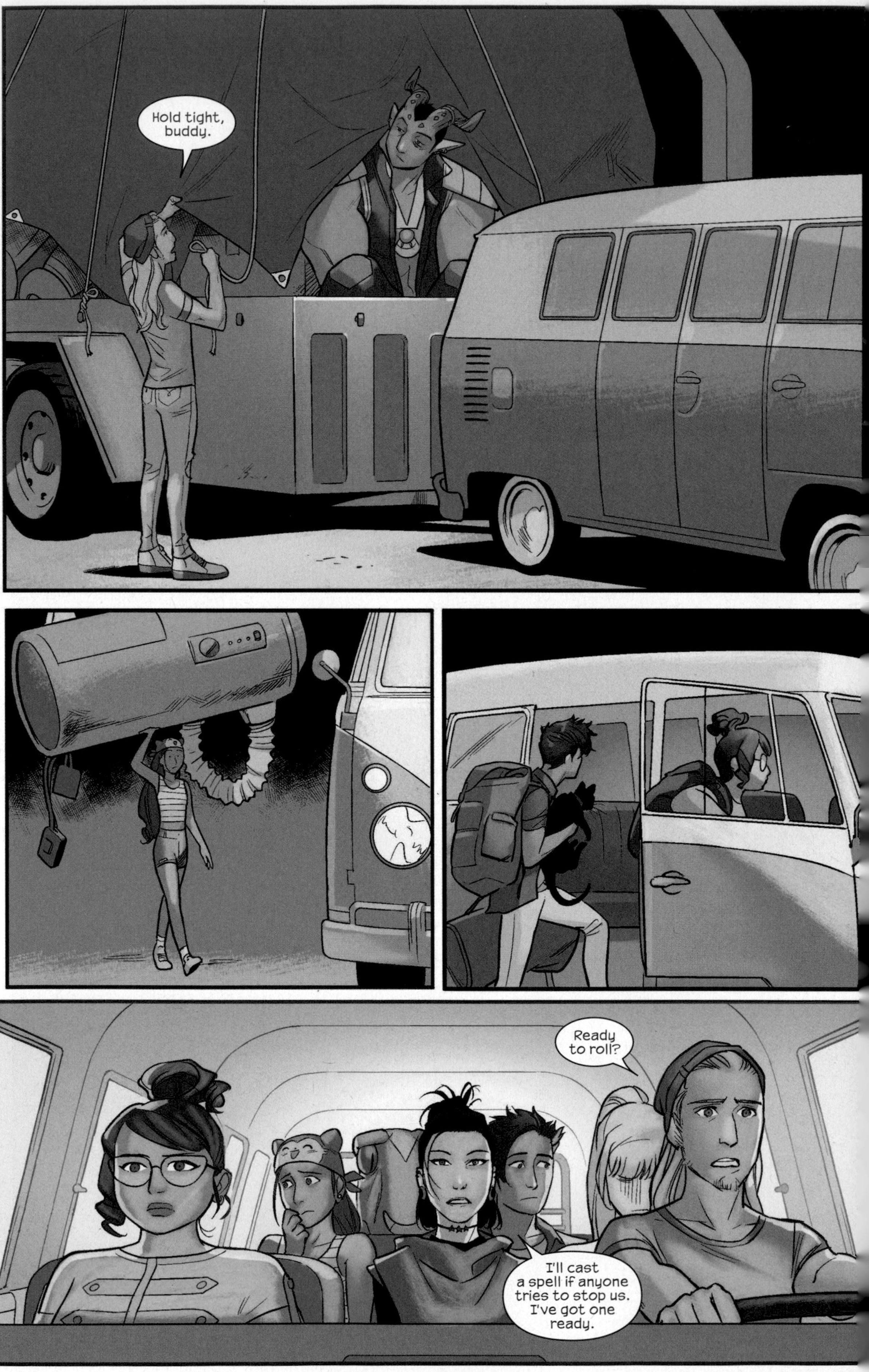

Hold tight, buddy.
Ready to roll?
I'll cast a spell if anyone tries to stop us. I've got one ready.

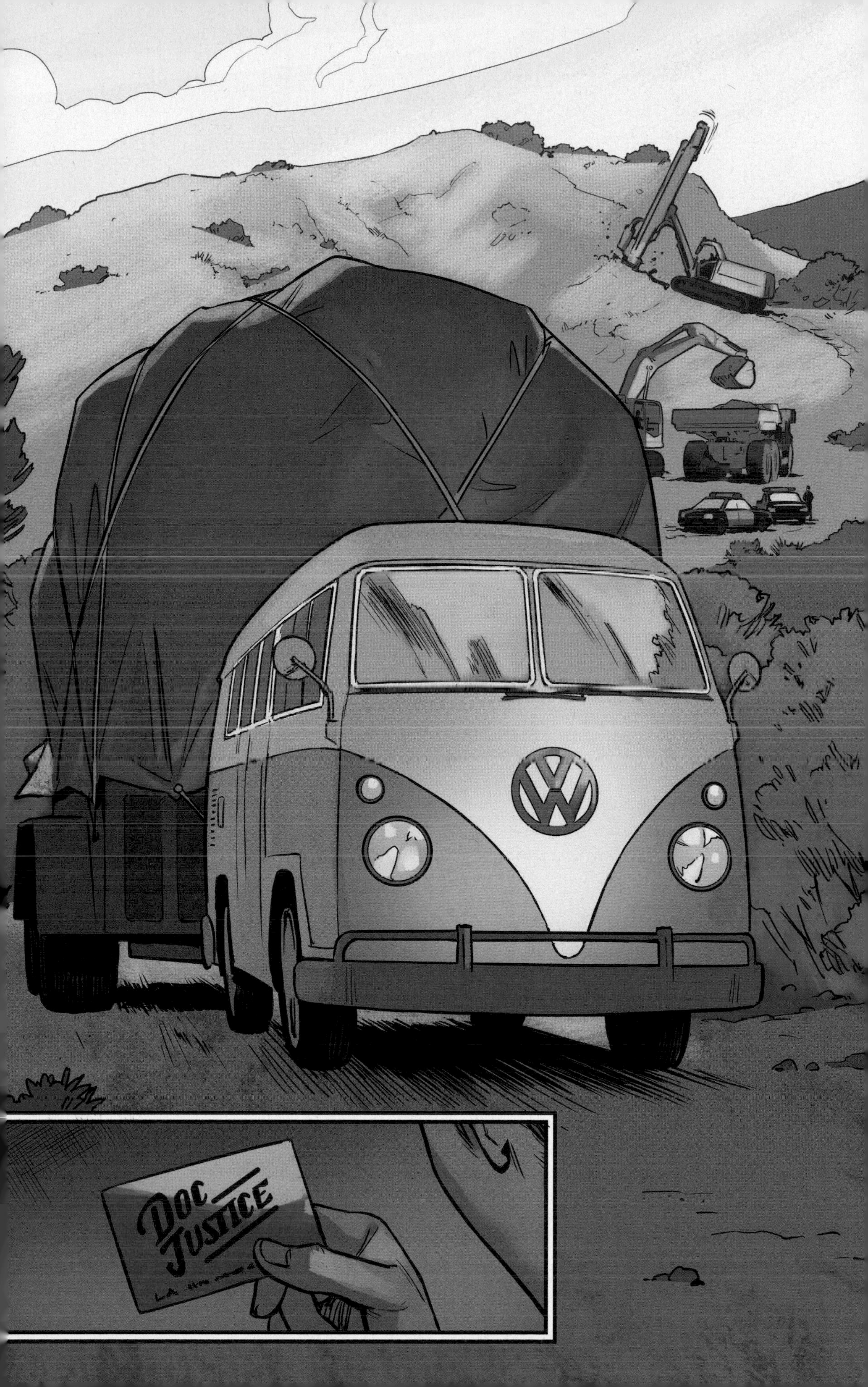
DOC JUSTICE

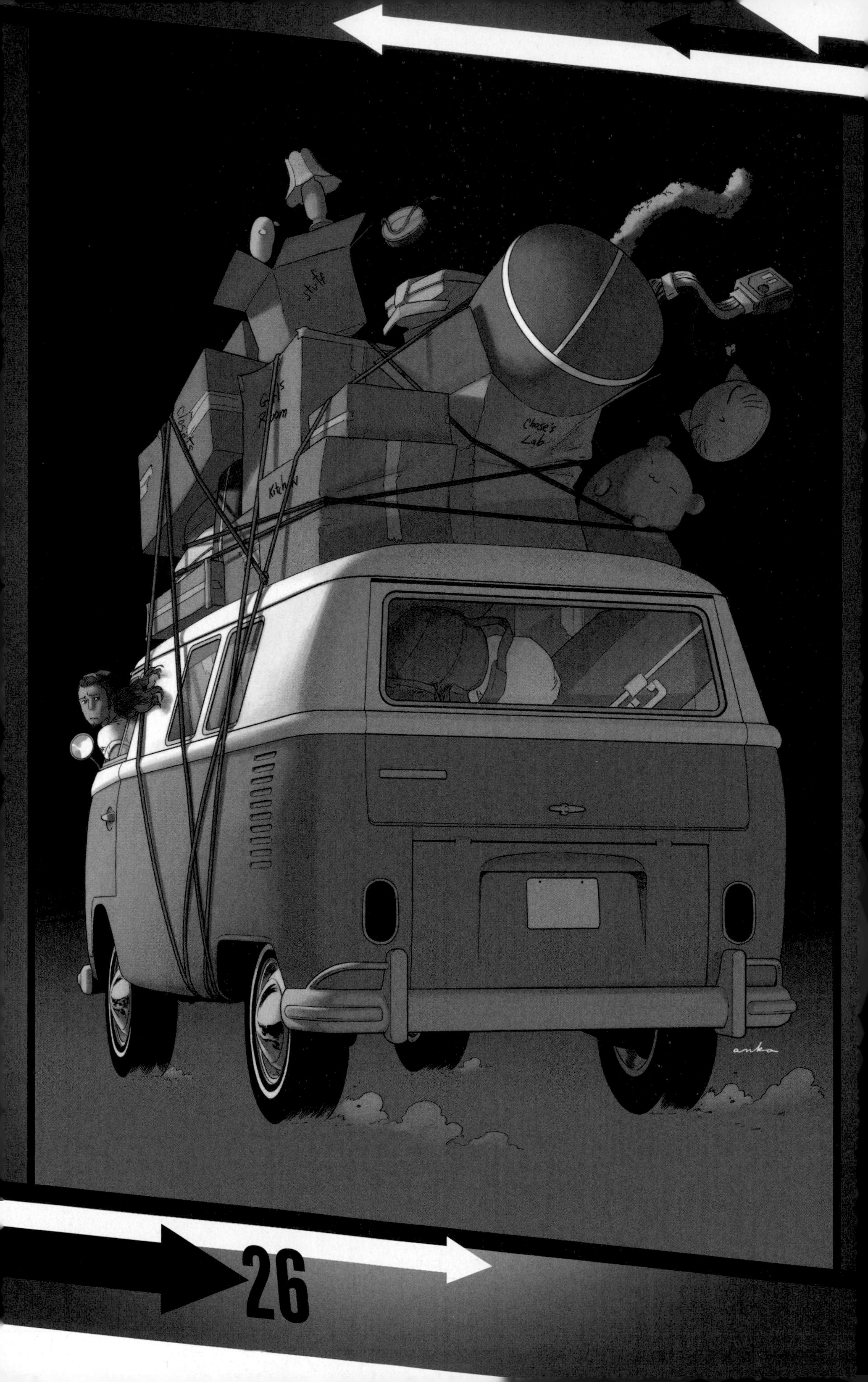
stuff
Room
Chase's Lab
Kitchen
anka
26

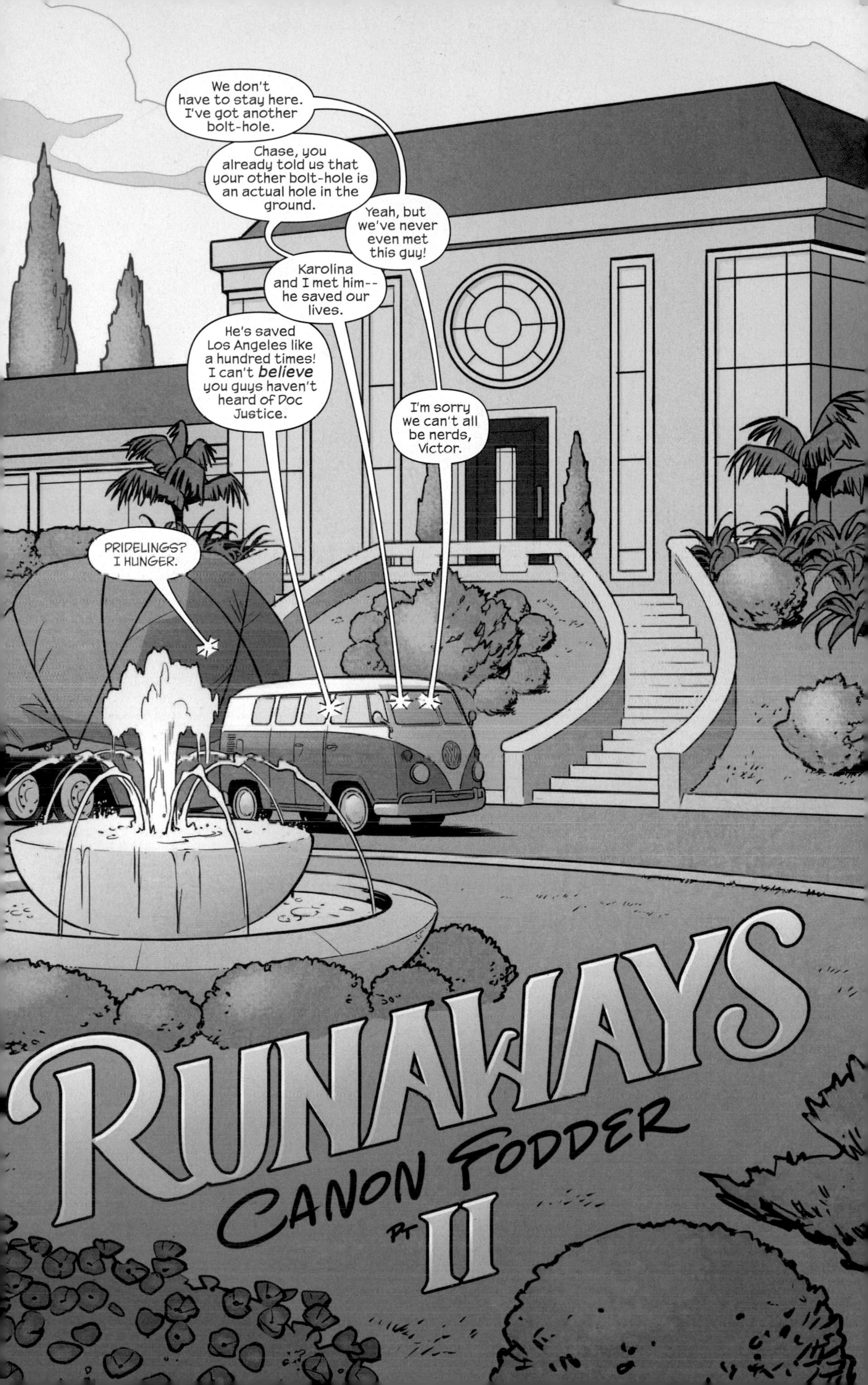
We don't have to stay here. I've got another bolt-hole.
Chase, you already told us that your other bolt-hole is an actual hole in the ground.
Yeah, but we've never even met this guy!
Karolina and I met him--he saved our lives.
He's saved Los Angeles like a hundred times! I can't *believe* you guys haven't heard of Doc Justice.
I'm sorry we can't all be nerds, Victor.
PRIDELINGS? I HUNGER.
RUNAWAYS
CANON FODDER
PT II

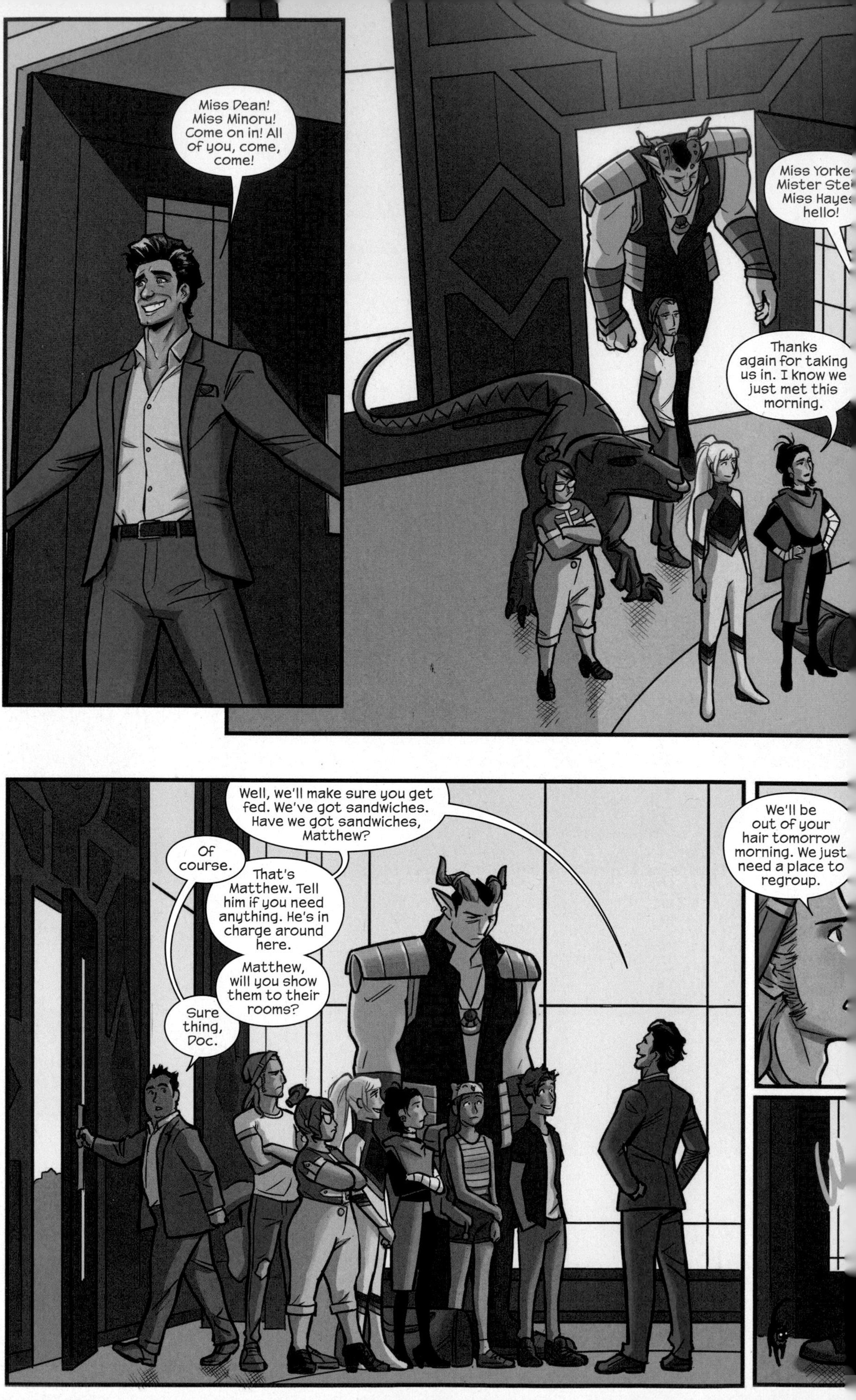

Miss Dean! Miss Minoru! Come on in! All of you, come, come!
Miss Yorke Mister Ste Miss Hayes hello!
Thanks again for taking us in. I know we just met this morning.
Well, we'll make sure you get fed. We've got sandwiches. Have we got sandwiches, Matthew?
Of course.
That's Matthew. Tell him if you need anything. He's in charge around here.
Matthew, will you show them to their rooms?
Sure thing, Doc.
We'll be out of your hair tomorrow morning. We just need a place to regroup.

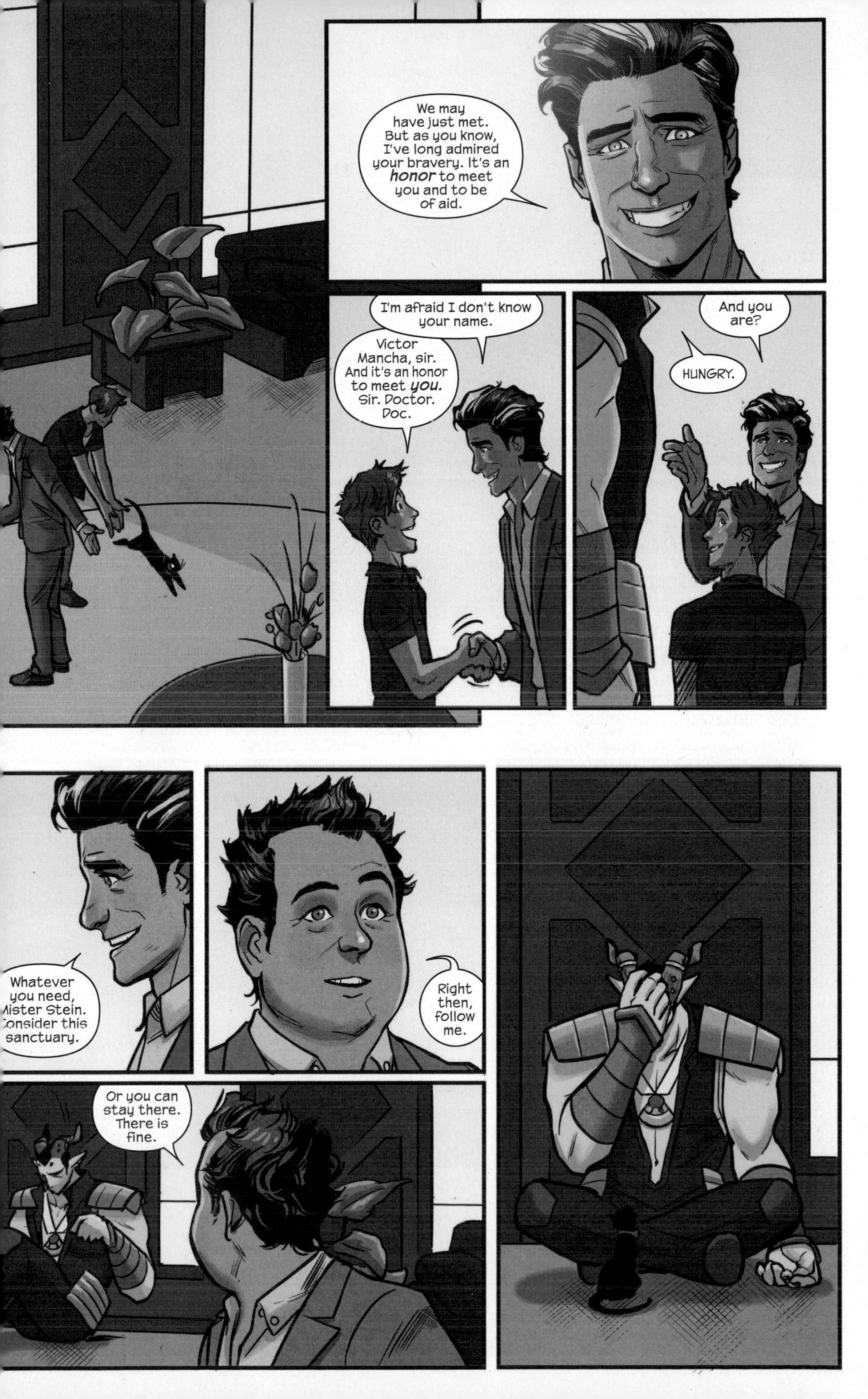
We may have just met. But as you know, I've long admired your bravery. It's an *honor* to meet you and to be of aid.
I'm afraid I don't know your name.
Victor Mancha, sir. And it's an honor to meet *you.* Sir. Doctor. Doc.
And you are?
HUNGRY.
Whatever you need, Mister Stein. Consider this sanctuary.
Right then, follow me.
Or you can stay there. There is fine.

Is this where we live now?

No, Molly. This is just for a day or two. Just until we figure out what's happening at the Hostel.

I'm so sorry--

Stop apologizing, Karrie. It might not have had anything to do with you. Maybe they were just... drilling.

But I should have told you guys what I was doing. It wasn't fair to endanger everyone--

Oh my God, Karolina, *shut* up.

You're not the first person in the world to do something sneaky and selfish.

How about you lighten up, Gert?

How about no?

It's okay, Nico, she's right. I'm centering myself again, I'm sorry.

For God's *sake*, Karrie, stop *apologizing.*

I'm sorry. *I'm sorry!*

You girls settling in all right?

girls' wir
boys stay
boys' w

The
REC R
is fo
recrea

Yes, just fine. Thank you.

The light in here is extraordinary.

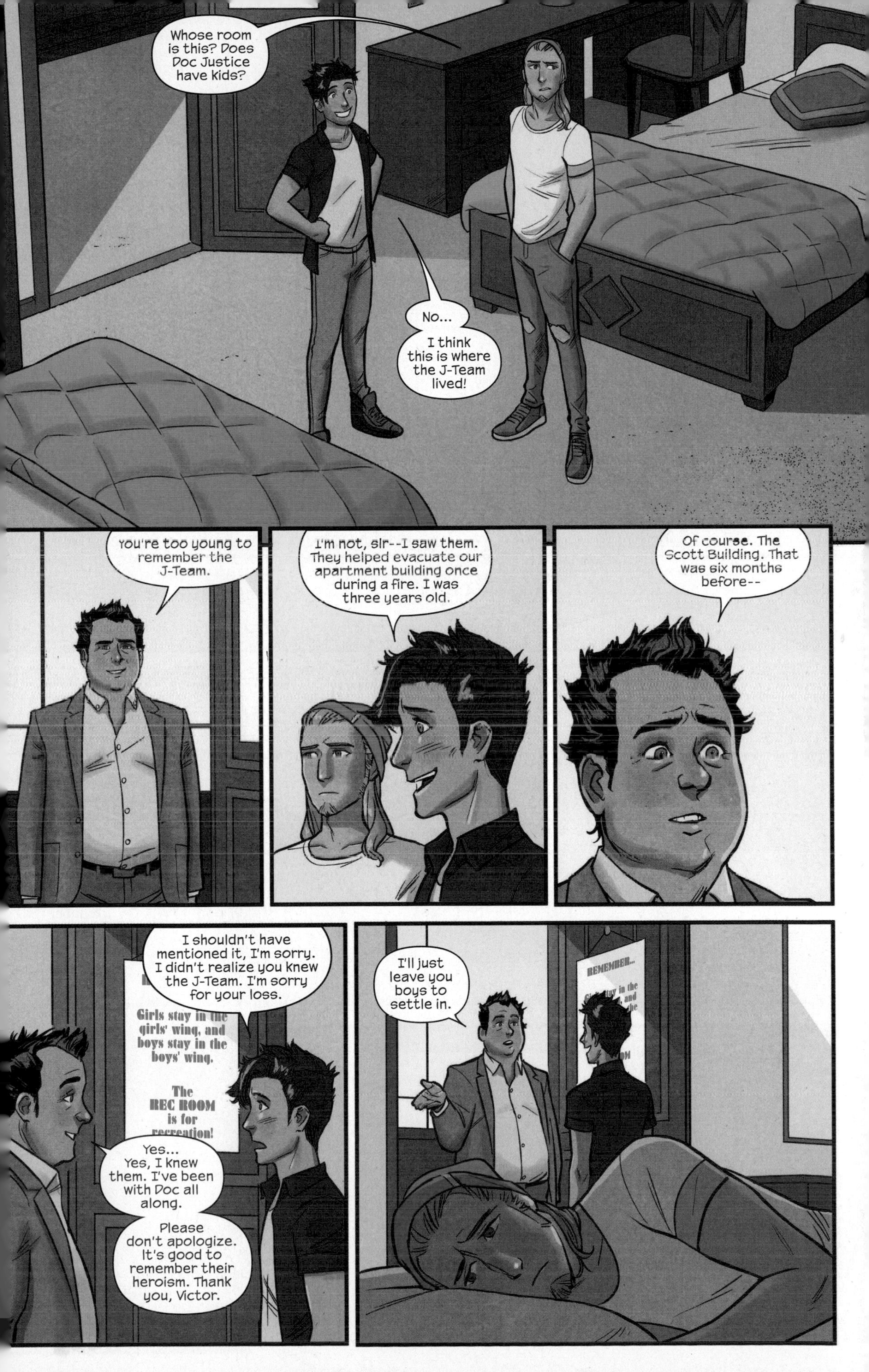
Whose room is this? Does Doc Justice have kids?
No... I think this is where the J-Team lived!
You're too young to remember the J-Team.
I'm not, sir--I saw them. They helped evacuate our apartment building once during a fire. I was three years old.
Of course. The Scott Building. That was six months before--
I shouldn't have mentioned it, I'm sorry. I didn't realize you knew the J-Team. I'm sorry for your loss.
Girls stay in the girls' wing, and boys stay in the boys' wing.
The REC ROOM is for recreation!
Yes... Yes, I knew them. I've been with Doc all along.
Please don't apologize. It's good to remember their heroism. Thank you, Victor.
I'll just leave you boys to settle in.
REMEMBER...

Well, the good news is--it looks like it's just a drainage project over in Bronson Canyon... They're not going to tear down a landmark.

The bad news is--the Public Works department is almost completely in the Pride's pocket. The project could all be a cover for flushing you out.

Um. The Pride is dead. We pretty much killed them.

Oh. Miss Yorkes...

It's true, your parents are dead.

But the crime network they left behind was far too entrenched, far too well organized to simply dissolve when they disappeared.

I think there's something I should show you

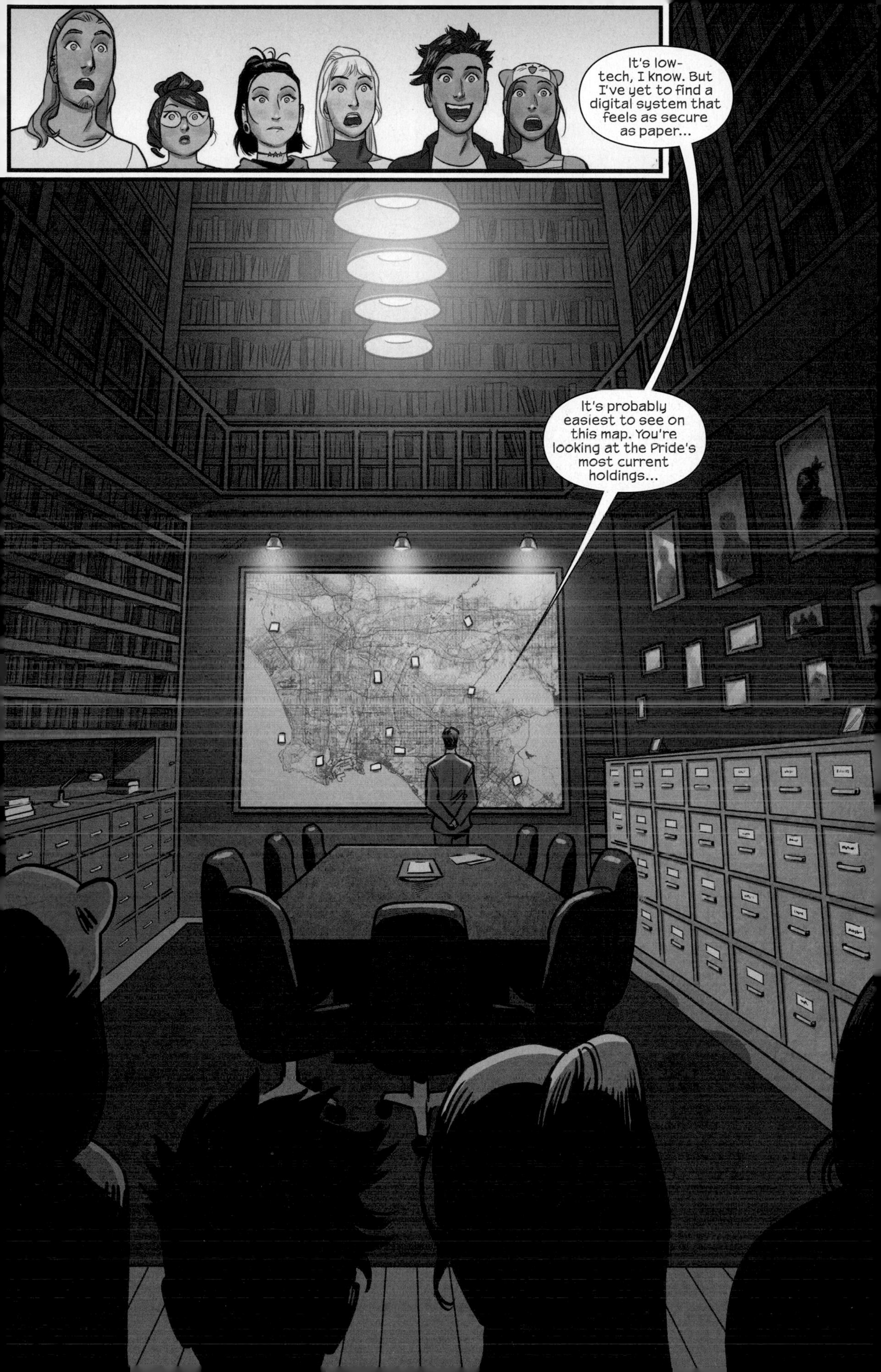
It's low-tech, I know. But I've yet to find a digital system that feels as secure as paper...
It's probably easiest to see on this map. You're looking at the Pride's most current holdings...

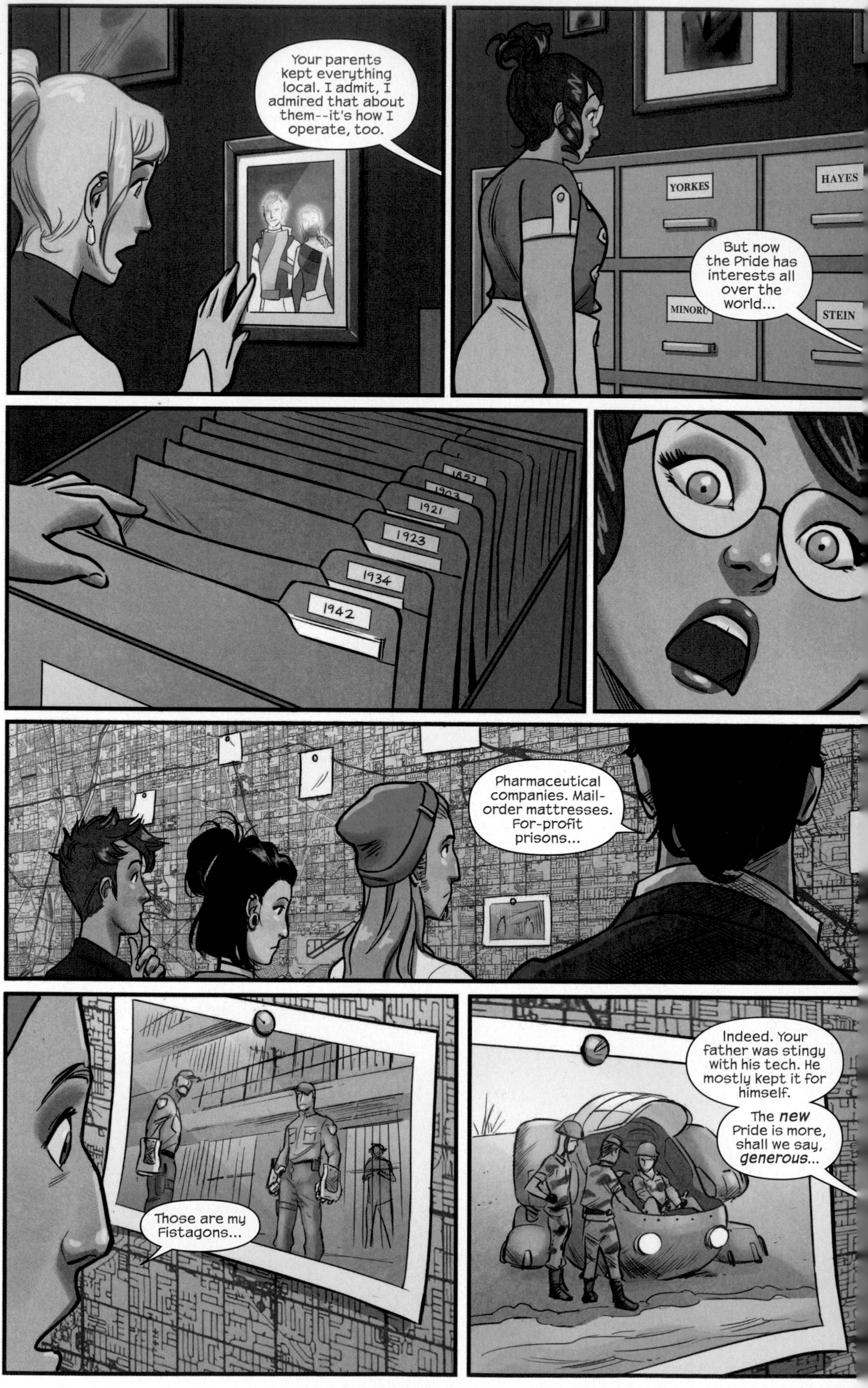
Your parents kept everything local. I admit, I admired that about them--it's how I operate, too.
YORKES
HAYES
MINORU
STEIN
But now the Pride has interests all over the world...
1853
1903
1921
1923
1934
1942
Pharmaceutical companies. Mail-order mattresses. For-profit prisons...
Those are my Fistagons...
Indeed. Your father was stingy with his tech. He mostly kept it for himself.
The *new* Pride is more, shall we say, ***generous***...

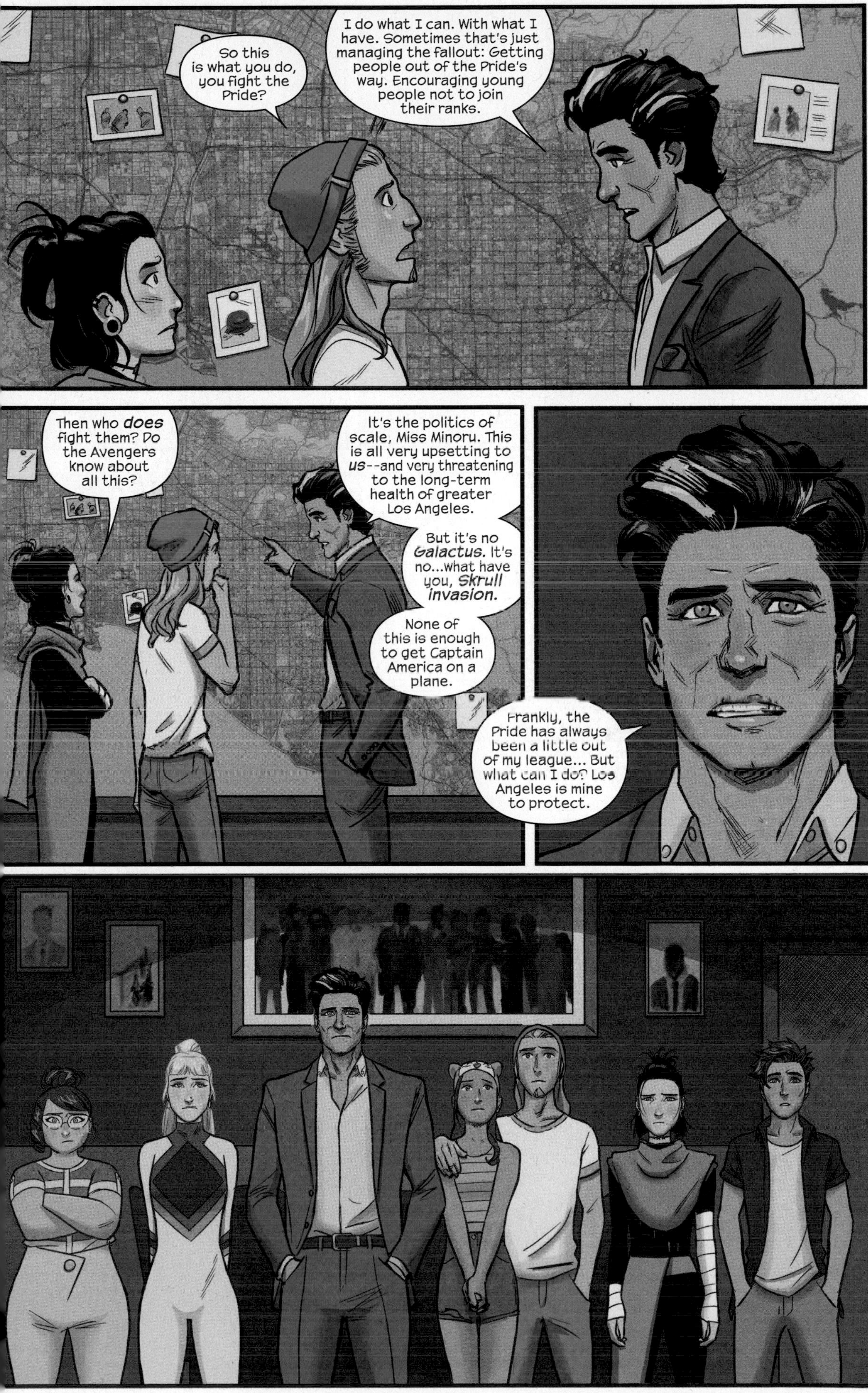

So this is what you do, you fight the Pride?
I do what I can. With what I have. Sometimes that's just managing the fallout: Getting people out of the Pride's way. Encouraging young people not to join their ranks.
Then who **does** fight them? Do the Avengers know about all this?
It's the politics of scale, Miss Minoru. This is all very upsetting to **us**--and very threatening to the long-term health of greater Los Angeles.
But it's no **Galactus.** It's no...what have you, **Skrull invasion.**
None of this is enough to get Captain America on a plane.
Frankly, the Pride has always been a little out of my league... But what can I do? Los Angeles is mine to protect.

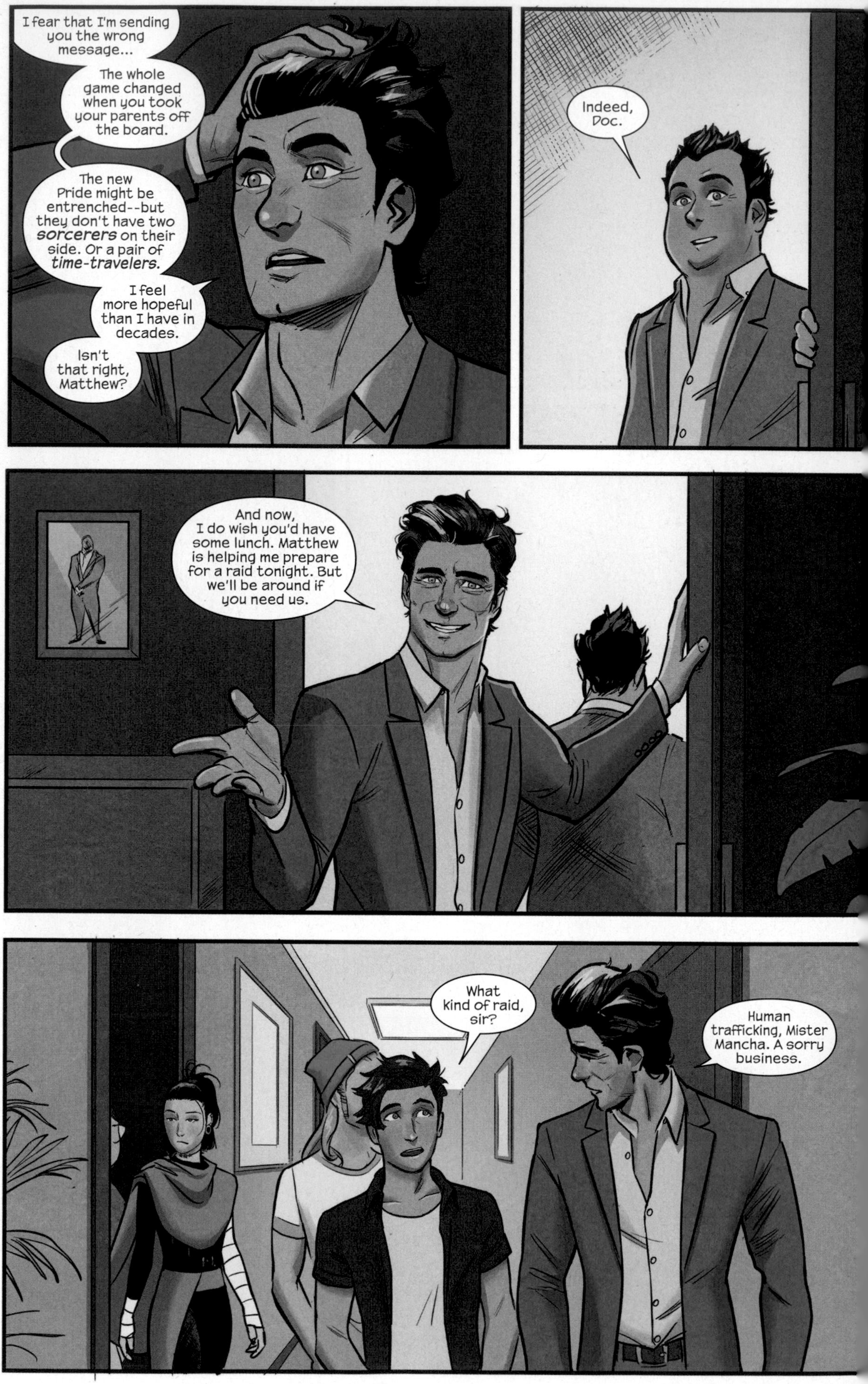
I fear that I'm sending you the wrong message...
The whole game changed when you took your parents off the board.
The new Pride might be entrenched--but they don't have two *sorcerers* on their side. Or a pair of *time-travelers.*
I feel more hopeful than I have in decades.
Isn't that right, Matthew?
Indeed, Doc.
And now, I do wish you'd have some lunch. Matthew is helping me prepare for a raid tonight. But we'll be around if you need us.
What kind of raid, sir?
Human trafficking, Mister Mancha. A sorry business.

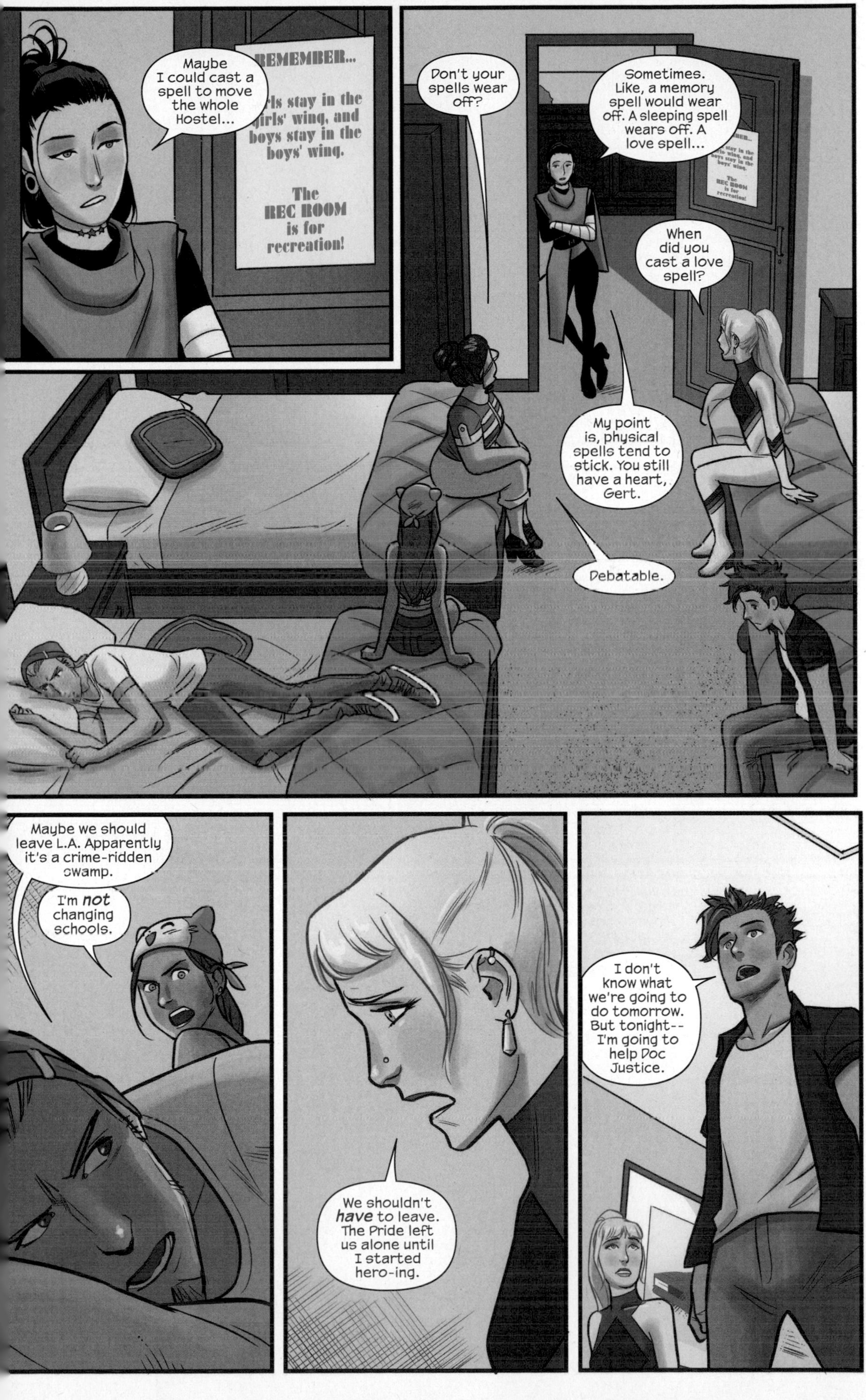
Maybe I could cast a spell to move the whole Hostel...
REMEMBER... Girls stay in the girls' wing, and boys stay in the boys' wing. The REC ROOM is for recreation!
Don't your spells wear off?
Sometimes. Like, a memory spell would wear off. A sleeping spell wears off. A love spell...
When did you cast a love spell?
My point is, physical spells tend to stick. You still have a heart, Gert.
Debatable.
Maybe we should leave L.A. Apparently it's a crime-ridden swamp.
I'm *not* changing schools.
We shouldn't *have* to leave. The Pride left us alone until I started hero-ing.
I don't know what we're going to do tomorrow. But tonight-- I'm going to help Doc Justice.

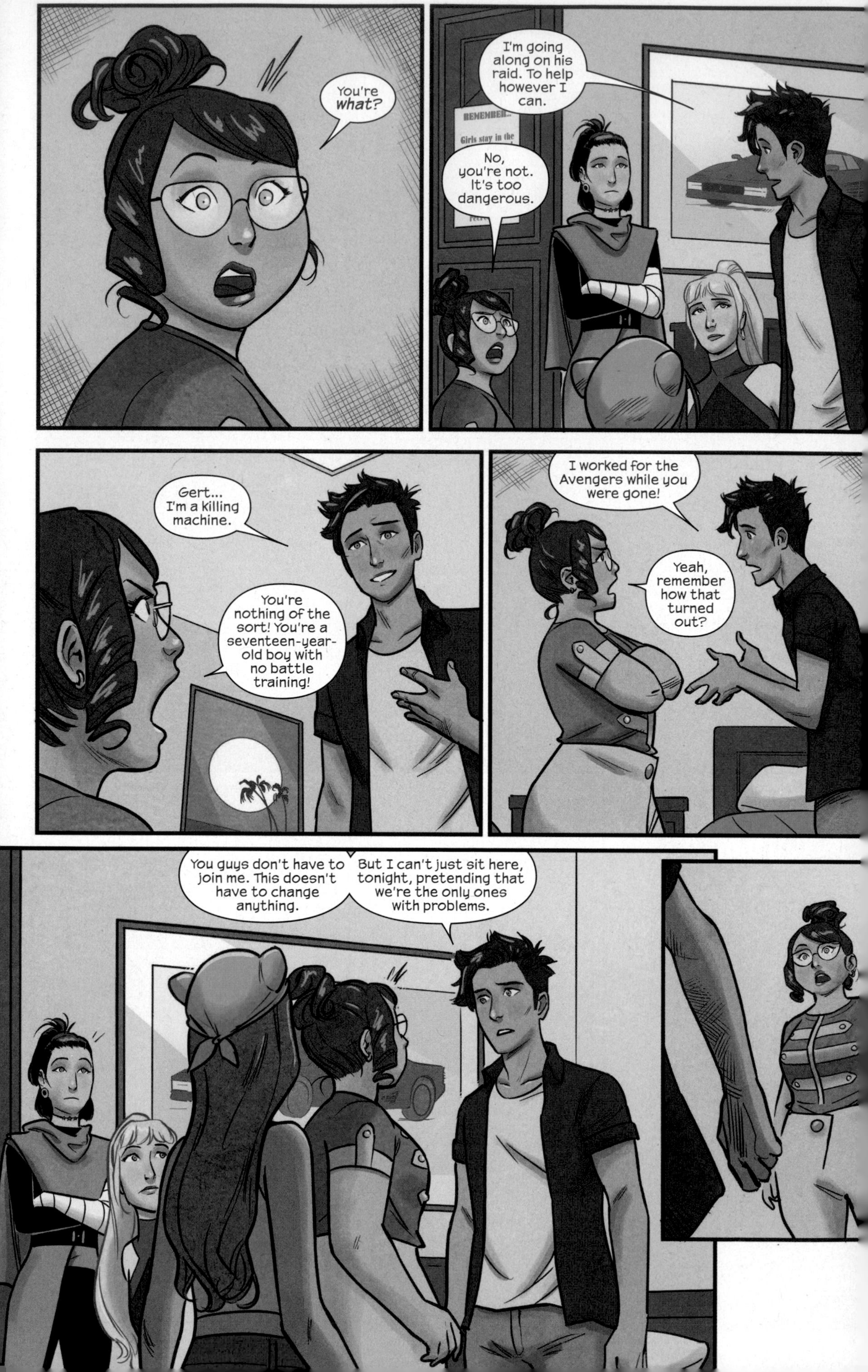
You're *what?*
I'm going along on his raid. To help however I can.
REMEMBER...
Girls stay in the
No, you're not. It's too dangerous.
Gert... I'm a killing machine.
You're nothing of the sort! You're a seventeen-year-old boy with no battle training!
I worked for the Avengers while you were gone!
Yeah, remember how that turned out?
You guys don't have to join me. This doesn't have to change anything.
But I can't just sit here, tonight, pretending that we're the only ones with problems.

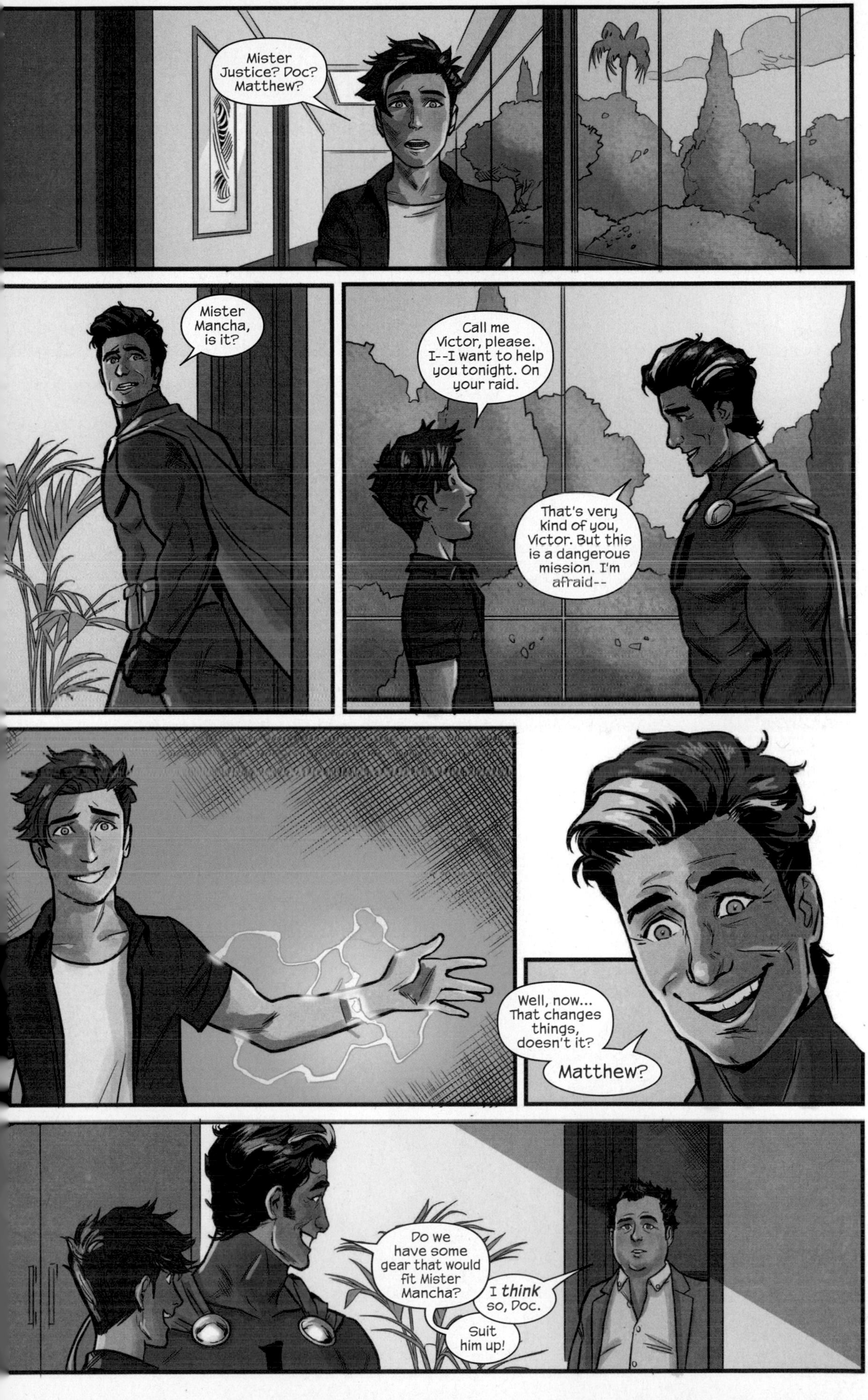
Mister Justice? Doc? Matthew?
Mister Mancha, is it?
Call me Victor, please. I--I want to help you tonight. On your raid.
That's very kind of you, Victor. But this is a dangerous mission. I'm afraid--
Well, now... That changes things, doesn't it?
Matthew?
Do we have some gear that would fit Mister Mancha?
I *think* so, Doc.
Suit him up!

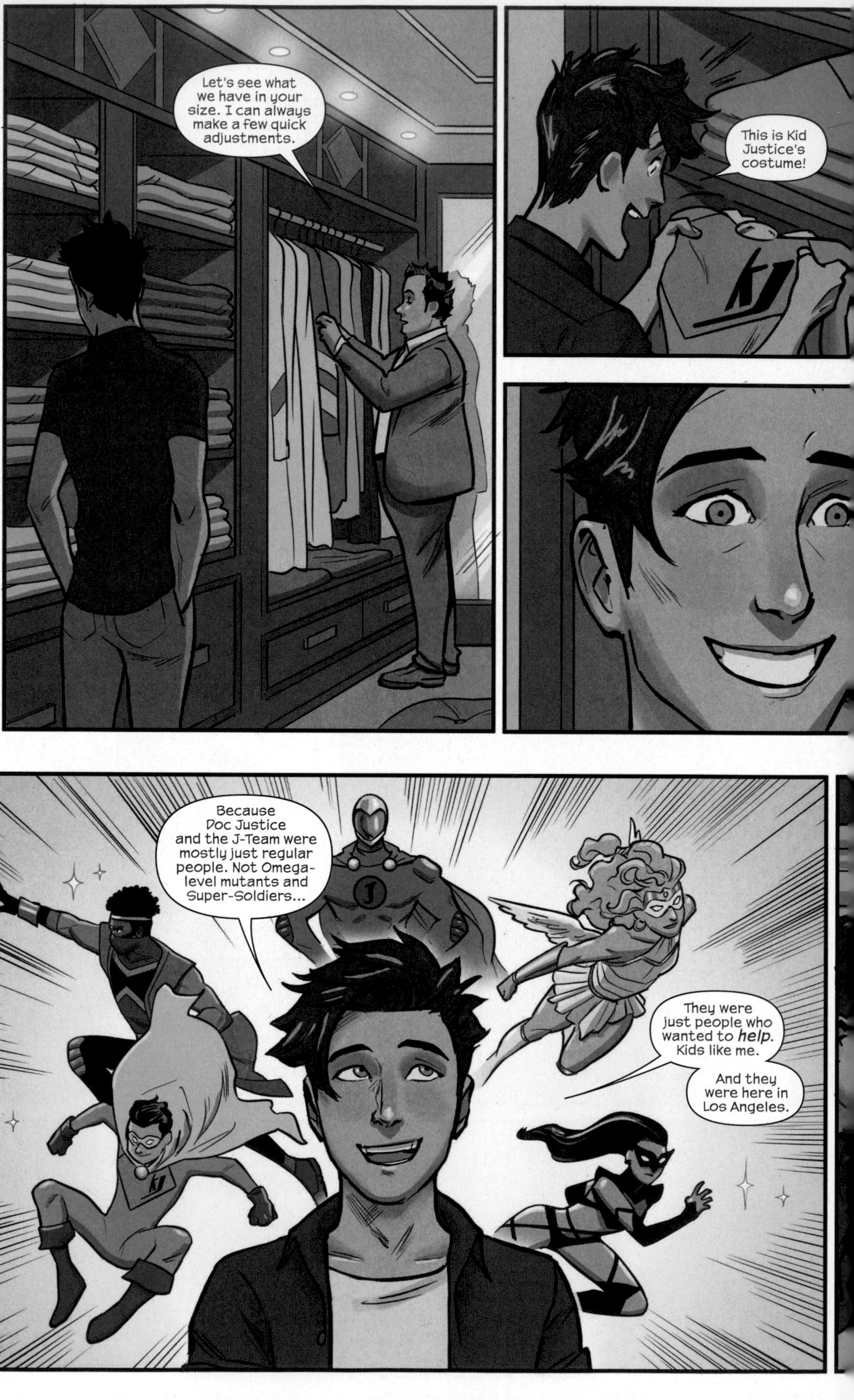
Let's see what we have in your size. I can always make a few quick adjustments.
This is Kid Justice's costume!
Because Doc Justice and the J-Team were mostly just regular people. Not Omega-level mutants and Super-Soldiers...
They were just people who wanted to *help*. Kids like me.
And they were here in Los Angeles.

Man in suit: Now, Mister Mancha, you are *definitely* too young to remember *that* iteration of the J-Team. Kid Justice was active back in the '80s.

Man in suit: One of them, yes...

Mancha: I'm kind of a nerd about hero stuff. I know all the J-Team members. I even know about J-Squad and that team Doc led in the '90s--

Man in suit: Justice for All. *Nobody* remembers Justice for All...

Mancha: I do. I mean, I don't *remember* it, but I read all about it.

Mancha: The J-team was my favorite.

Man in suit: Mister Mancha... In a world with Avengers and X-Men, why would the *J-Team* be your favorite?

Mancha: I could never imagine joining the Avengers...

Mancha: But I thought maybe I could be on the *J-Team* someday.

Man in suit: Well, I'd hardly call you "regular," Mister Mancha. But welcome to the J-Team.

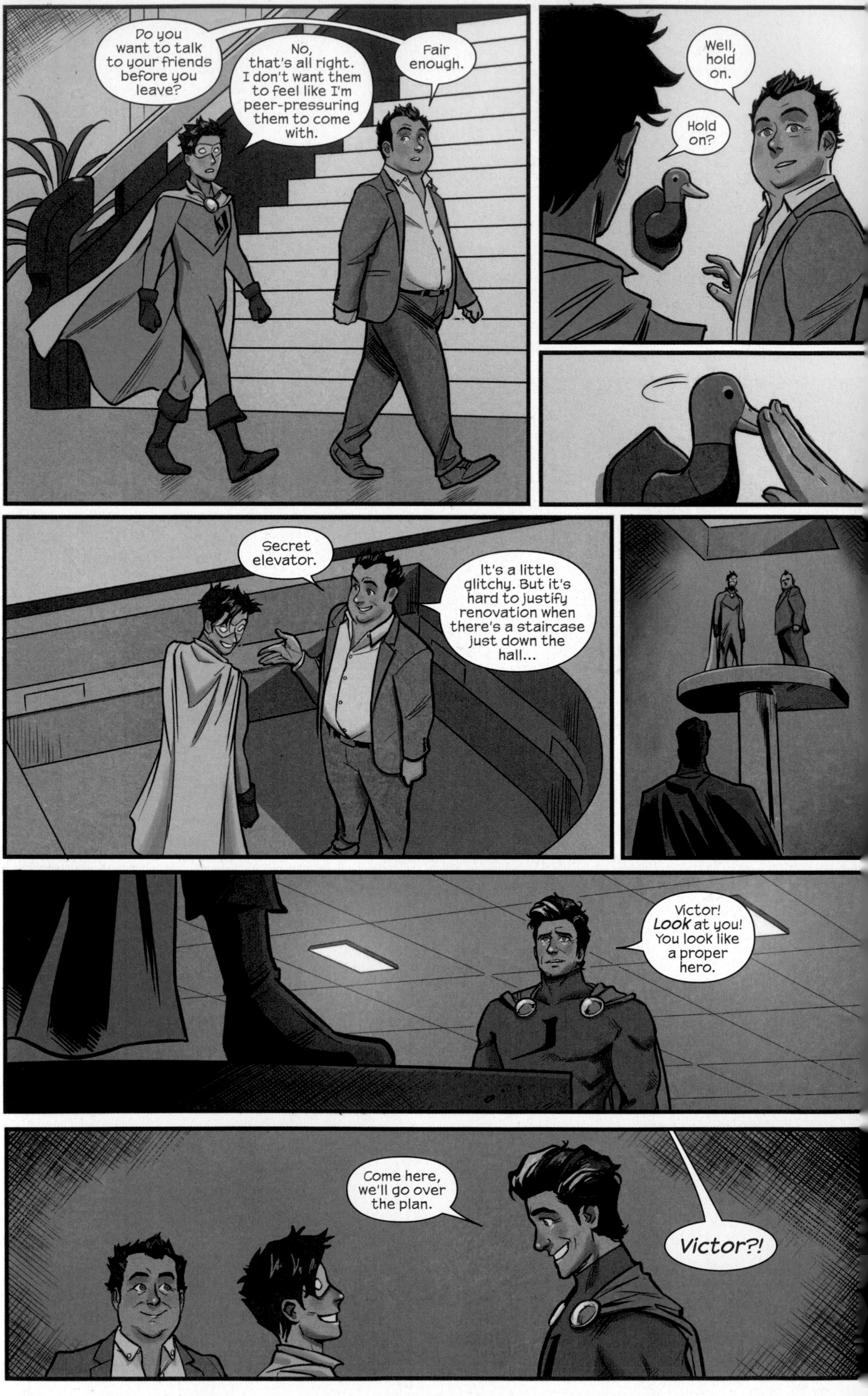
Do you want to talk to your friends before you leave?
No, that's all right. I don't want them to feel like I'm peer-pressuring them to come with.
Fair enough.
Well, hold on.
Hold on?
Secret elevator.
It's a little glitchy. But it's hard to justify renovation when there's a staircase just down the hall...
Victor! *Look* at you! You look like a proper hero.
Come here, we'll go over the plan.
Victor?!

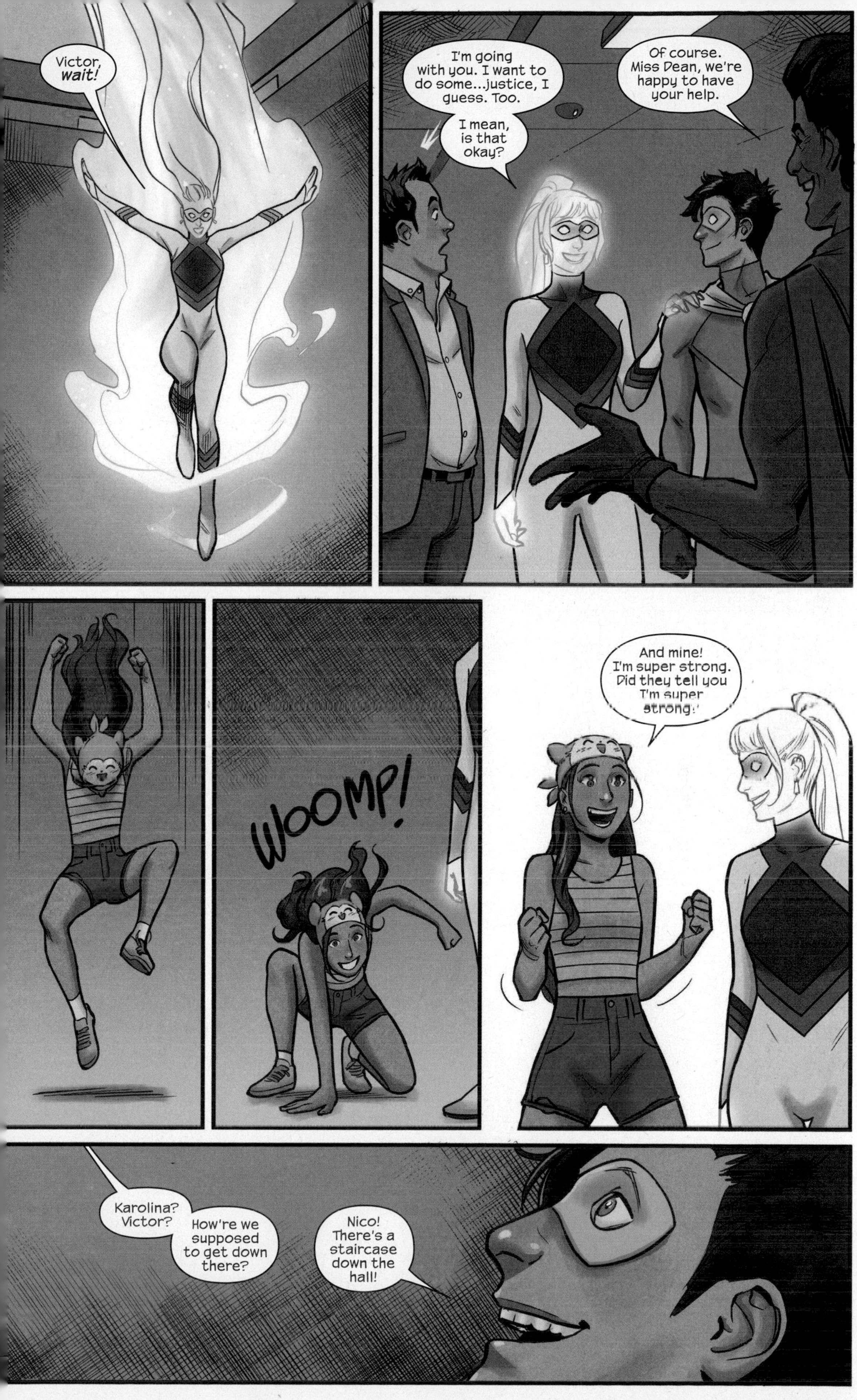
Victor, *wait!*
I'm going with you. I want to do some...justice, I guess. Too.
I mean, is that okay?
Of course. Miss Dean, we're happy to have your help.
WOOMP!
And mine! I'm super strong. Did they tell you I'm super strong?
Karolina? Victor?
How're we supposed to get down there?
Nico! There's a staircase down the hall!

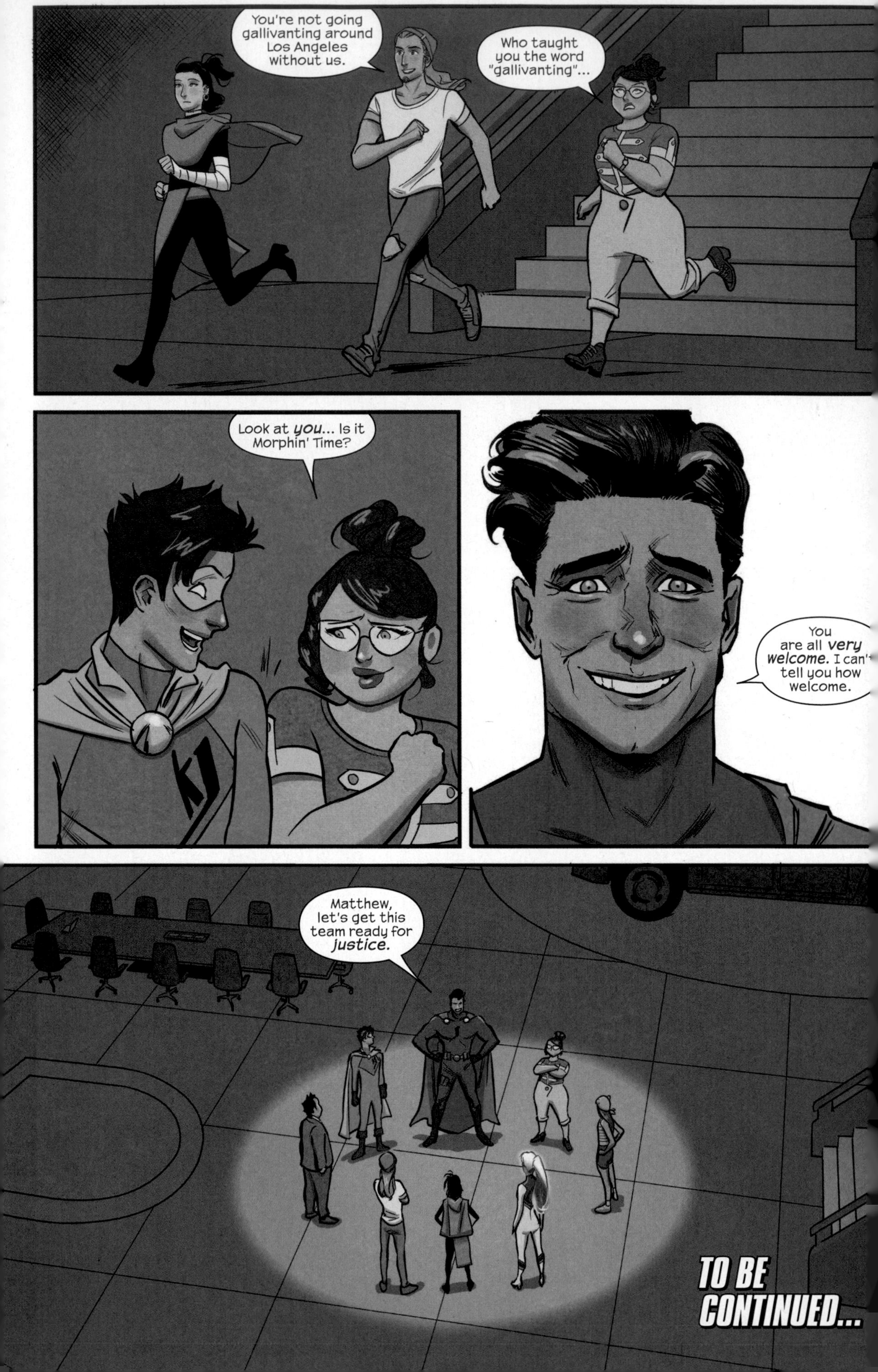
You're not going gallivanting around Los Angeles without us.
Who taught you the word "gallivanting"...
Look at you... Is it Morphin' Time?
You are all very welcome. I can't tell you how welcome.
Matthew, let's get this team ready for justice.
TO BE CONTINUED...

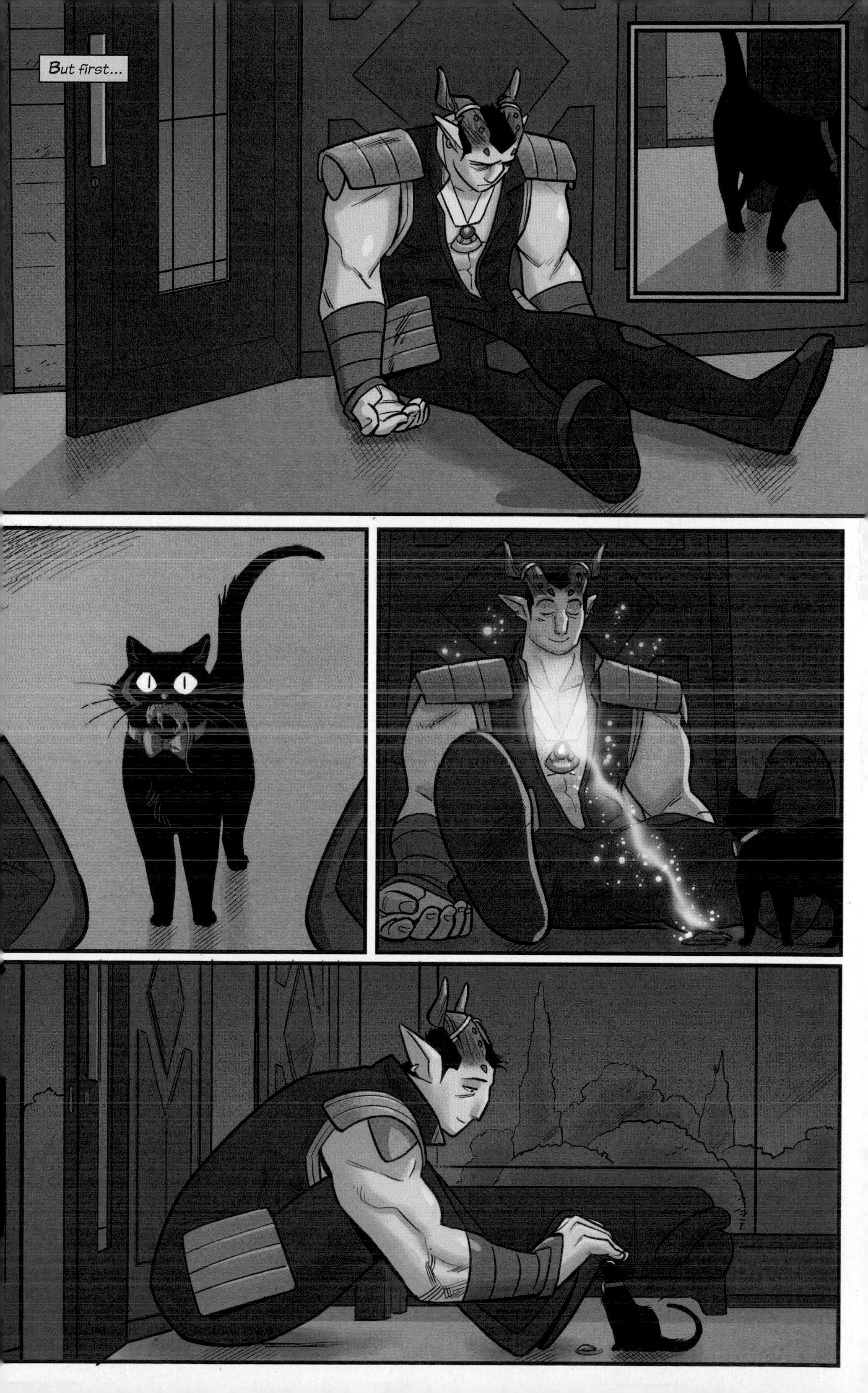
But first...

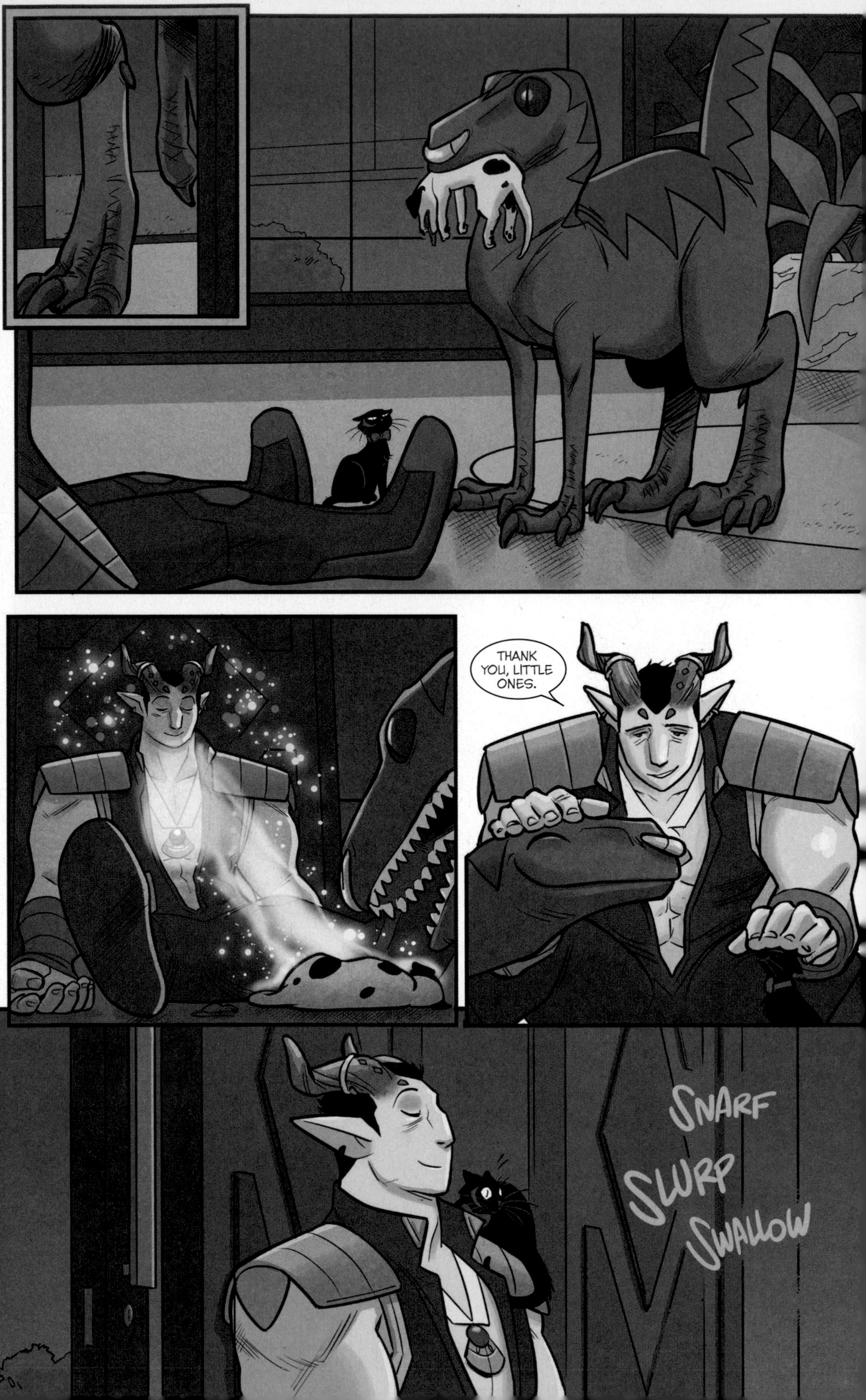
THANK YOU, LITTLE ONES.
SNARF
SLURP
SWALLOW

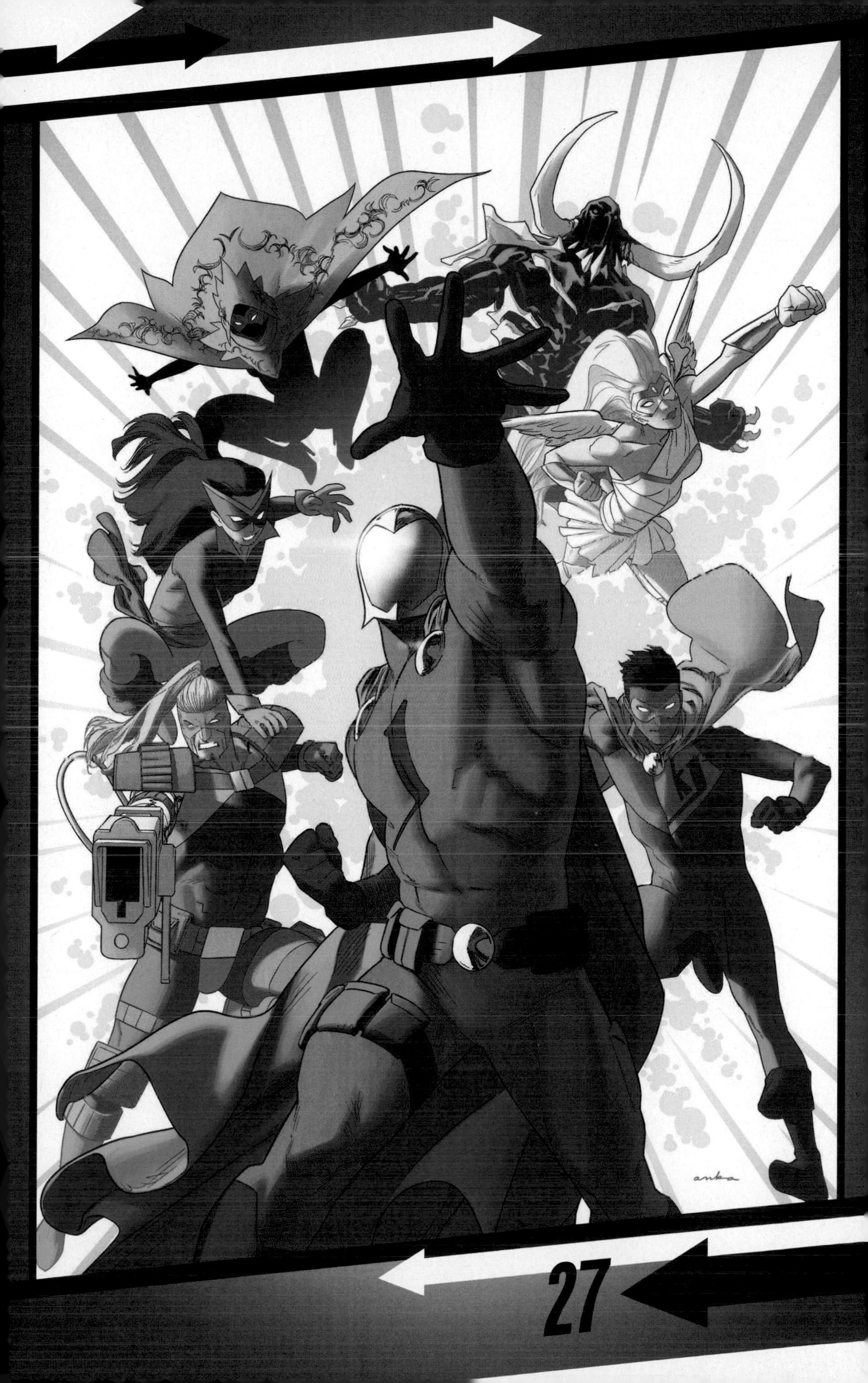
anka

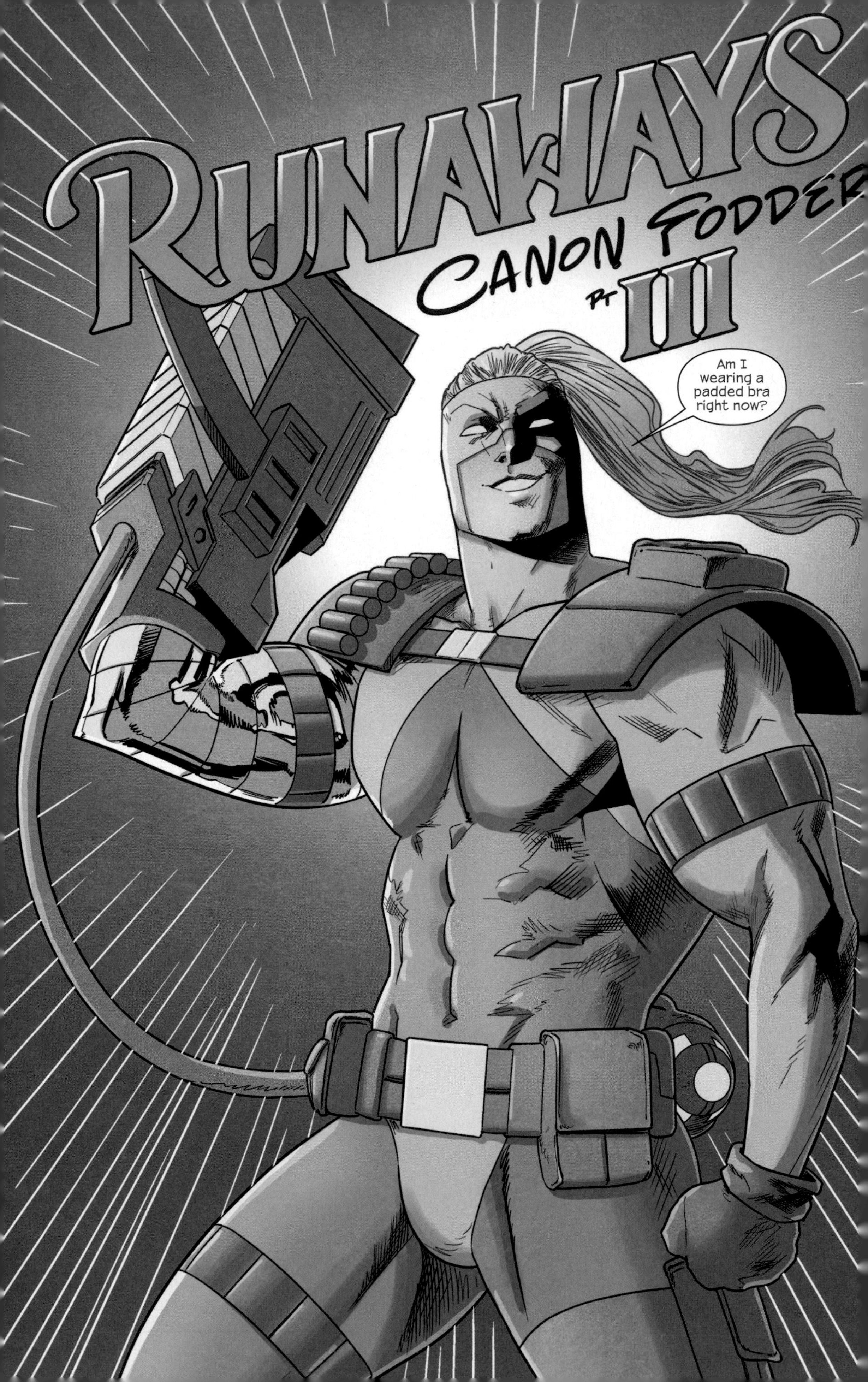
RUNAWAYS
CANON FODDER
PT III
Am I wearing a padded bra right now?

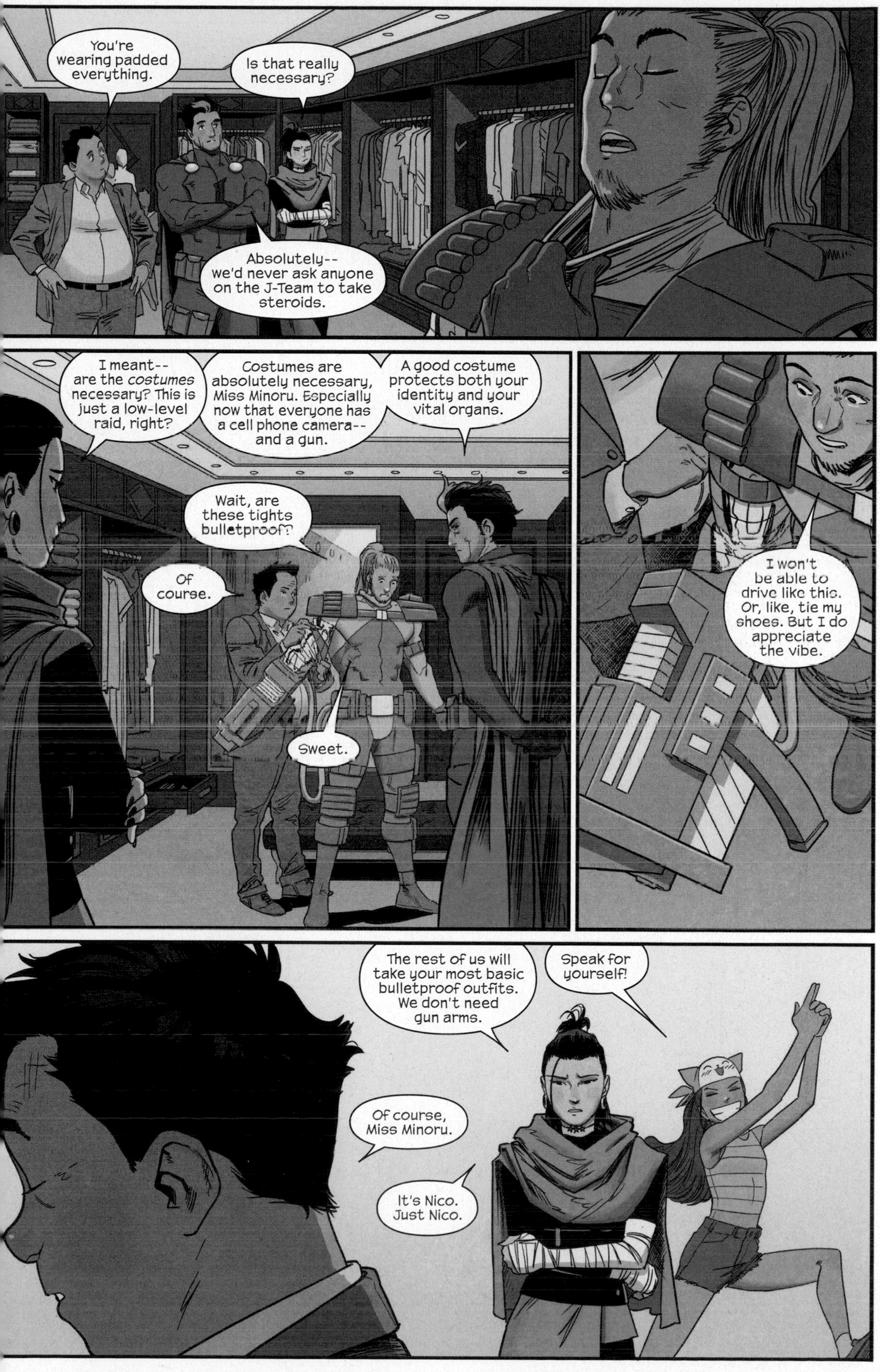
You're wearing padded everything.
Is that really necessary?
Absolutely-- we'd never ask anyone on the J-Team to take steroids.
I meant-- are the *costumes* necessary? This is just a low-level raid, right?
Costumes are absolutely necessary, Miss Minoru. Especially now that everyone has a cell phone camera-- and a gun.
A good costume protects both your identity and your vital organs.
Wait, are these tights bulletproof?
Of course.
Sweet.
I won't be able to drive like this. Or, like, tie my shoes. But I do appreciate the vibe.
The rest of us will take your most basic bulletproof outfits. We don't need gun arms.
Speak for yourself!
Of course, Miss Minoru.
It's Nico. Just Nico.

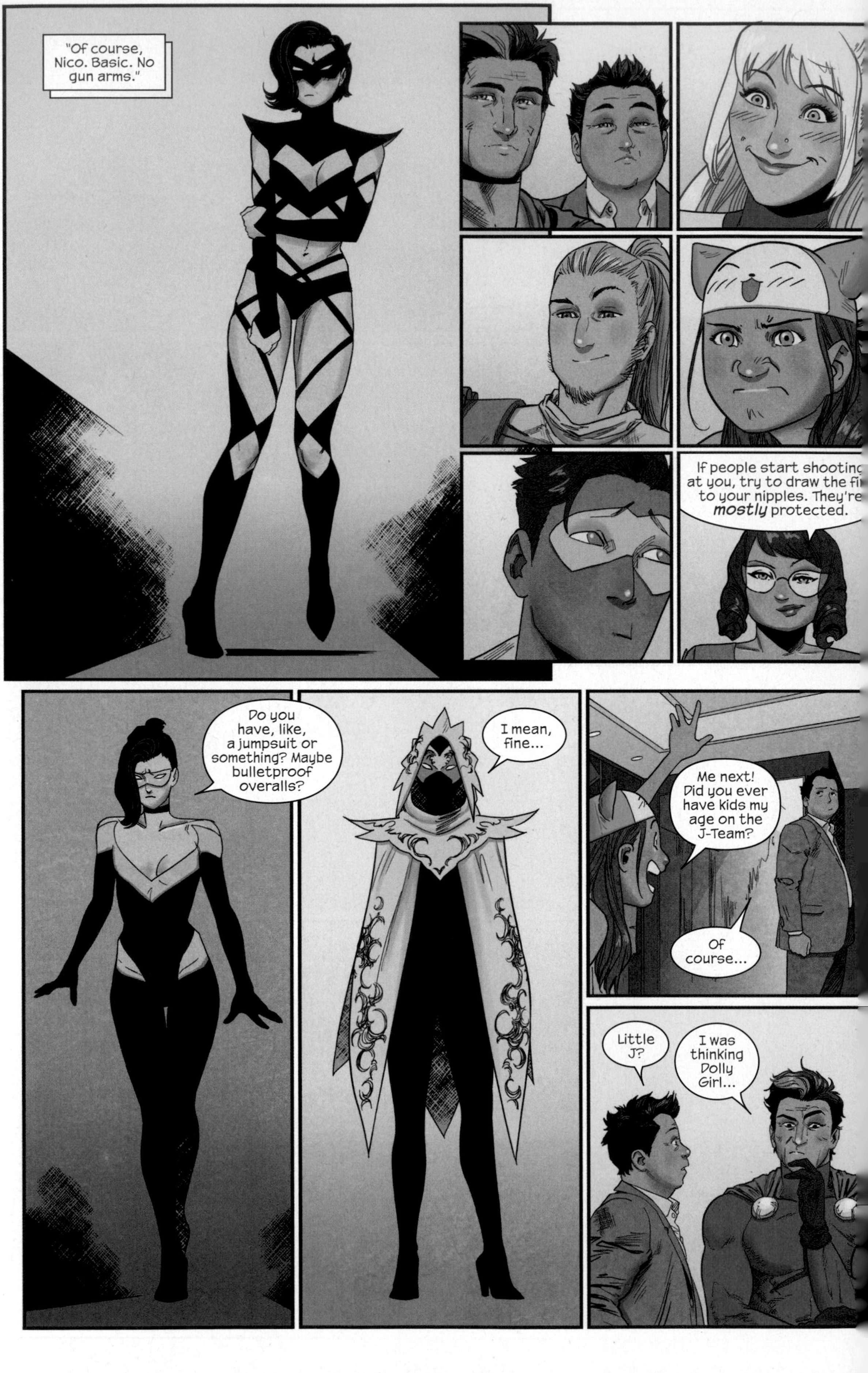
"Of course, Nico. Basic. No gun arms."
If people start shootinc at you, try to draw the fi to your nipples. They're *mostly* protected.
Do you have, like, a jumpsuit or something? Maybe bulletproof overalls?
I mean, fine...
Me next! Did you ever have kids my age on the J-Team?
Of course...
Little J?
I was thinking Dolly Girl...

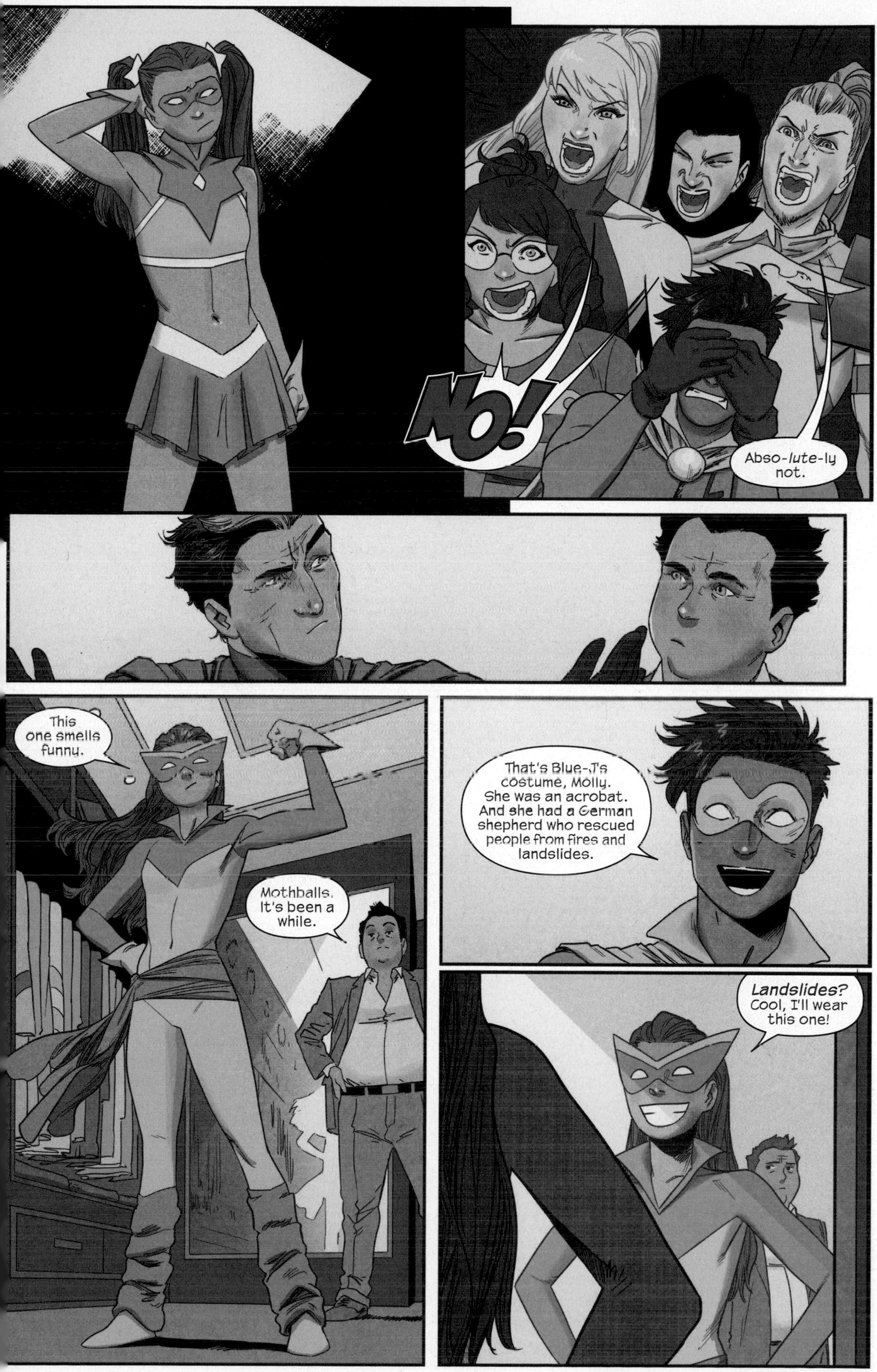
NO!
Abso-*lute*-ly not.
This one smells funny.
Mothballs. It's been a while.
That's Blue-J's costume, Molly. She was an acrobat. And she had a German shepherd who rescued people from fires and landslides.
Landslides? Cool, I'll wear this one!

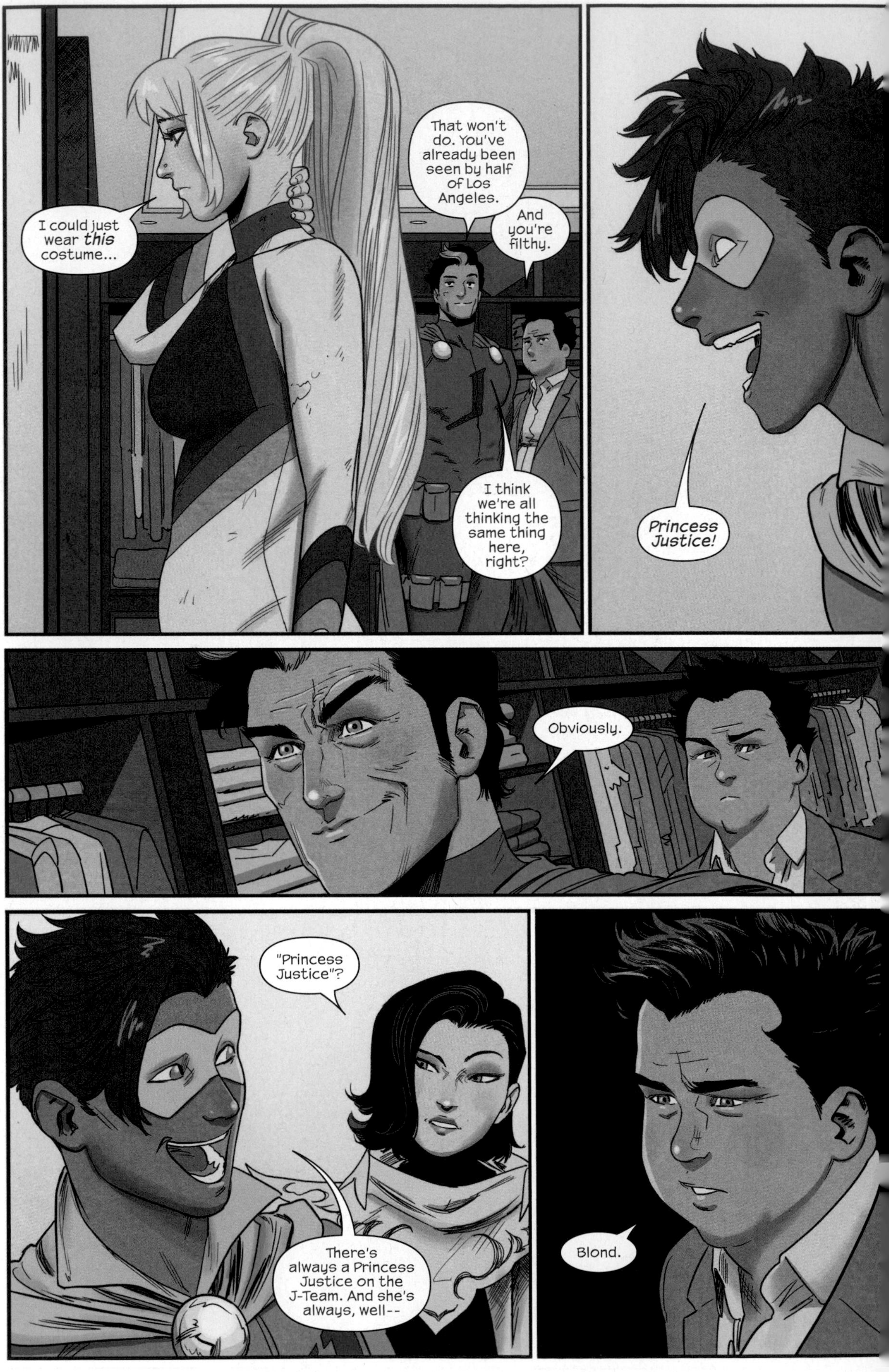
I could just wear *this* costume...
That won't do. You've already been seen by half of Los Angeles.
And you're filthy.
I think we're all thinking the same thing here, right?
Princess Justice!
Obviously.
"Princess Justice"?
There's always a Princess Justice on the J-Team. And she's always, well--
Blond.

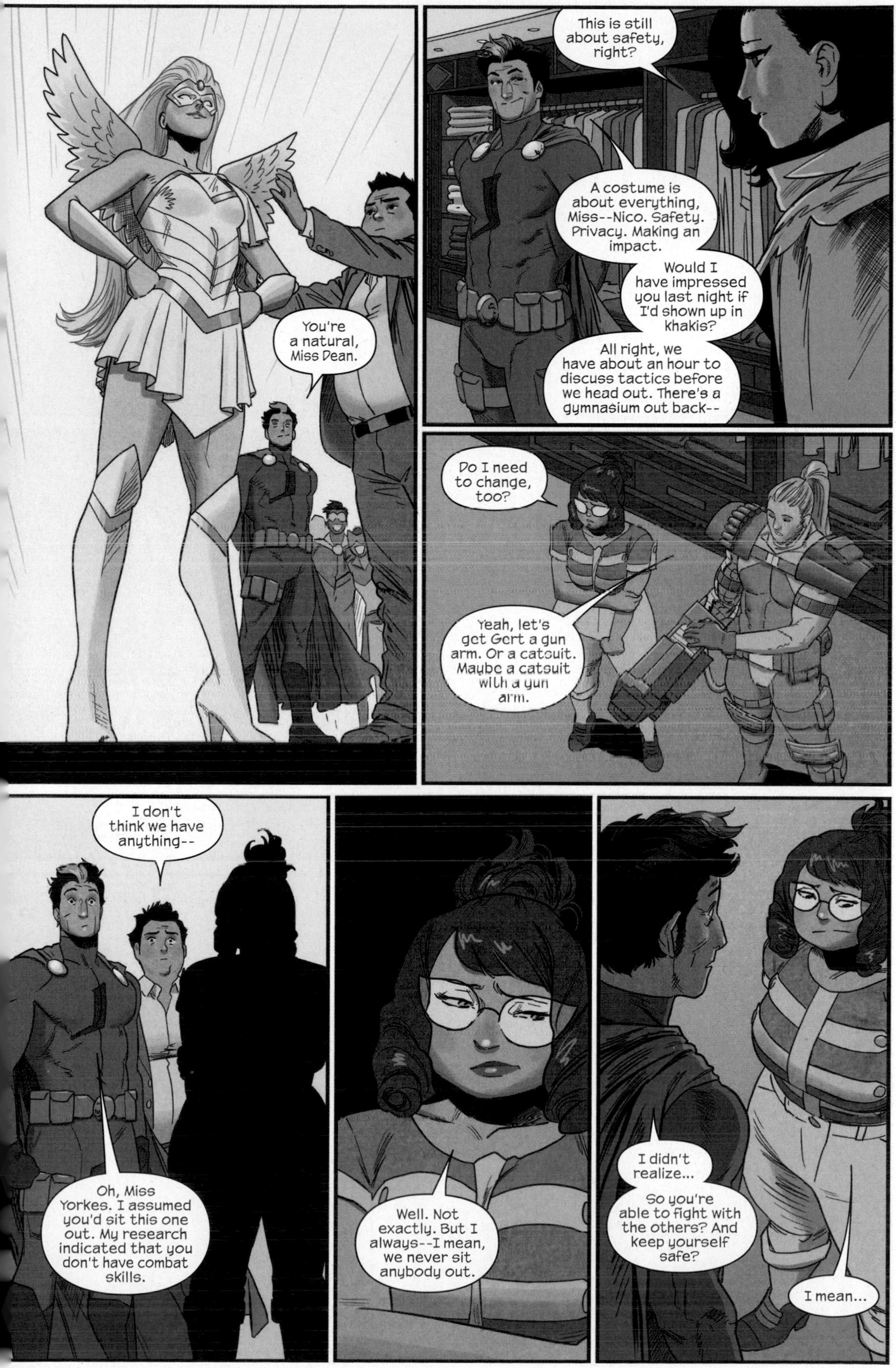
You're a natural, Miss Dean.
This is still about safety, right?
A costume is about everything, Miss--Nico. Safety. Privacy. Making an impact.
Would I have impressed you last night if I'd shown up in khakis?
All right, we have about an hour to discuss tactics before we head out. There's a gymnasium out back--
Do I need to change, too?
Yeah, let's get Gert a gun arm. Or a catsuit. Maybe a catsuit with a gun arm.
I don't think we have anything--
Oh, Miss Yorkes. I assumed you'd sit this one out. My research indicated that you don't have combat skills.
Well. Not exactly. But I always--I mean, we never sit anybody out.
I didn't realize...
So you're able to fight with the others? And keep yourself safe?
I mean...

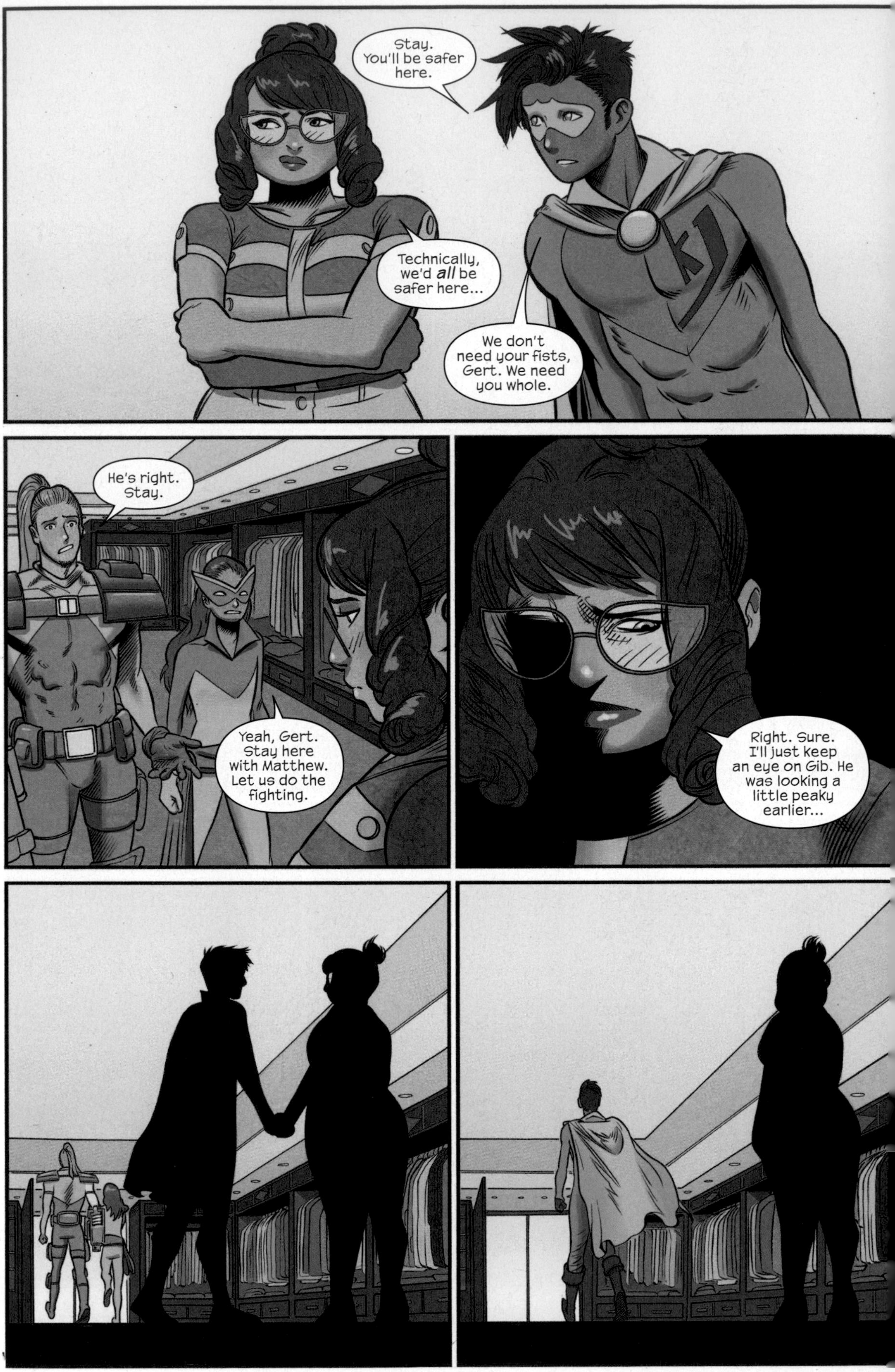
Stay. You'll be safer here.
Technically, we'd *all* be safer here...
We don't need your fists, Gert. We need you whole.
He's right. Stay.
Yeah, Gert. Stay here with Matthew. Let us do the fighting.
Right. Sure. I'll just keep an eye on Gib. He was looking a little peaky earlier...

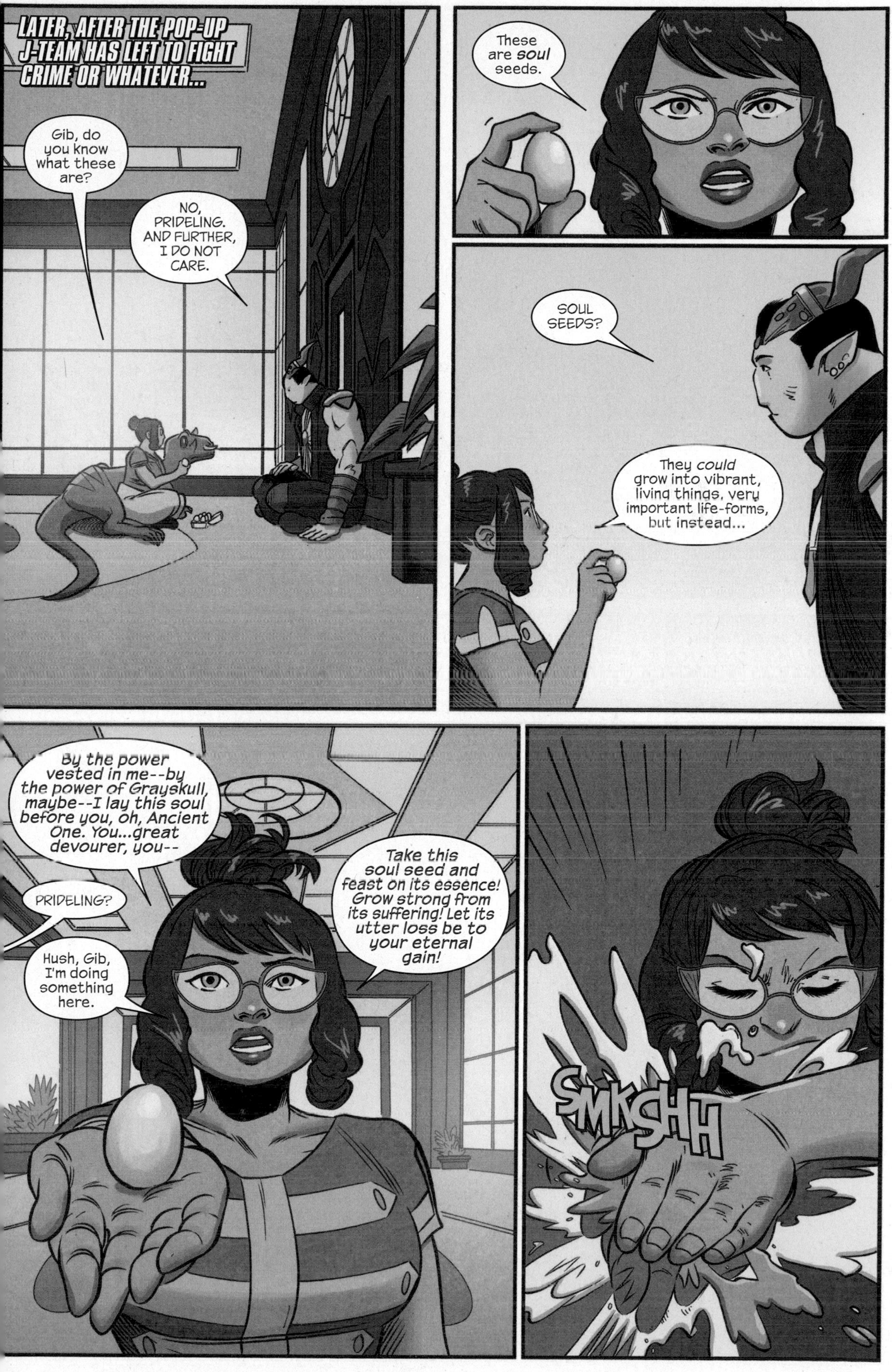
LATER, AFTER THE POP-UP J-TEAM HAS LEFT TO FIGHT CRIME OR WHATEVER...
Gib, do you know what these are?
NO, PRIDELING. AND FURTHER, I DO NOT CARE.
These are soul seeds.
SOUL SEEDS?
They could grow into vibrant, living things, very important life-forms, but instead...
By the power vested in me--by the power of Grayskull, maybe--I lay this soul before you, oh, Ancient One. You...great devourer, you--
PRIDELING?
Hush, Gib, I'm doing something here.
Take this soul seed and feast on its essence! Grow strong from its suffering! Let its utter loss be to your eternal gain!
SMKSHH

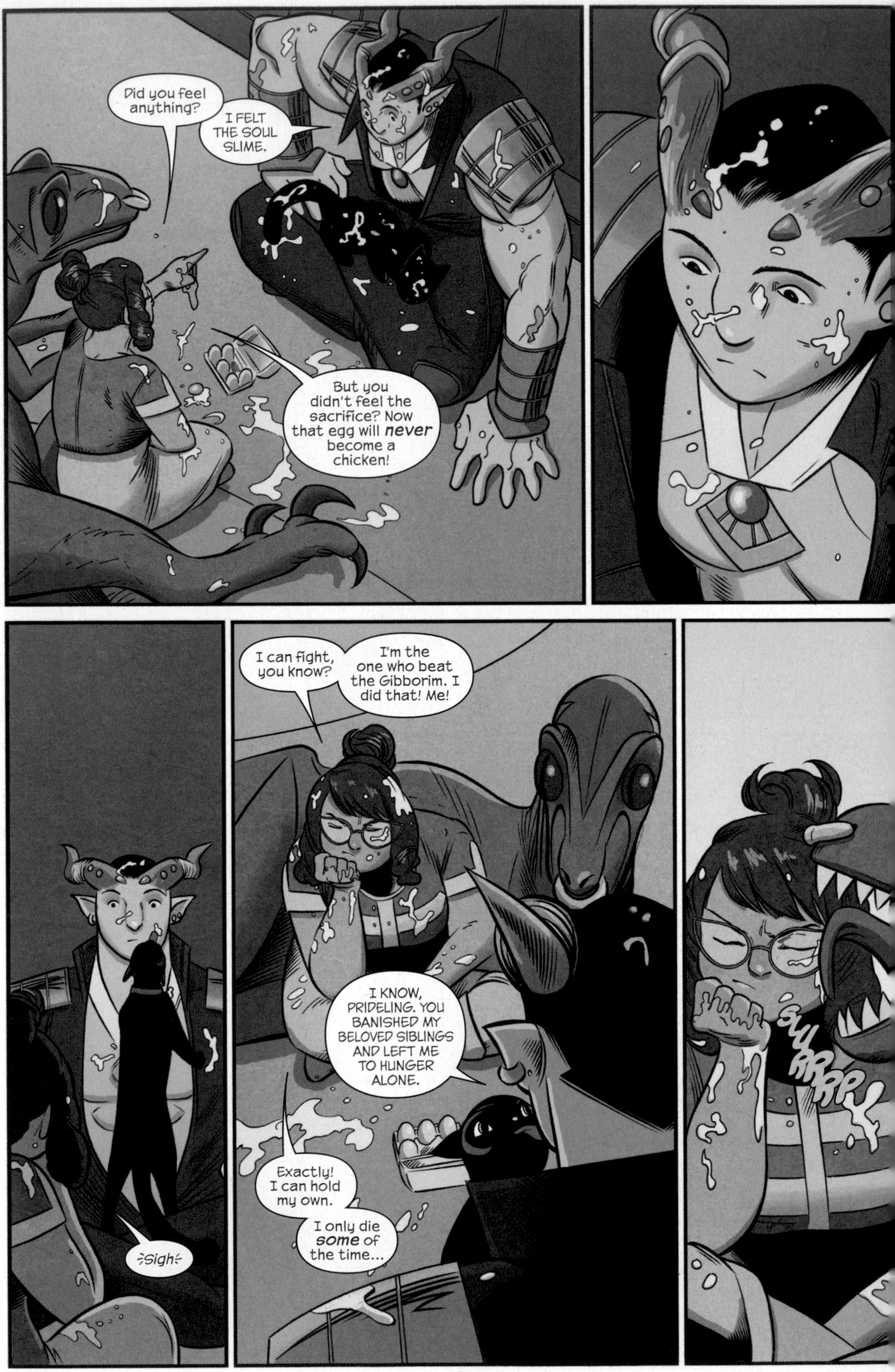

Did you feel anything?
I FELT THE SOUL SLIME.
But you didn't feel the sacrifice? Now that egg will *never* become a chicken!
I can fight, you know?
I'm the one who beat the Gibborim. I did that! Me!
I KNOW, PRIDELING. YOU BANISHED MY BELOVED SIBLINGS AND LEFT ME TO HUNGER ALONE.
Exactly! I can hold my own.
I only die *some* of the time...
Sigh
SLURRRP!

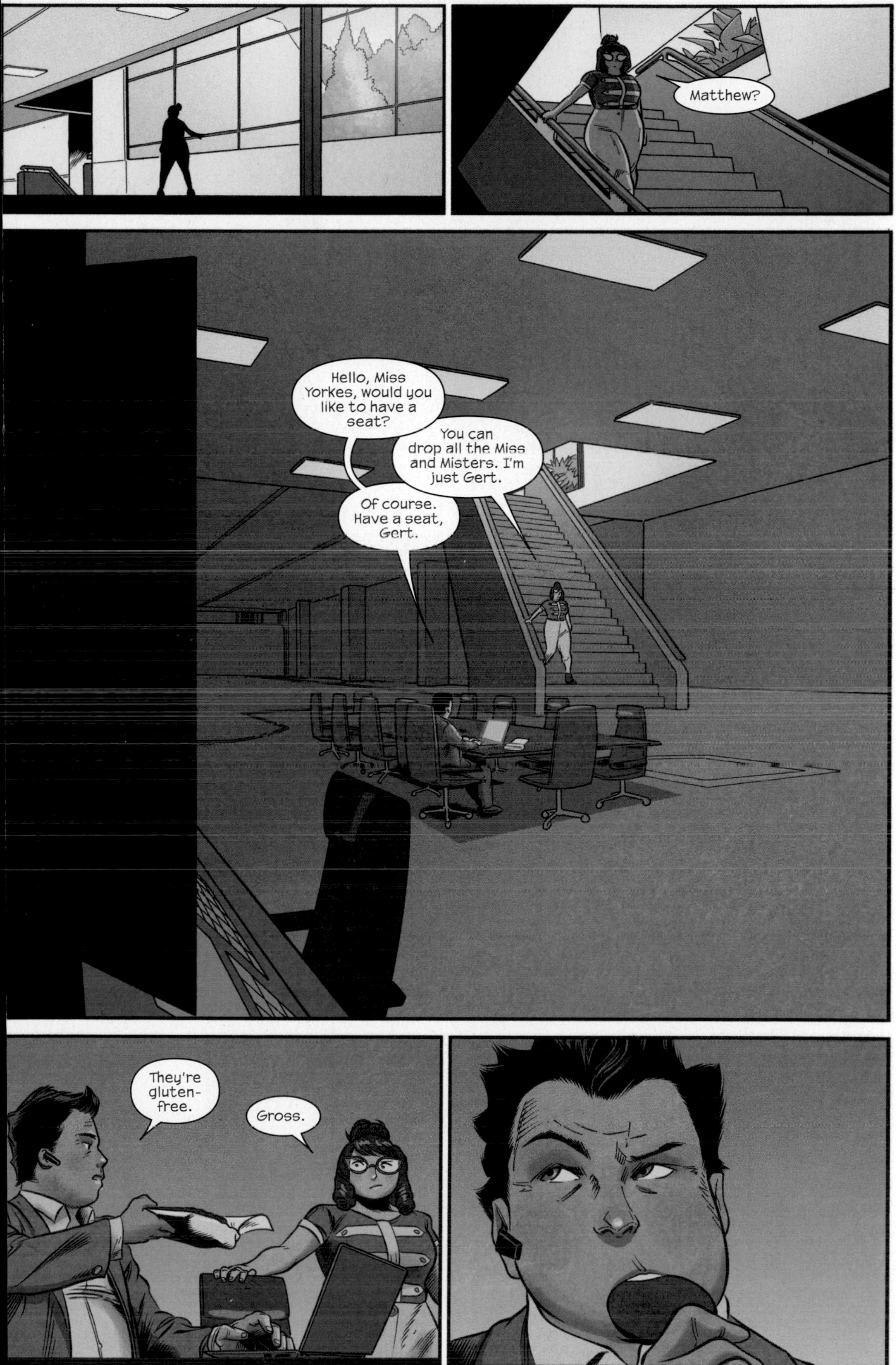
Matthew?
Hello, Miss Yorkes, would you like to have a seat?
You can drop all the Miss and Misters. I'm just Gert.
Of course. Have a seat, Gert.
They're gluten-free.
Gross.

Are you monitoring the mission?

On audio, at the moment.

Why aren't you using HAL 9000 over there?

It's hardly worth turning it on; I can do more on my laptop these days... You could do more on your cell phone.

I don't have a cell phone.

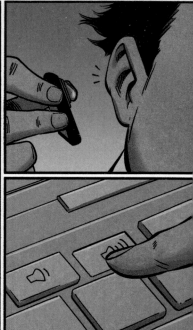

Five minutes from target...

They haven't even started?

Traffic.

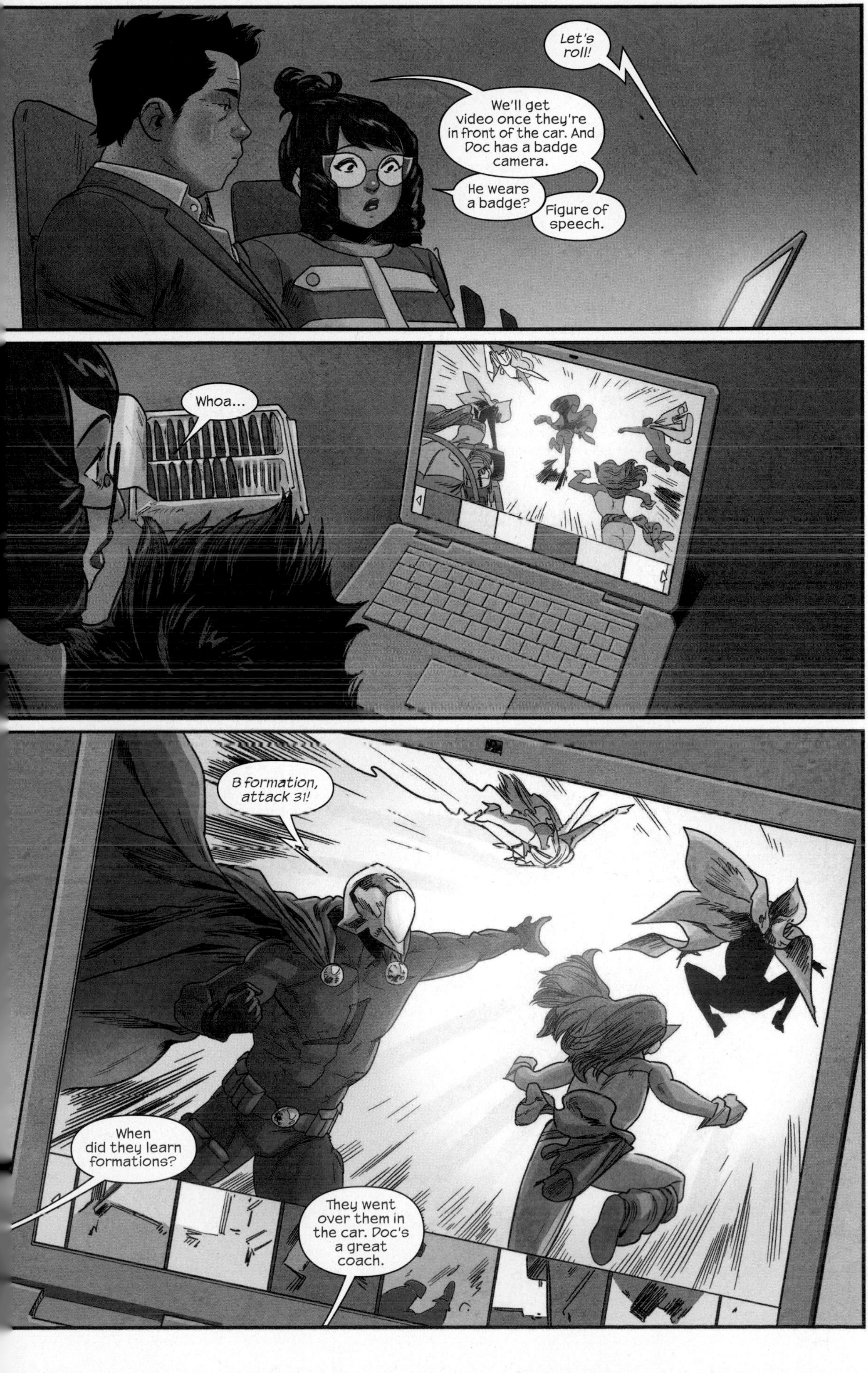
Let's roll!
We'll get video once they're in front of the car. And Doc has a badge camera.
He wears a badge?
Figure of speech.
Whoa...
B formation, attack 31!
When did they learn formations?
They went over them in the car. Doc's a great coach.

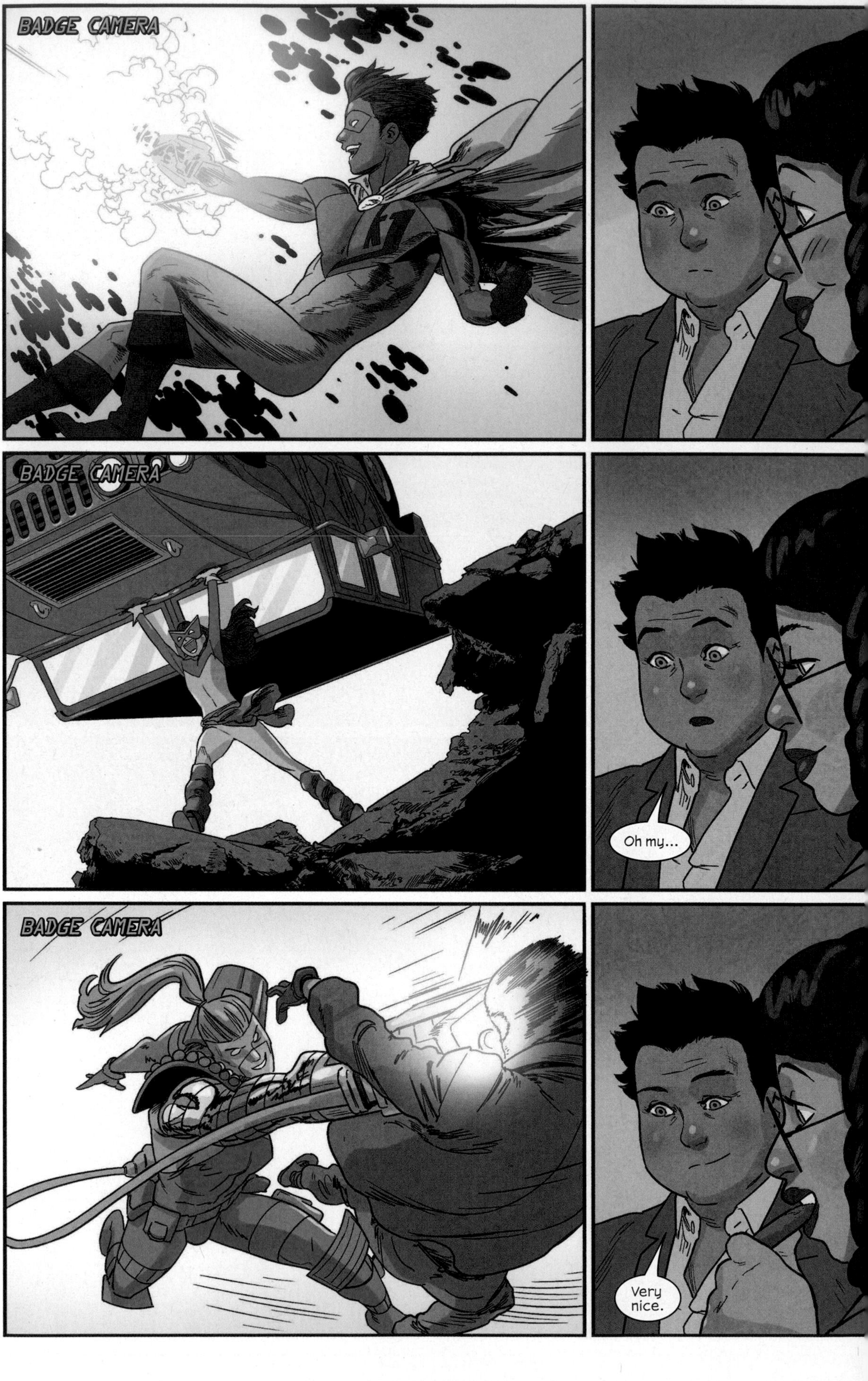
BADGE CAMERA
BADGE CAMERA
Oh my...
BADGE CAMERA
Very nice.

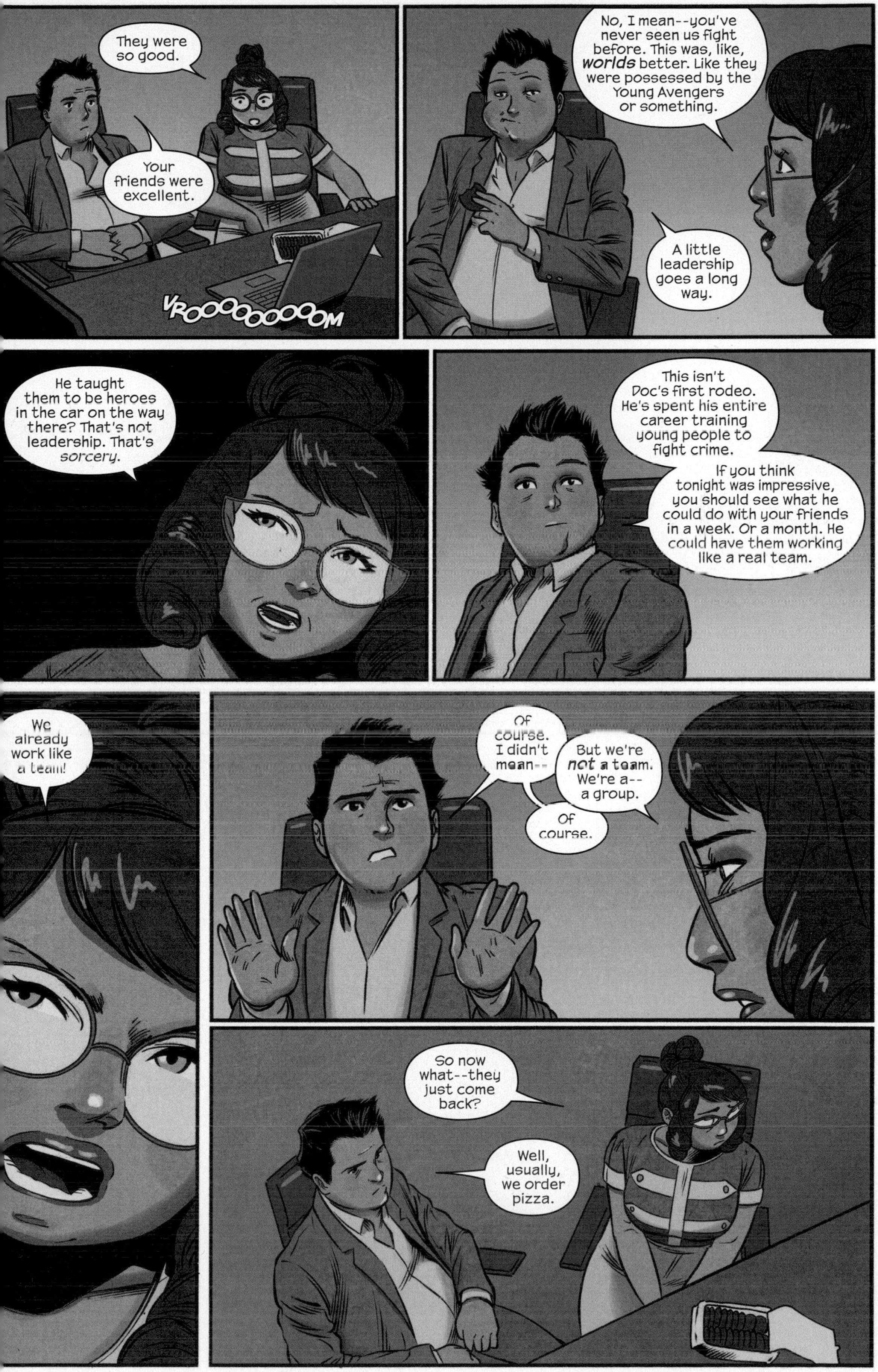

They were so good.
Your friends were excellent.
VROOOOOOOOOM
No, I mean--you've never seen us fight before. This was, like, *worlds* better. Like they were possessed by the Young Avengers or something.
A little leadership goes a long way.
He taught them to be heroes in the car on the way there? That's not leadership. That's *sorcery*.
This isn't Doc's first rodeo. He's spent his entire career training young people to fight crime.
If you think tonight was impressive, you should see what he could do with your friends in a week. Or a month. He could have them working like a real team.
We already work like a team!
Of course. I didn't mean--
But we're *not* a team. We're a-- a group.
Of course.
So now what--they just come back?
Well, usually, we order pizza.

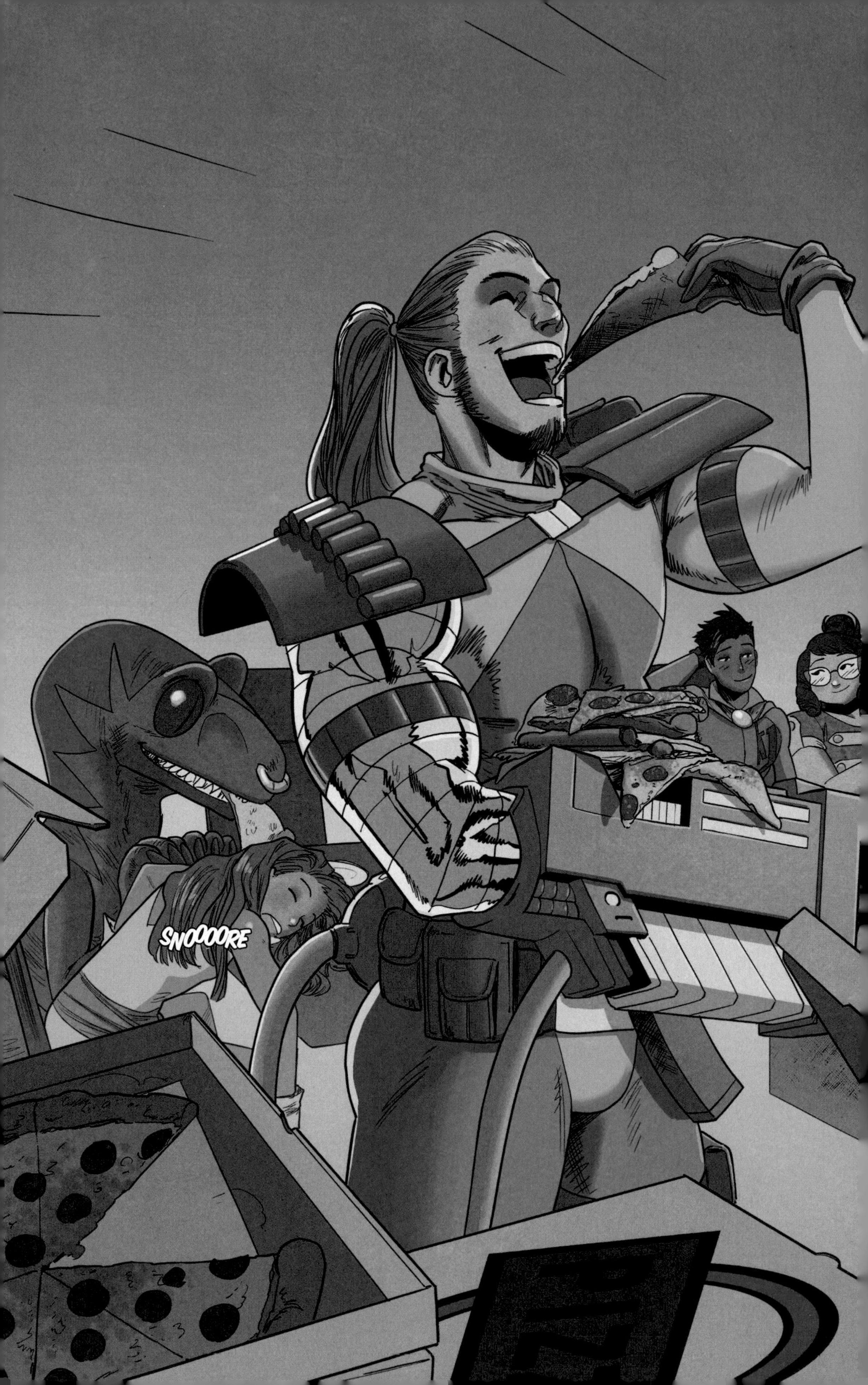
SNOOOORE

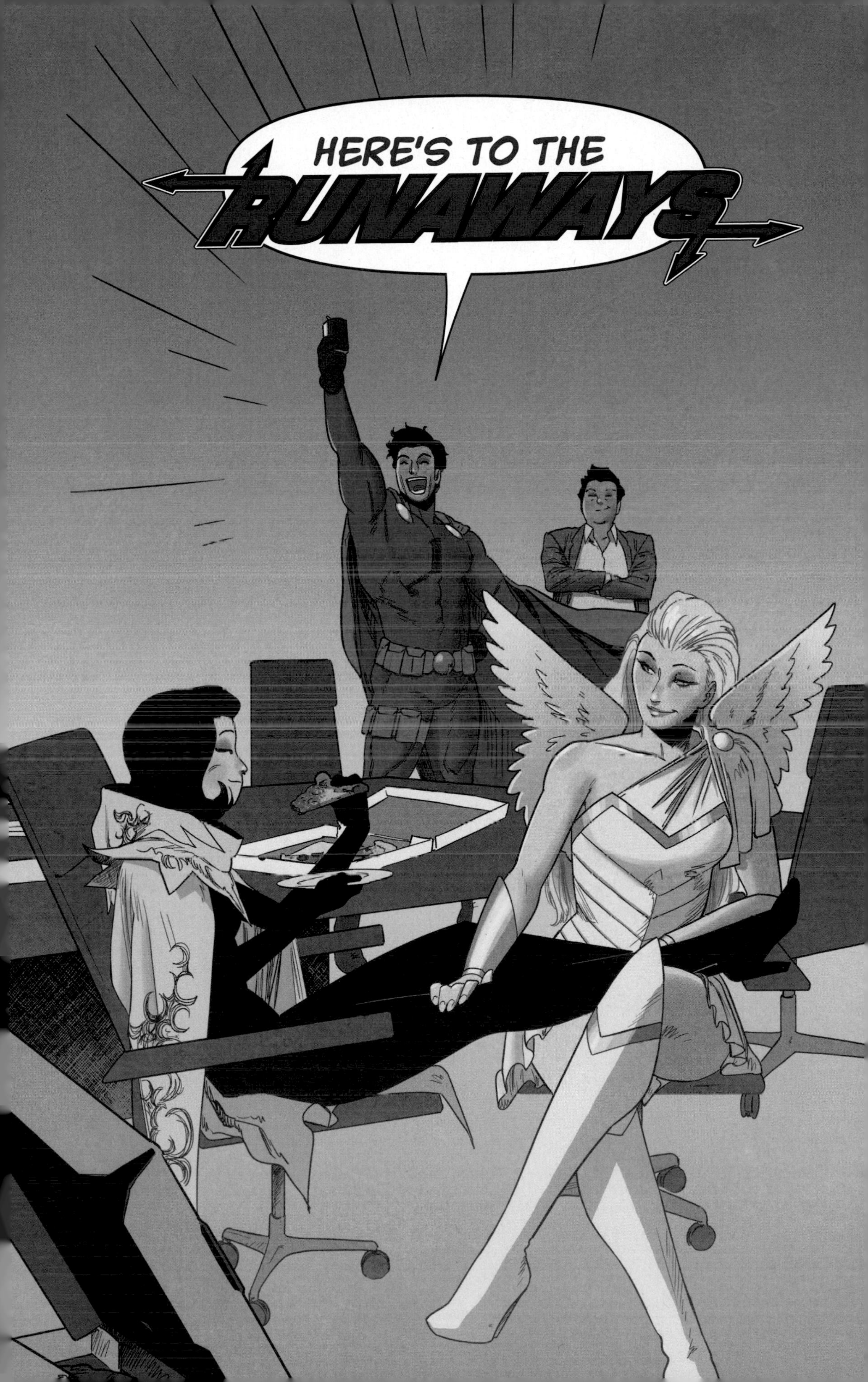
HERE'S TO THE RUNAWAYS

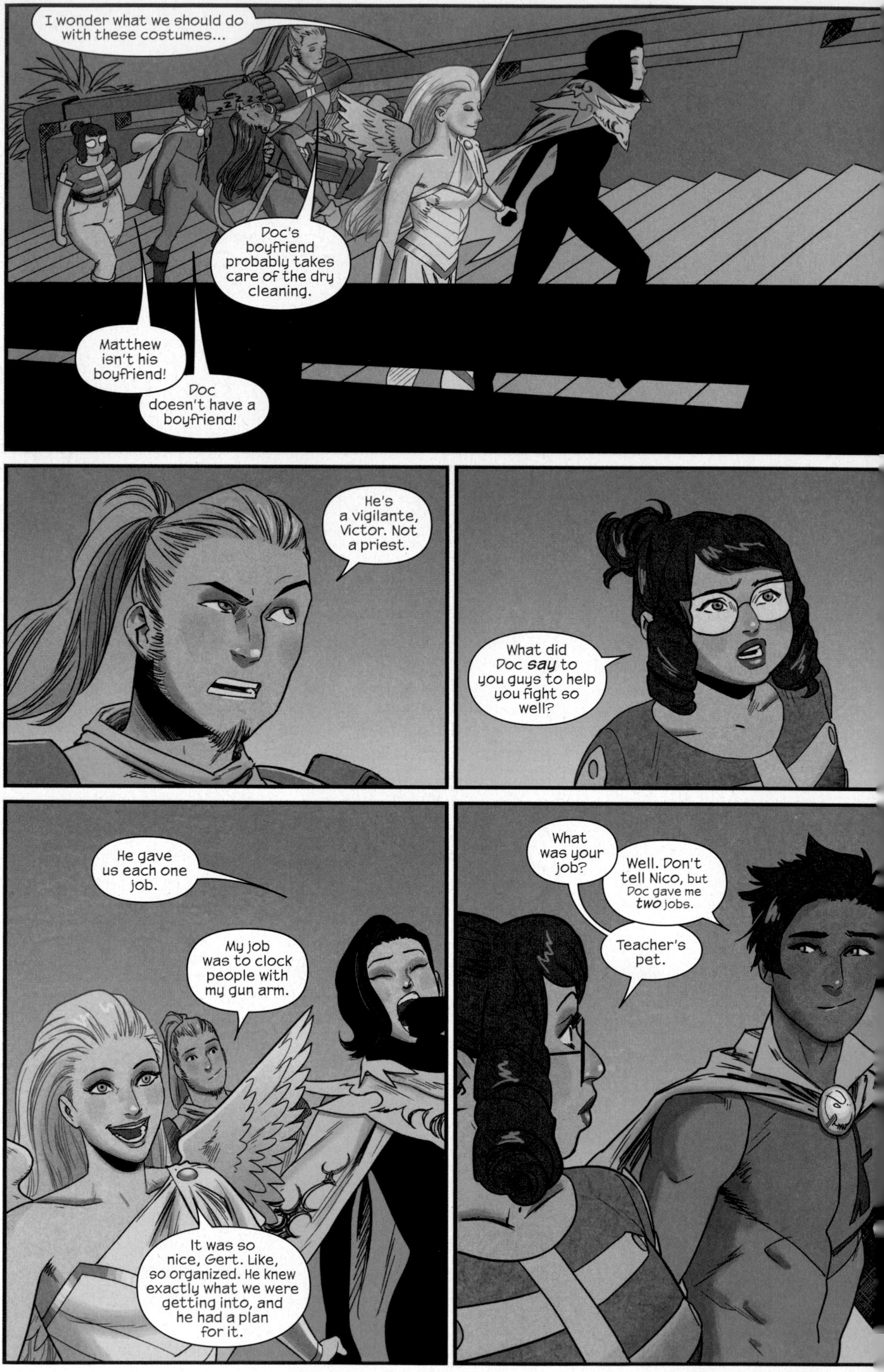
I wonder what we should do with these costumes...
Doc's boyfriend probably takes care of the dry cleaning.
Matthew isn't his boyfriend!
Doc doesn't have a boyfriend!
He's a vigilante, Victor. Not a priest.
What did Doc say to you guys to help you fight so well?
He gave us each one job.
My job was to clock people with my gun arm.
It was so nice, Gert. Like, so organized. He knew exactly what we were getting into, and he had a plan for it.
What was your job?
Well. Don't tell Nico, but Doc gave me two jobs.
Teacher's pet.

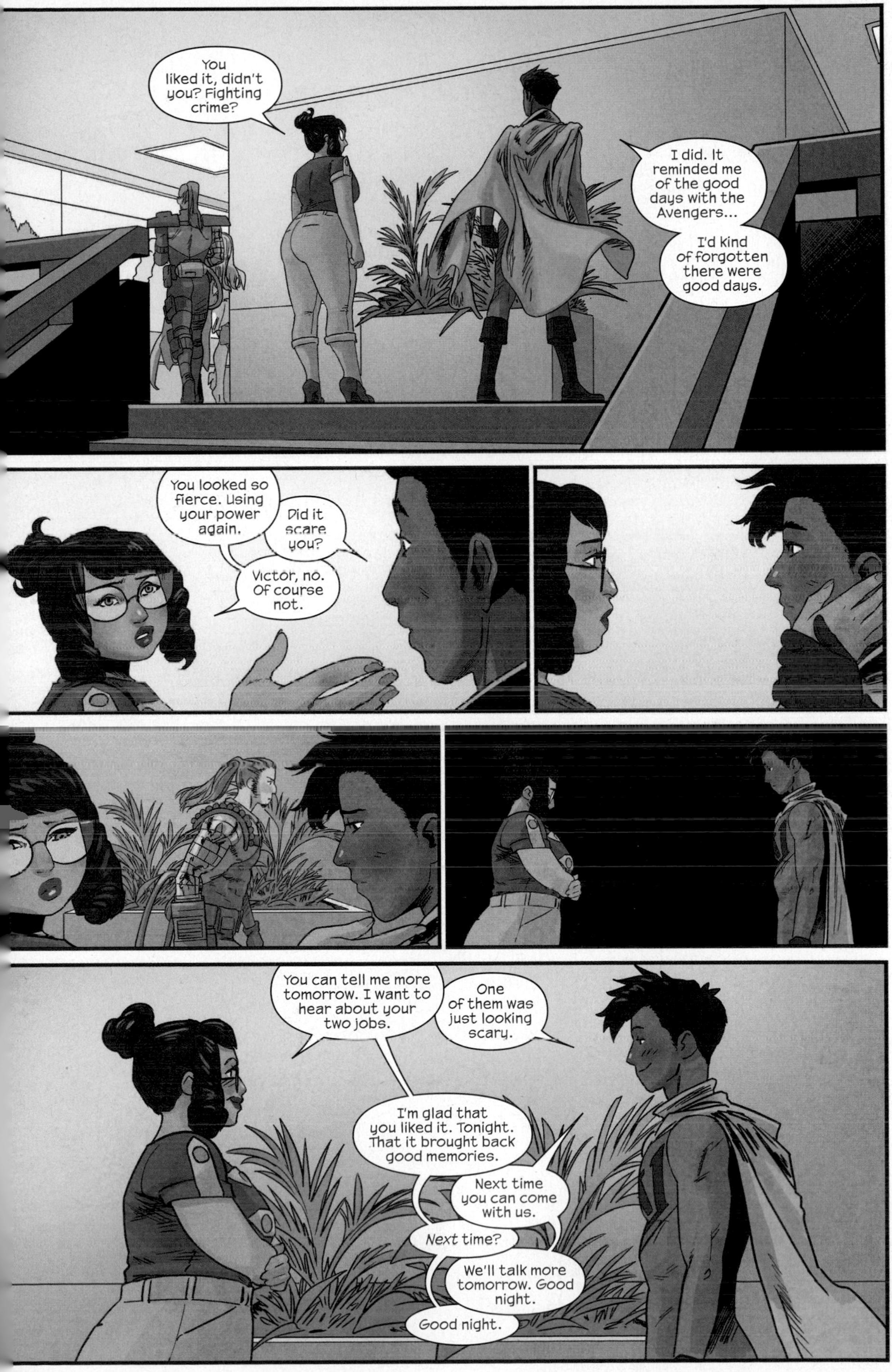
You liked it, didn't you? Fighting crime?
I did. It reminded me of the good days with the Avengers...
I'd kind of forgotten there were good days.
You looked so fierce. Using your power again.
Did it scare you?
Victor, no. Of course not.
You can tell me more tomorrow. I want to hear about your two jobs.
One of them was just looking scary.
I'm glad that you liked it. Tonight. That it brought back good memories.
Next time you can come with us.
Next time?
We'll talk more tomorrow. Good night.
Good night.

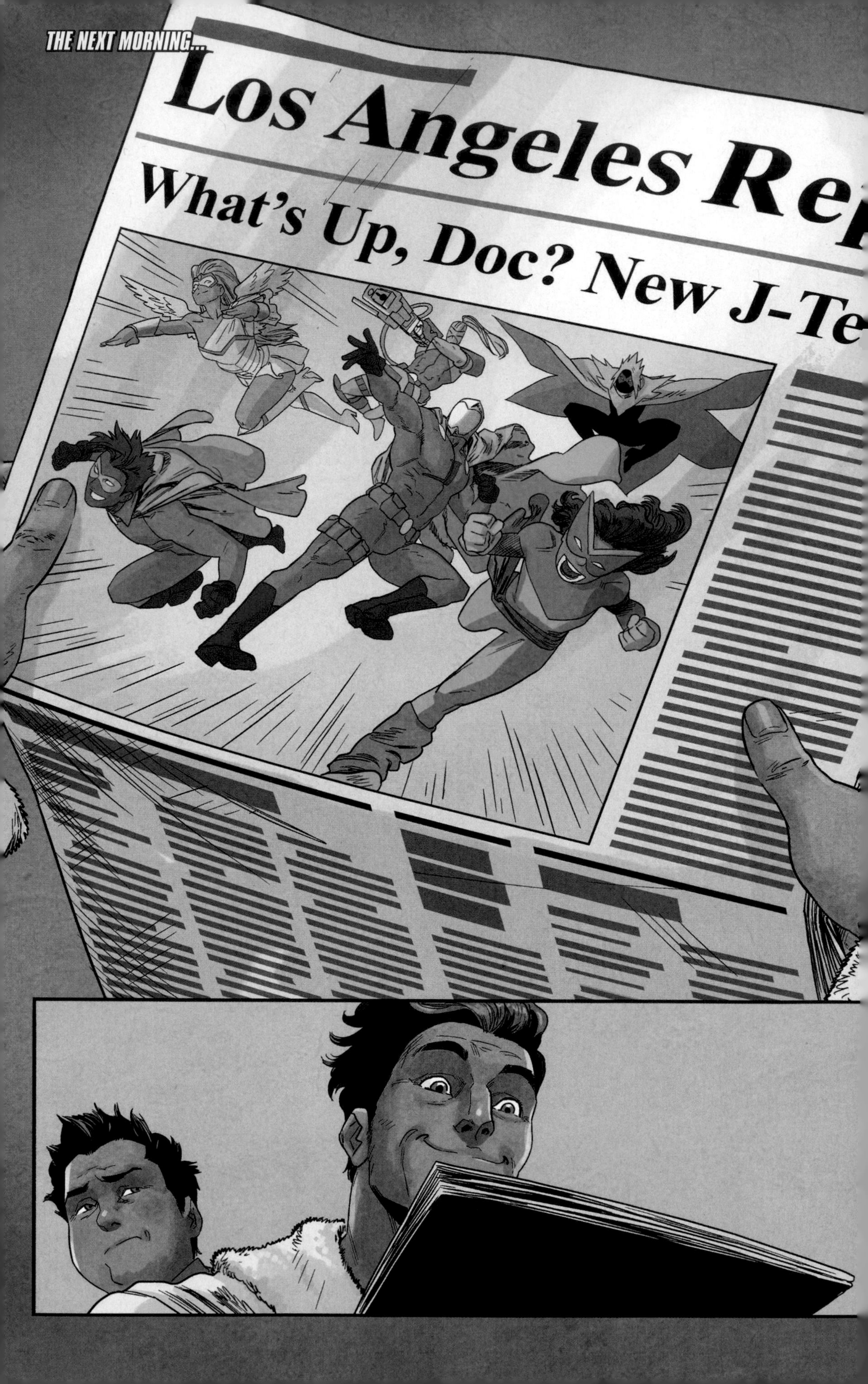
THE NEXT MORNING...
Los Angeles Re
What's Up, Doc? New J-Te

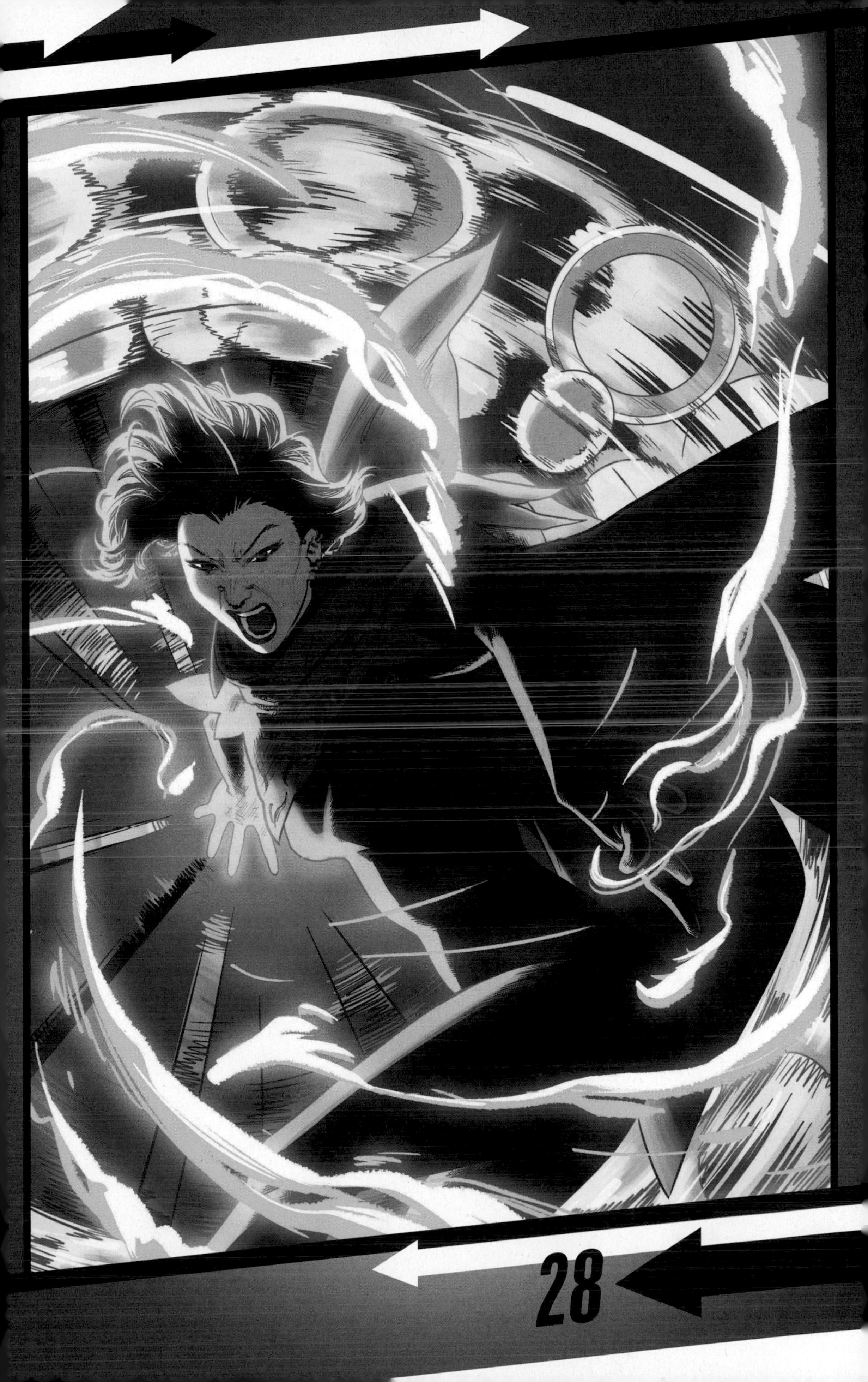

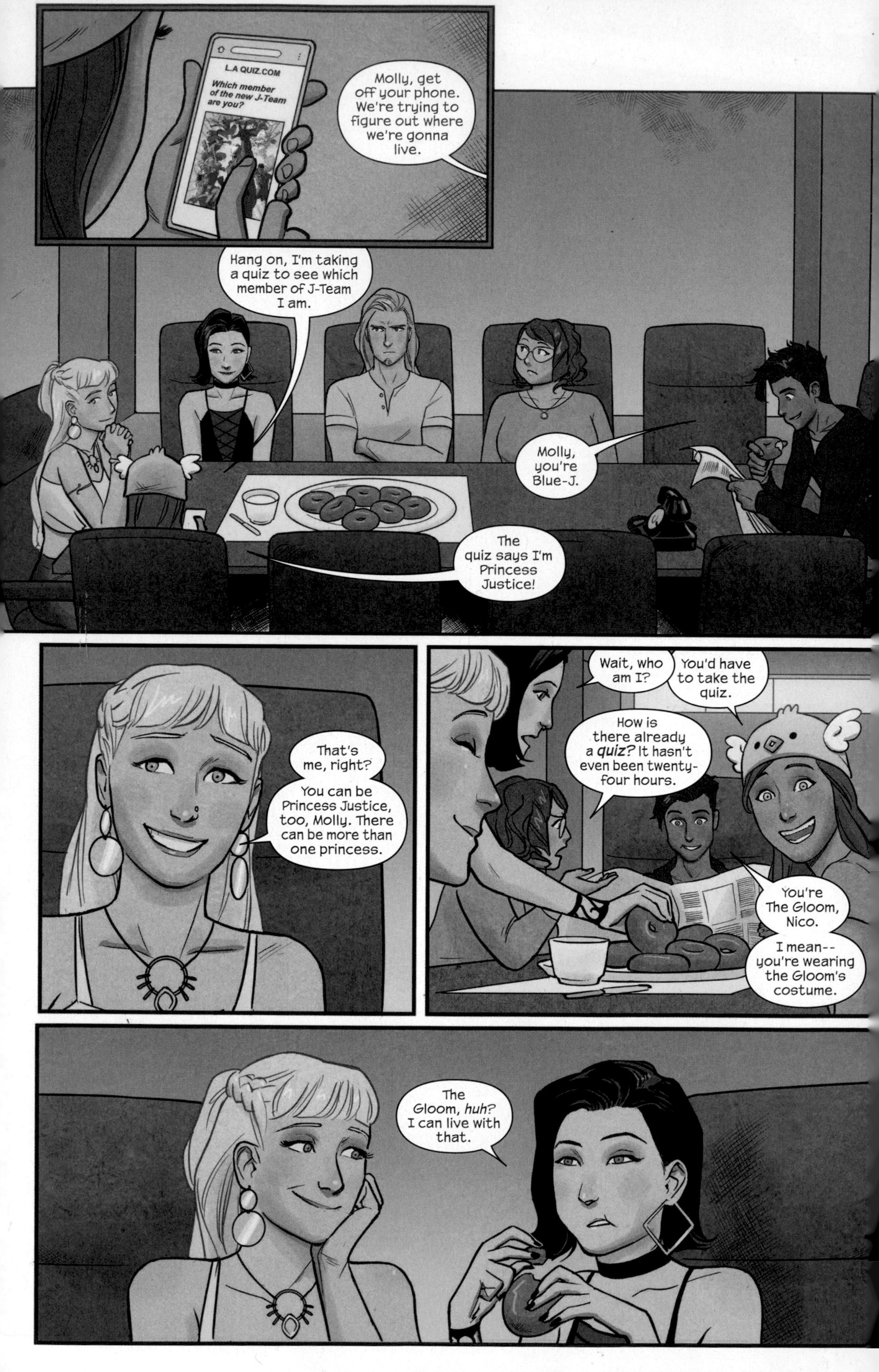
L.A QUIZ.COM
Which member of the new J-Team are you?
Molly, get off your phone. We're trying to figure out where we're gonna live.
Hang on, I'm taking a quiz to see which member of J-Team I am.
Molly, you're Blue-J.
The quiz says I'm Princess Justice!
That's me, right?
You can be Princess Justice, too, Molly. There can be more than one princess.
Wait, who am I?
You'd have to take the quiz.
How is there already a *quiz?* It hasn't even been twenty-four hours.
You're The Gloom, Nico.
I mean-- you're wearing the Gloom's costume.
The Gloom, *huh?* I can live with that.

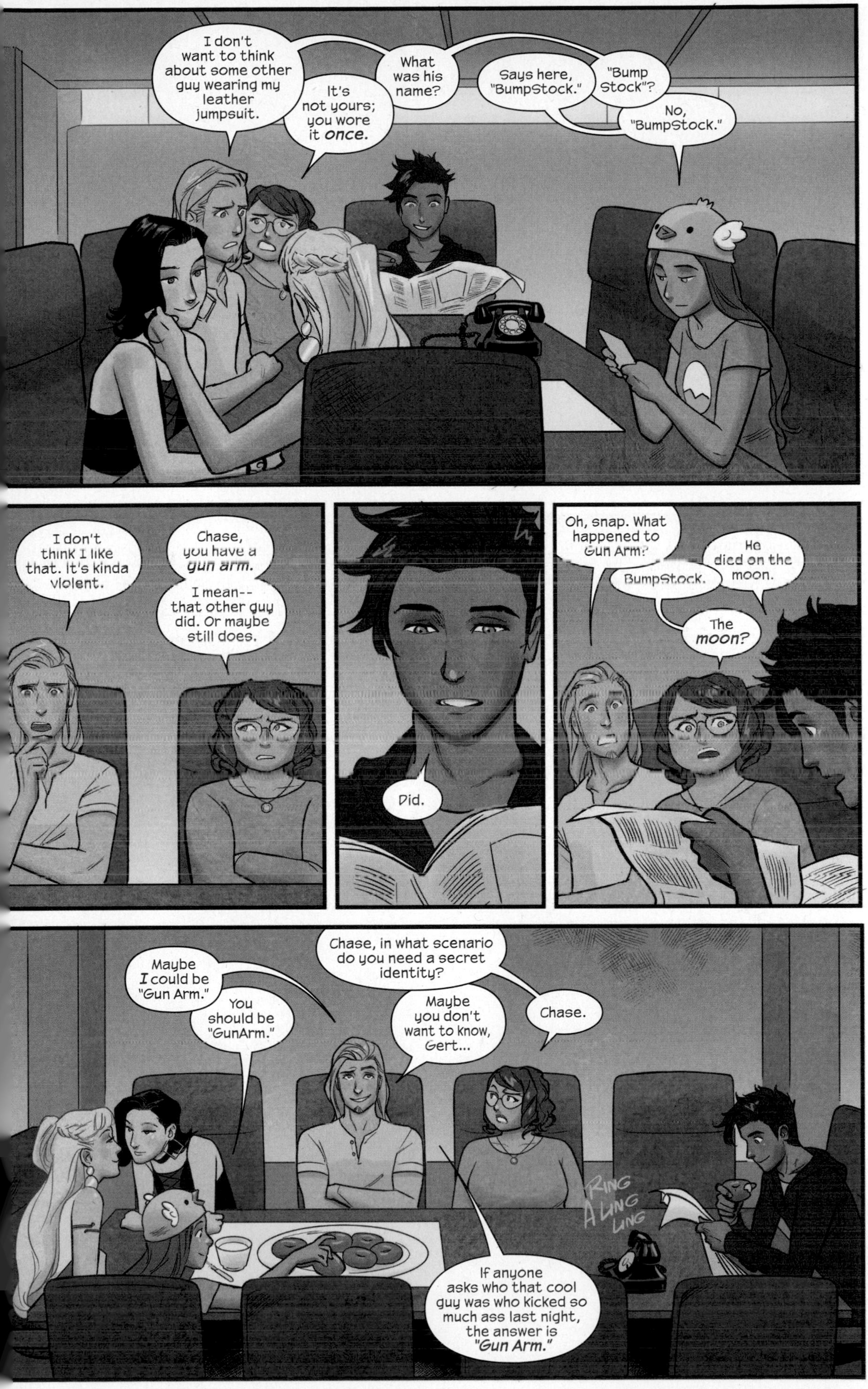

I don't want to think about some other guy wearing my leather jumpsuit.
It's not yours; you wore it *once.*
What was his name?
Says here, "BumpStock."
"Bump Stock"?
No, "BumpStock."
I don't think I like that. It's kinda violent.
Chase, you have a *gun arm.*
I mean-- that other guy did. Or maybe still does.
Did.
Oh, snap. What happened to Gun Arm?
BumpStock.
He died on the moon.
The *moon?*
Maybe *I* could be "Gun Arm."
You should be "GunArm."
Chase, in what scenario do you need a secret identity?
Maybe you don't want to know, Gert...
Chase.
RING A LING LING
If anyone asks who that cool guy was who kicked so much ass last night, the answer is *"Gun Arm."*

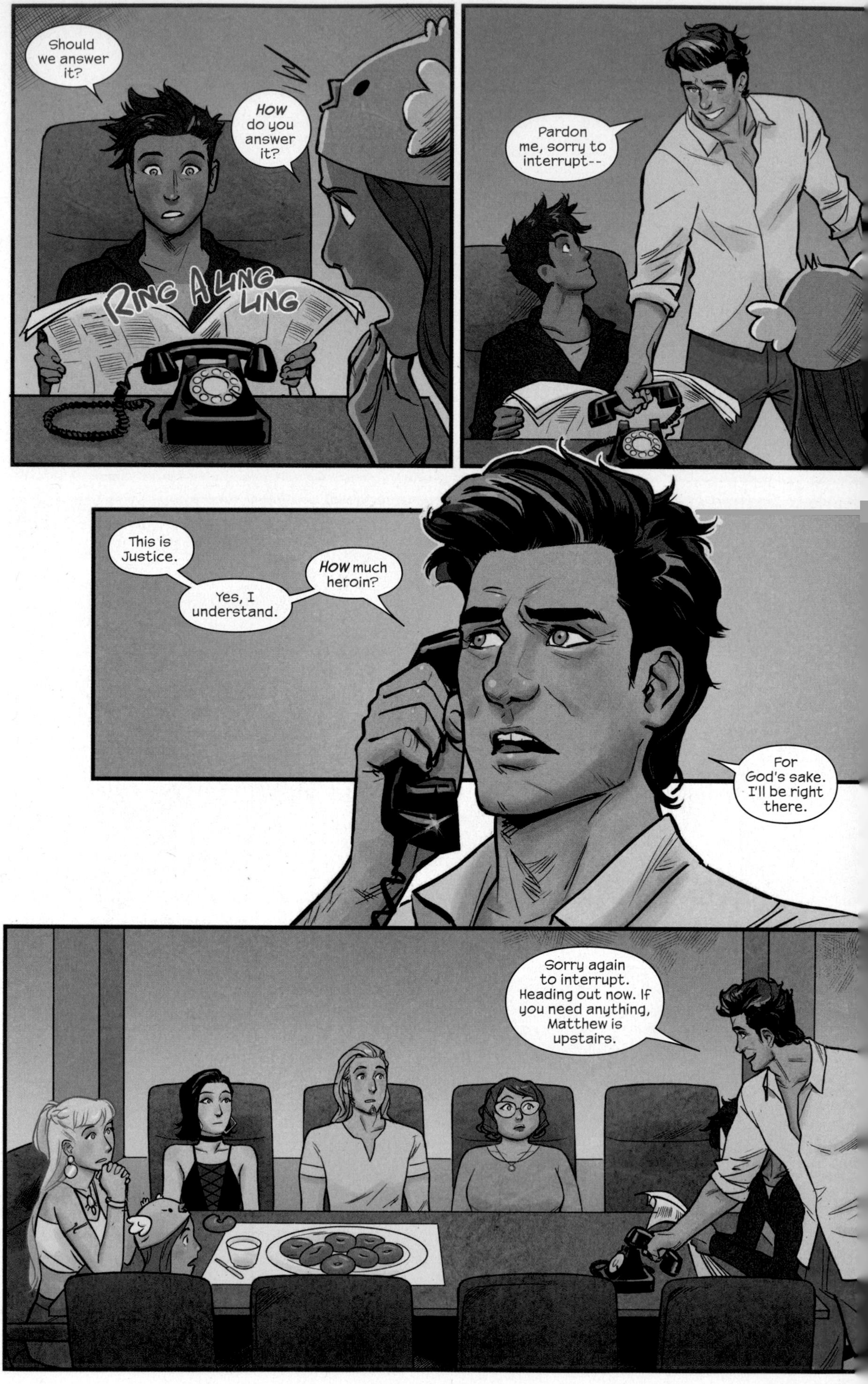

Should we answer it?
HOW do you answer it?
RING A LING LING
Pardon me, sorry to interrupt--
This is Justice.
Yes, I understand.
HOW much heroin?
For God's sake. I'll be right there.
Sorry again to interrupt. Heading out now. If you need anything, Matthew is upstairs.

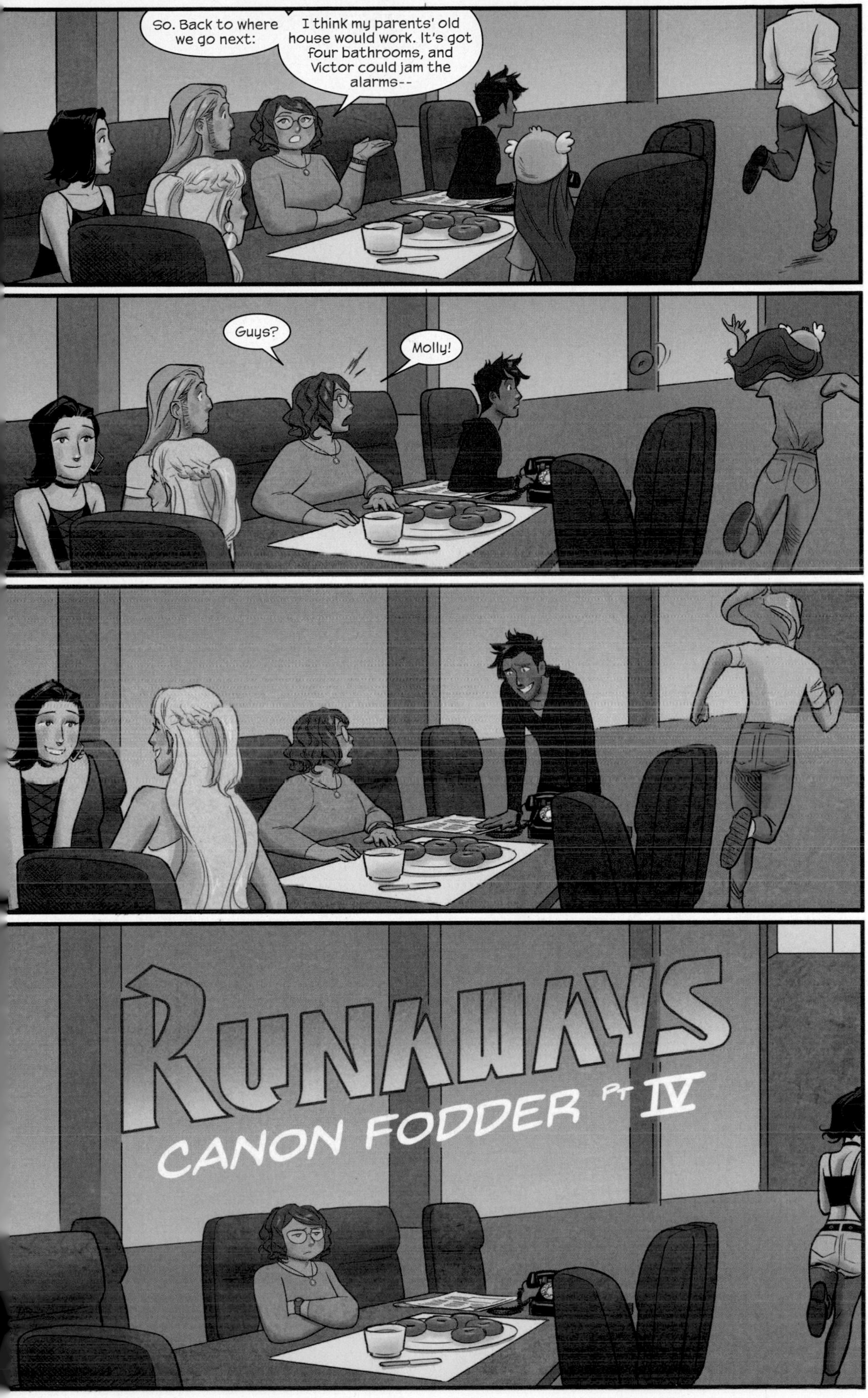
So. Back to where we go next:
I think my parents' old house would work. It's got four bathrooms, and Victor could jam the alarms--
Guys?
Molly!
RUNAWAYS
CANON FODDER PT IV

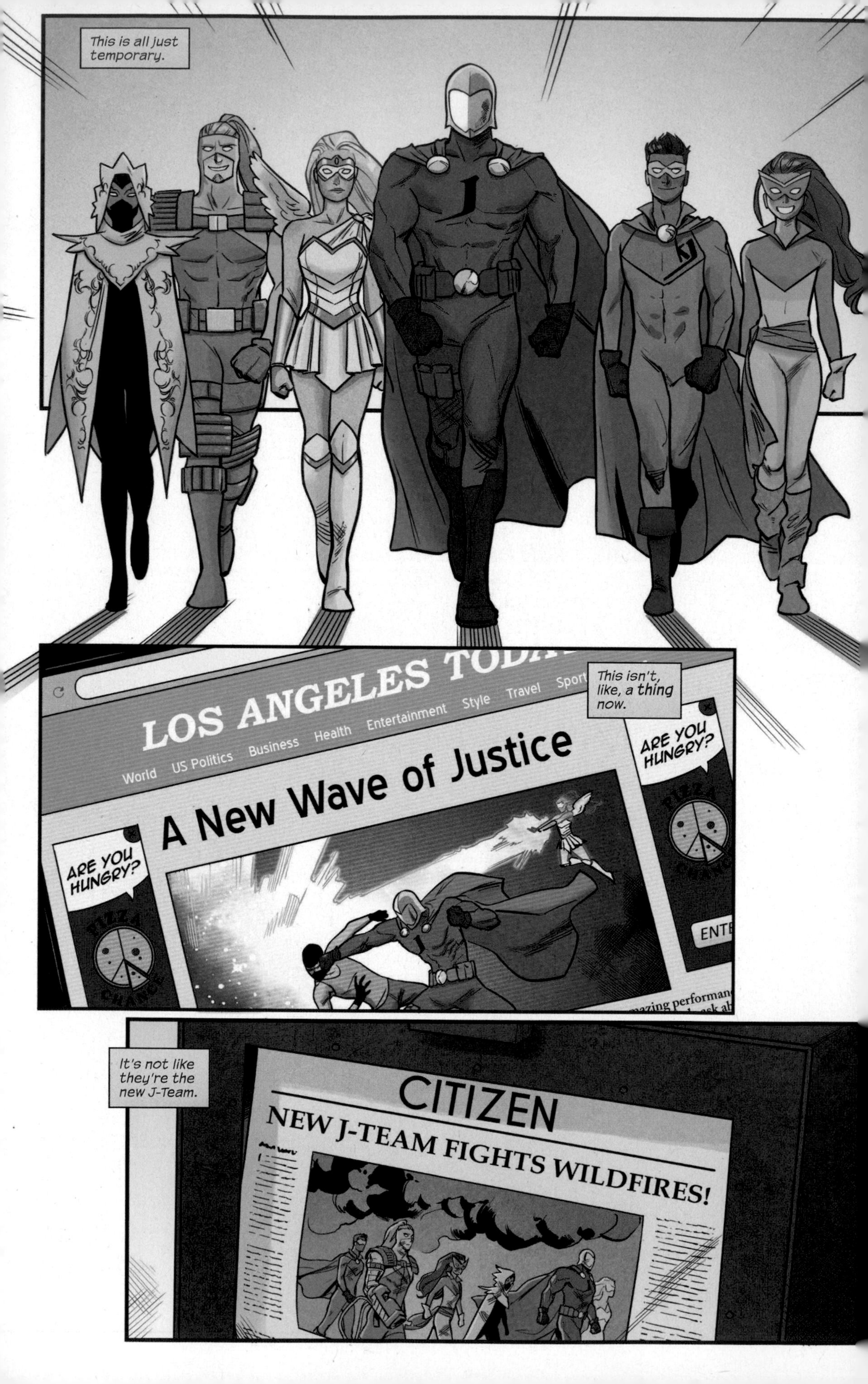
This is all just temporary.
LOS ANGELES TODA
World US Politics Business Health Entertainment Style Travel Sport
This isn't, like, a thing now.
A New Wave of Justice
ARE YOU HUNGRY?
PIZZA CHANCE
ARE YOU HUNGRY?
It's not like they're the new J-Team.
CITIZEN
NEW J-TEAM FIGHTS WILDFIRES!

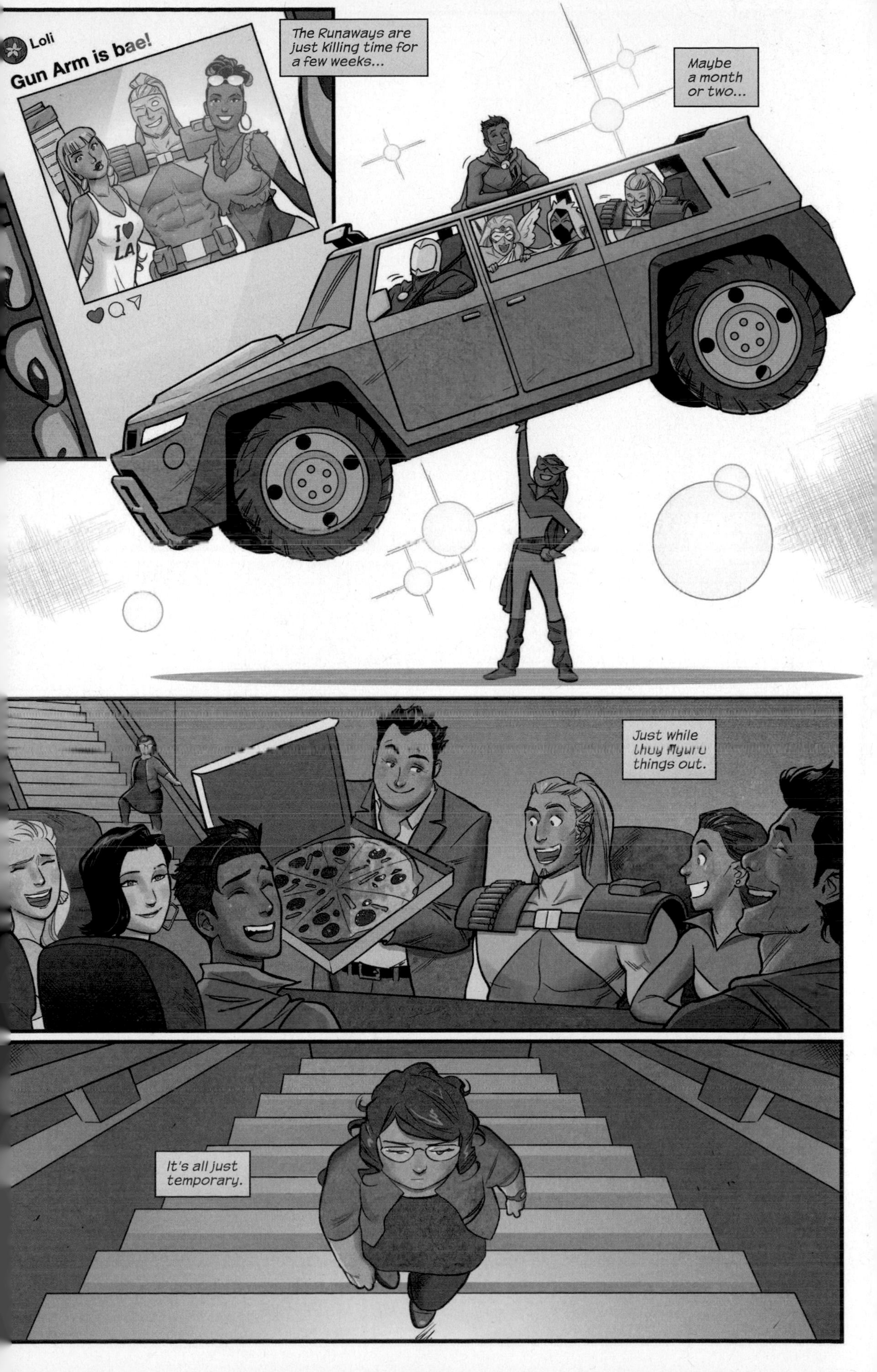
Loli
Gun Arm is bae!
I ♥ LA
The Runaways are just killing time for a few weeks...
Maybe a month or two...
Just while they figure things out.
It's all just temporary.

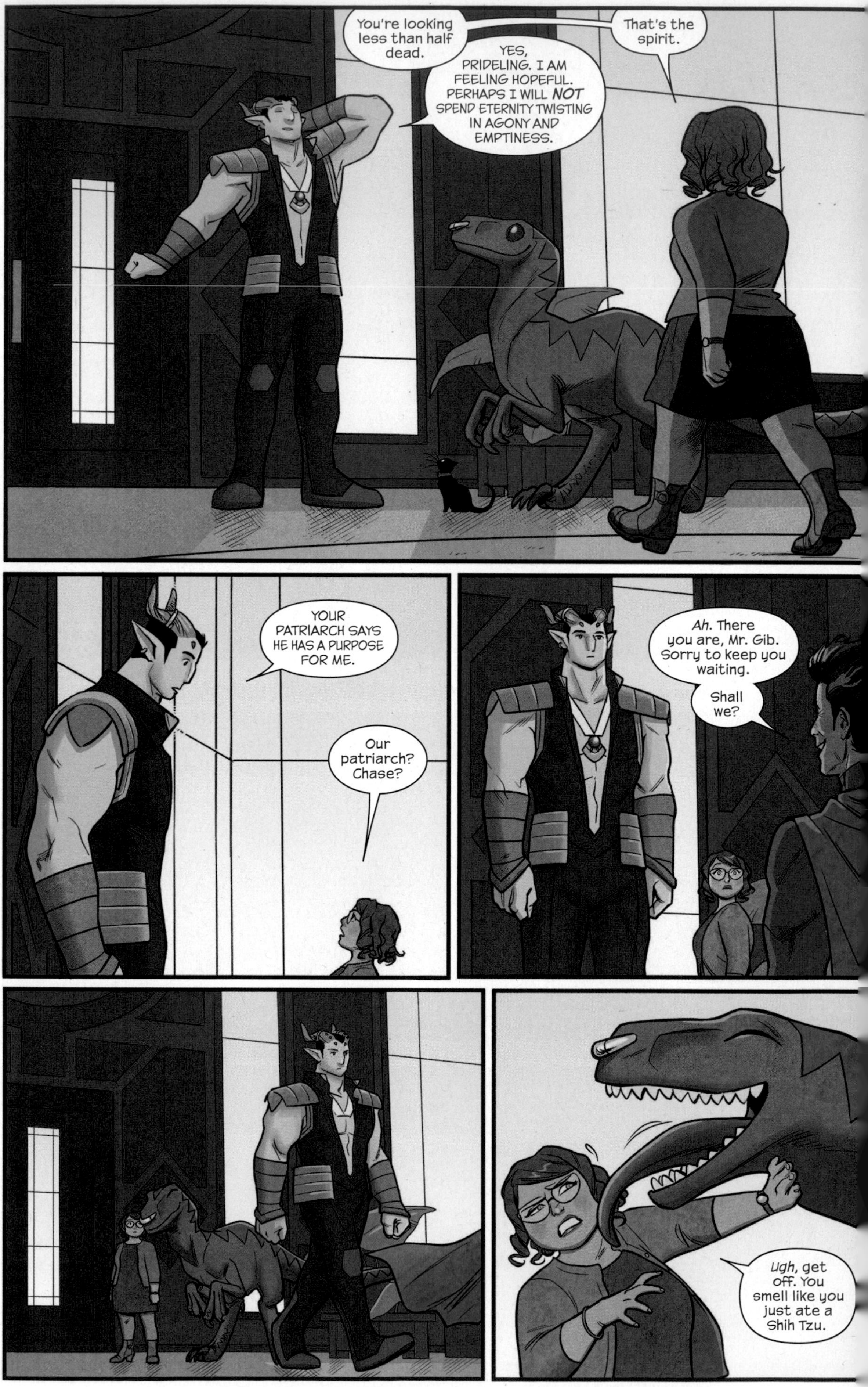

You're looking less than half dead.
YES, PRIDELING. I AM FEELING HOPEFUL. PERHAPS I WILL *NOT* SPEND ETERNITY TWISTING IN AGONY AND EMPTINESS.
That's the spirit.
YOUR PATRIARCH SAYS HE HAS A PURPOSE FOR ME.
Our patriarch? Chase?
Ah. There you are, Mr. Gib. Sorry to keep you waiting.
Shall we?
Ugh, get off. You smell like you just ate a Shih Tzu.

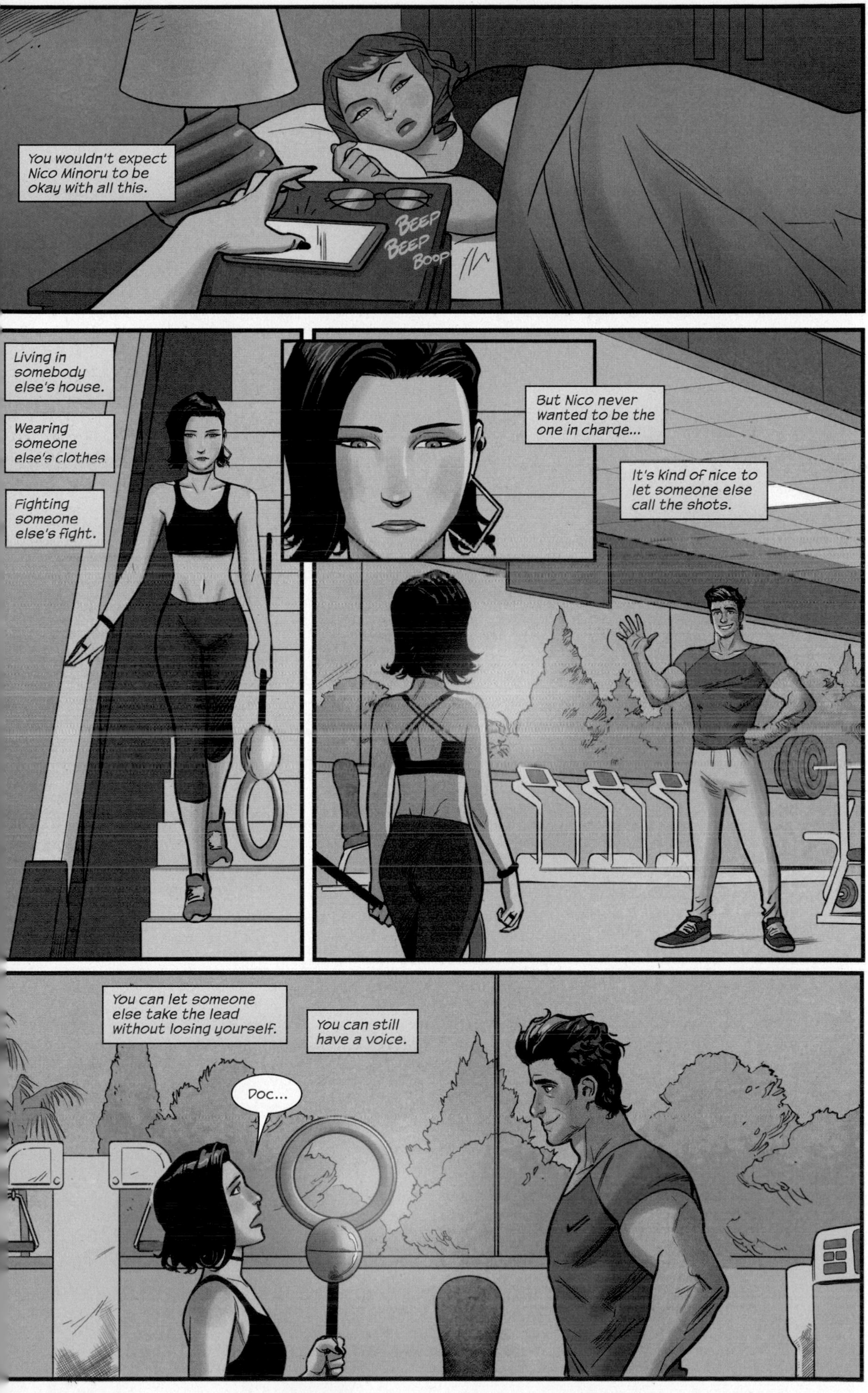
You wouldn't expect Nico Minoru to be okay with all this.
BEEP BEEP BOOP
Living in somebody else's house.
Wearing someone else's clothes.
Fighting someone else's fight.
But Nico never wanted to be the one in charge...
It's kind of nice to let someone else call the shots.
You can let someone else take the lead without losing yourself.
You can still have a voice.
Doc...

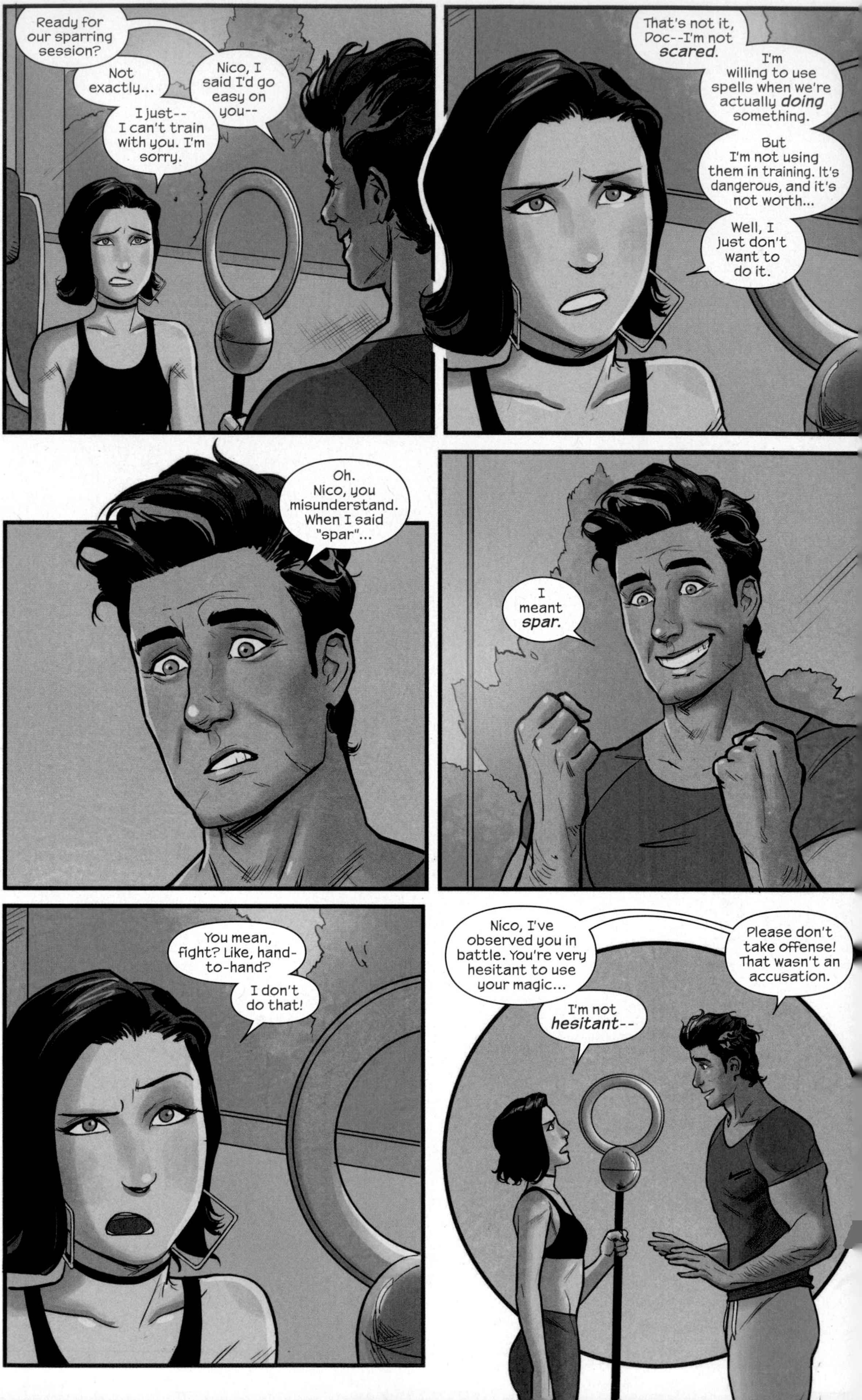
Ready for our sparring session?
Not exactly...
I just-- I can't train with you. I'm sorry.
Nico, I said I'd go easy on you--
That's not it, Doc--I'm not scared.
I'm willing to use spells when we're actually doing something.
But I'm not using them in training. It's dangerous, and it's not worth...
Well, I just don't want to do it.
Oh. Nico, you misunderstand. When I said "spar"...
I meant spar.
You mean, fight? Like, hand-to-hand?
I don't do that!
Nico, I've observed you in battle. You're very hesitant to use your magic...
I'm not hesitant--
Please don't take offense! That wasn't an accusation.

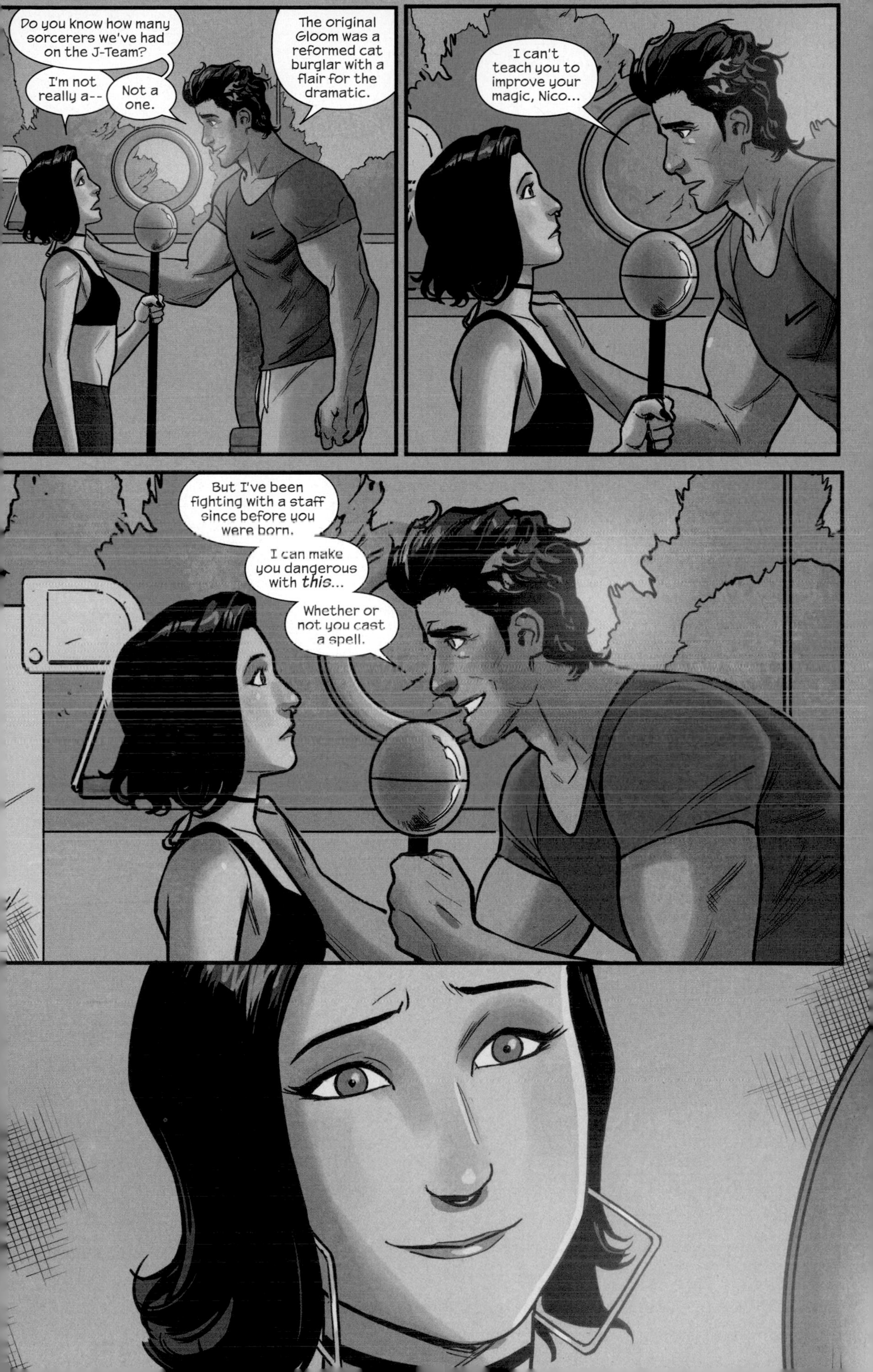
Do you know how many sorcerers we've had on the J-Team?
I'm not really a--
Not a one.
The original Gloom was a reformed cat burglar with a flair for the dramatic.
I can't teach you to improve your magic, Nico...
But I've been fighting with a staff since before you were born.
I can make you dangerous with *this*...
Whether or not you cast a spell.

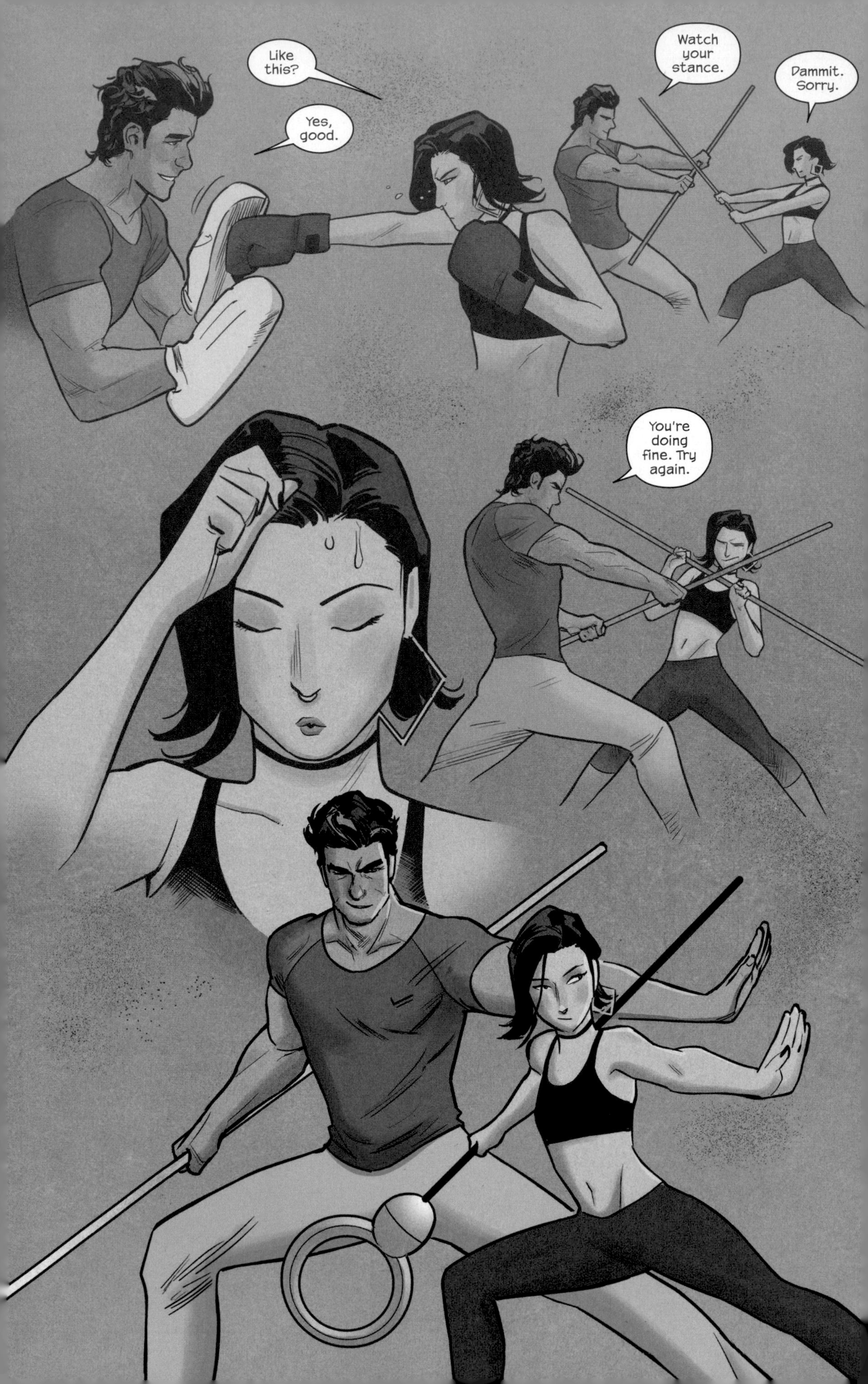

Like this?
Yes, good.
Watch your stance.
Dammit. Sorry.
You're doing fine. Try again.

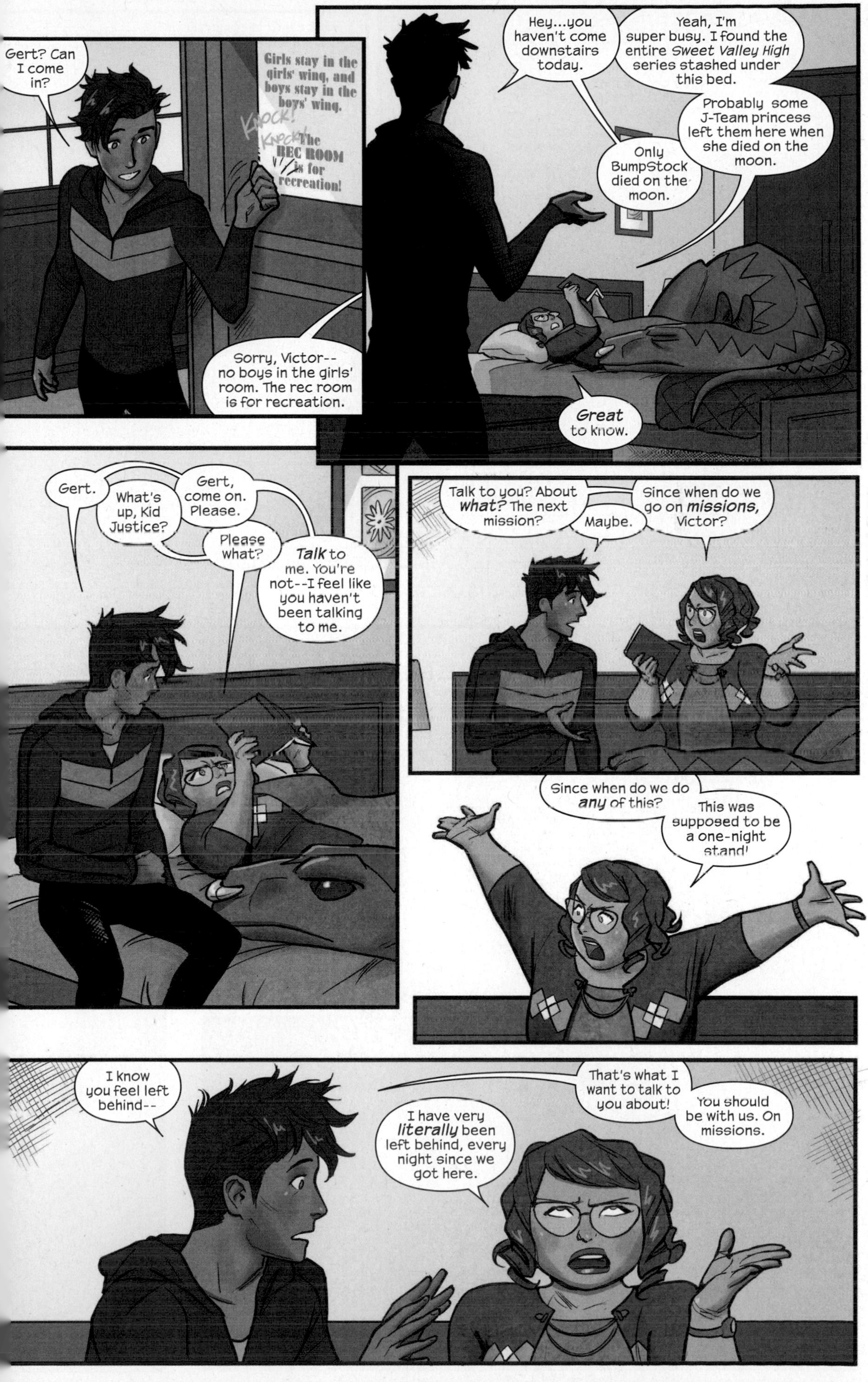
Gert? Can I come in?
Girls stay in the girls' wing, and boys stay in the boys' wing. The REC ROOM is for recreation!
KNOCK! KNOCK!
Sorry, Victor--no boys in the girls' room. The rec room is for recreation.
Hey...you haven't come downstairs today.
Yeah, I'm super busy. I found the entire Sweet Valley High series stashed under this bed.
Probably some J-Team princess left them here when she died on the moon.
Only BumpStock died on the moon.
Great to know.
Gert.
What's up, Kid Justice?
Gert, come on. Please.
Please what?
Talk to me. You're not--I feel like you haven't been talking to me.
Talk to you? About what? The next mission?
Maybe.
Since when do we go on missions, Victor?
Since when do we do any of this?
This was supposed to be a one-night stand!
I know you feel left behind--
I have very literally been left behind, every night since we got here.
That's what I want to talk to you about!
You should be with us. On missions.

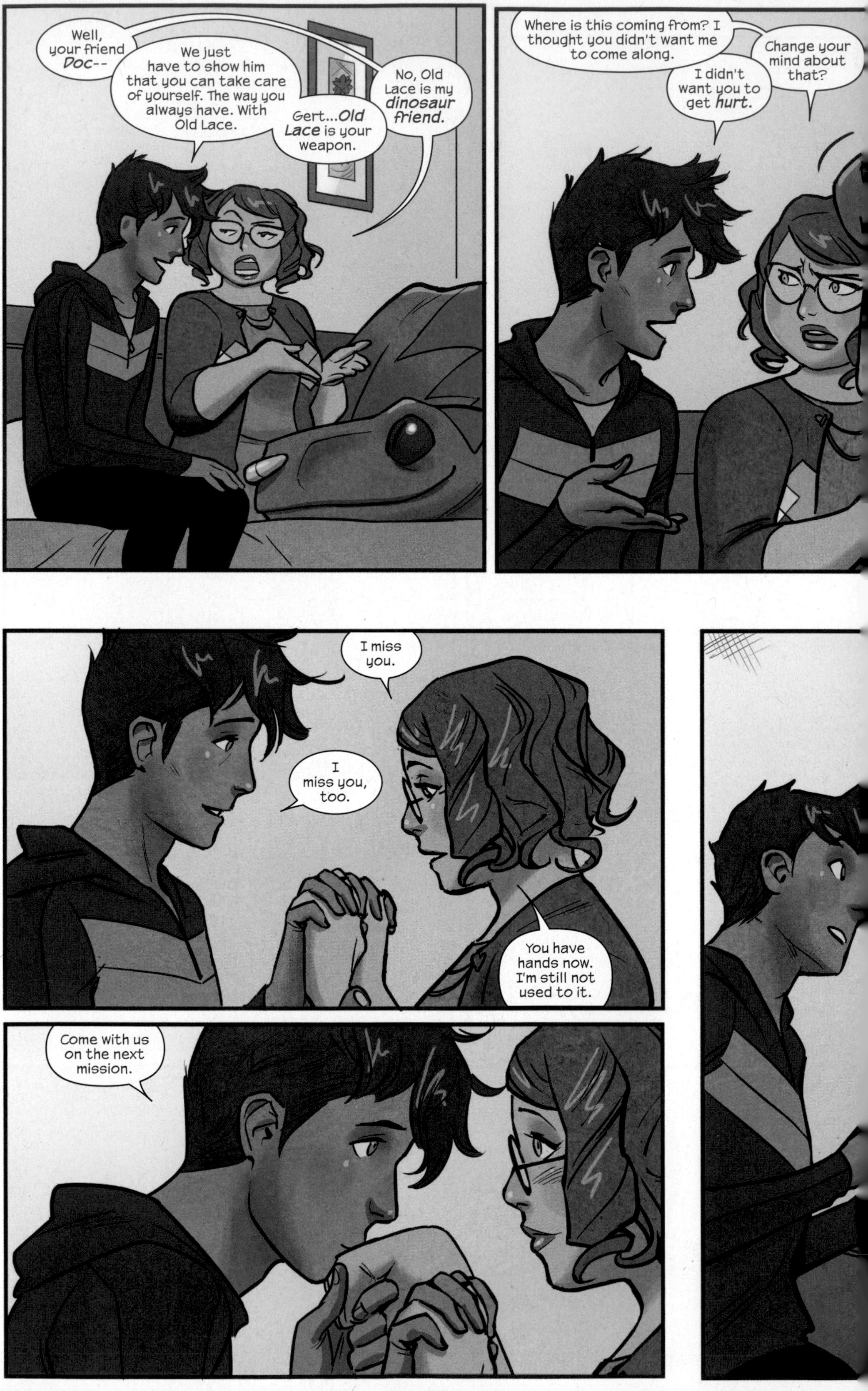
Well, your friend Doc--
We just have to show him that you can take care of yourself. The way you always have. With Old Lace.
No, Old Lace is my dinosaur friend.
Gert...Old Lace is your weapon.
Where is this coming from? I thought you didn't want me to come along.
Change your mind about that?
I didn't want you to get hurt.
I miss you.
I miss you, too.
You have hands now. I'm still not used to it.
Come with us on the next mission.

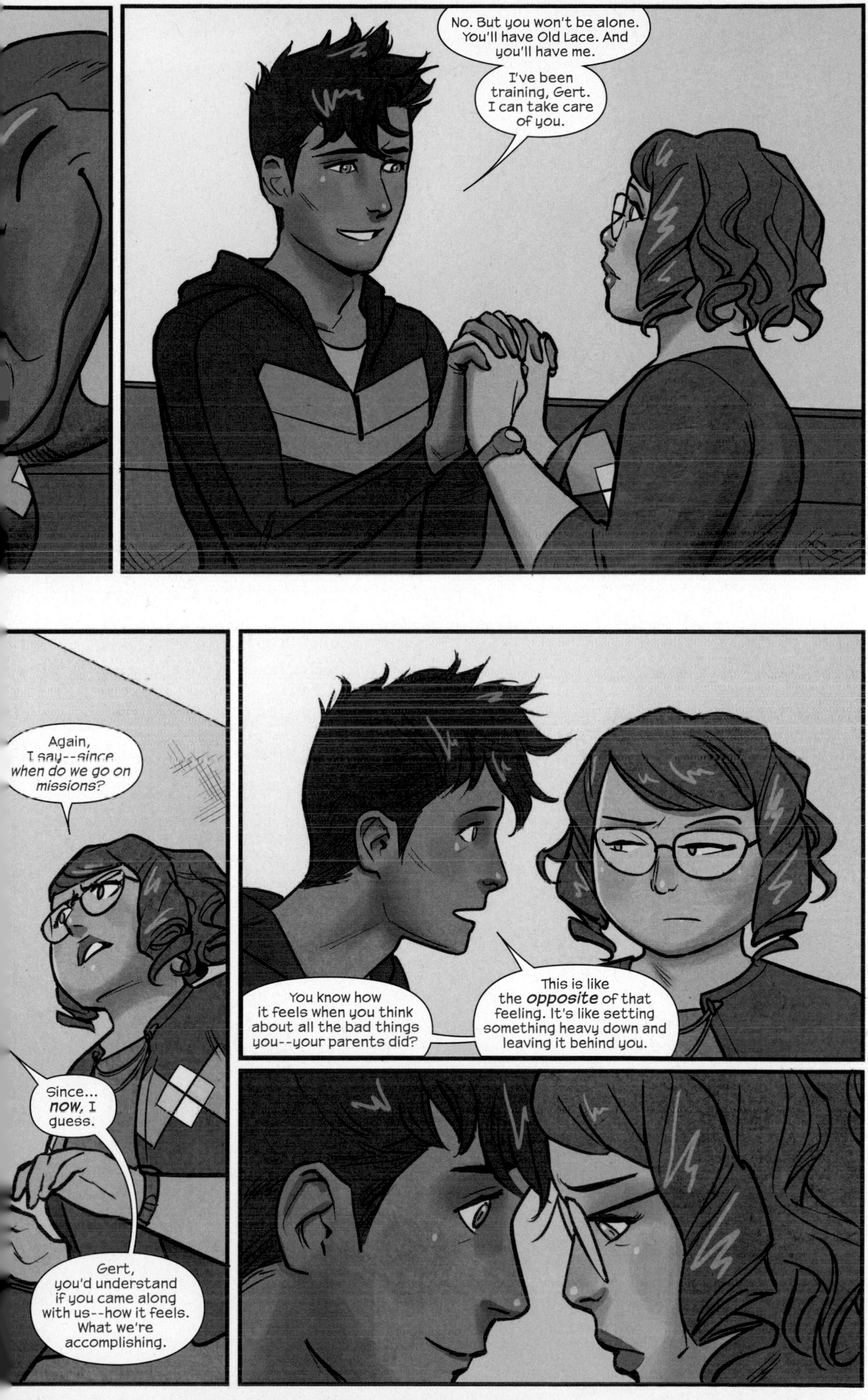
No. But you won't be alone. You'll have Old Lace. And you'll have me.
I've been training, Gert. I can take care of you.
Again, I say--since when do we go on missions?
Since... *now,* I guess.
Gert, you'd understand if you came along with us--how it feels. What we're accomplishing.
You know how it feels when you think about all the bad things you--your parents did?
This is like the *opposite* of that feeling. It's like setting something heavy down and leaving it behind you.

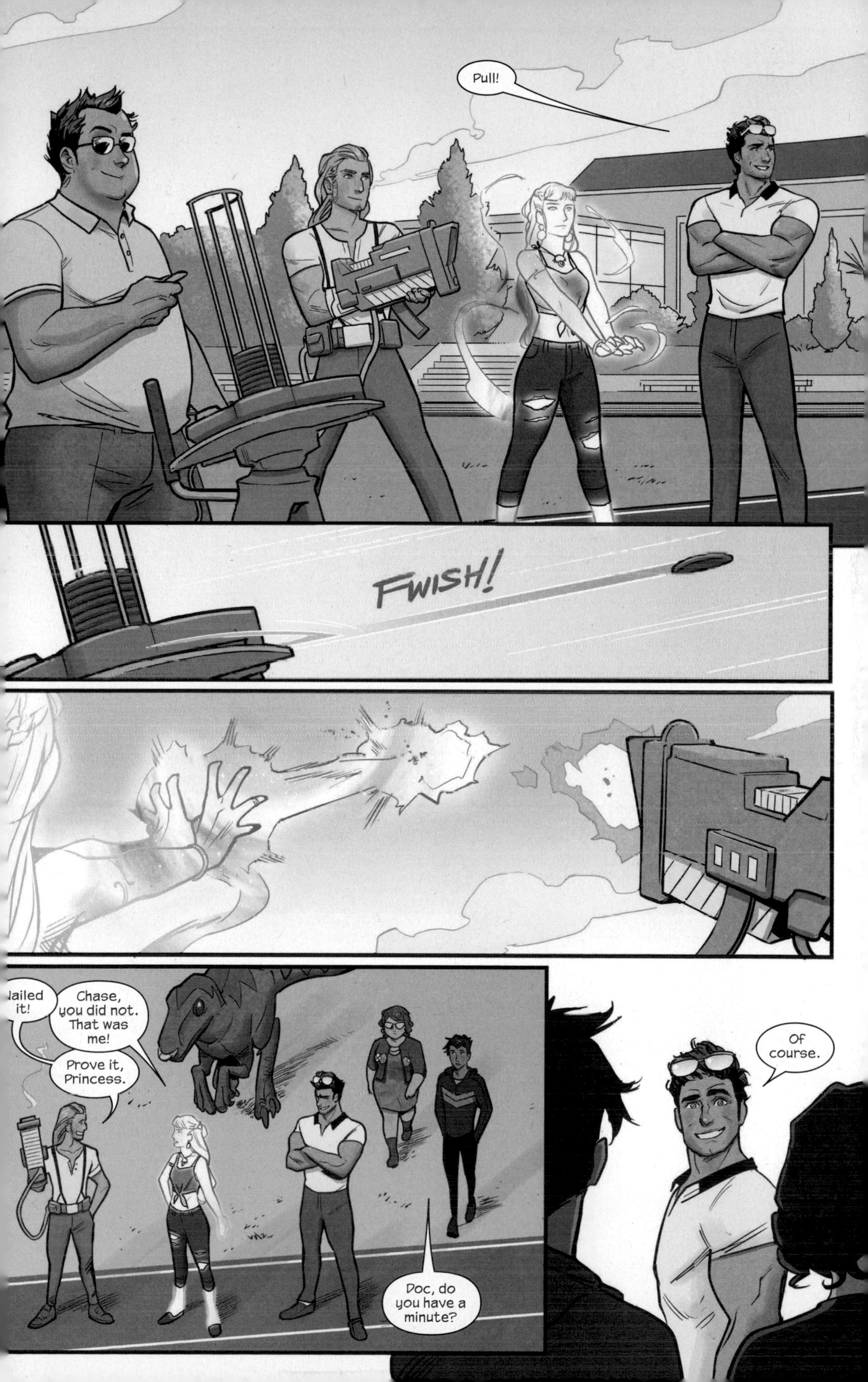
Pull!
FWISH!
Nailed it!
Chase, you did not. That was me!
Prove it, Princess.
Doc, do you have a minute?
Of course.

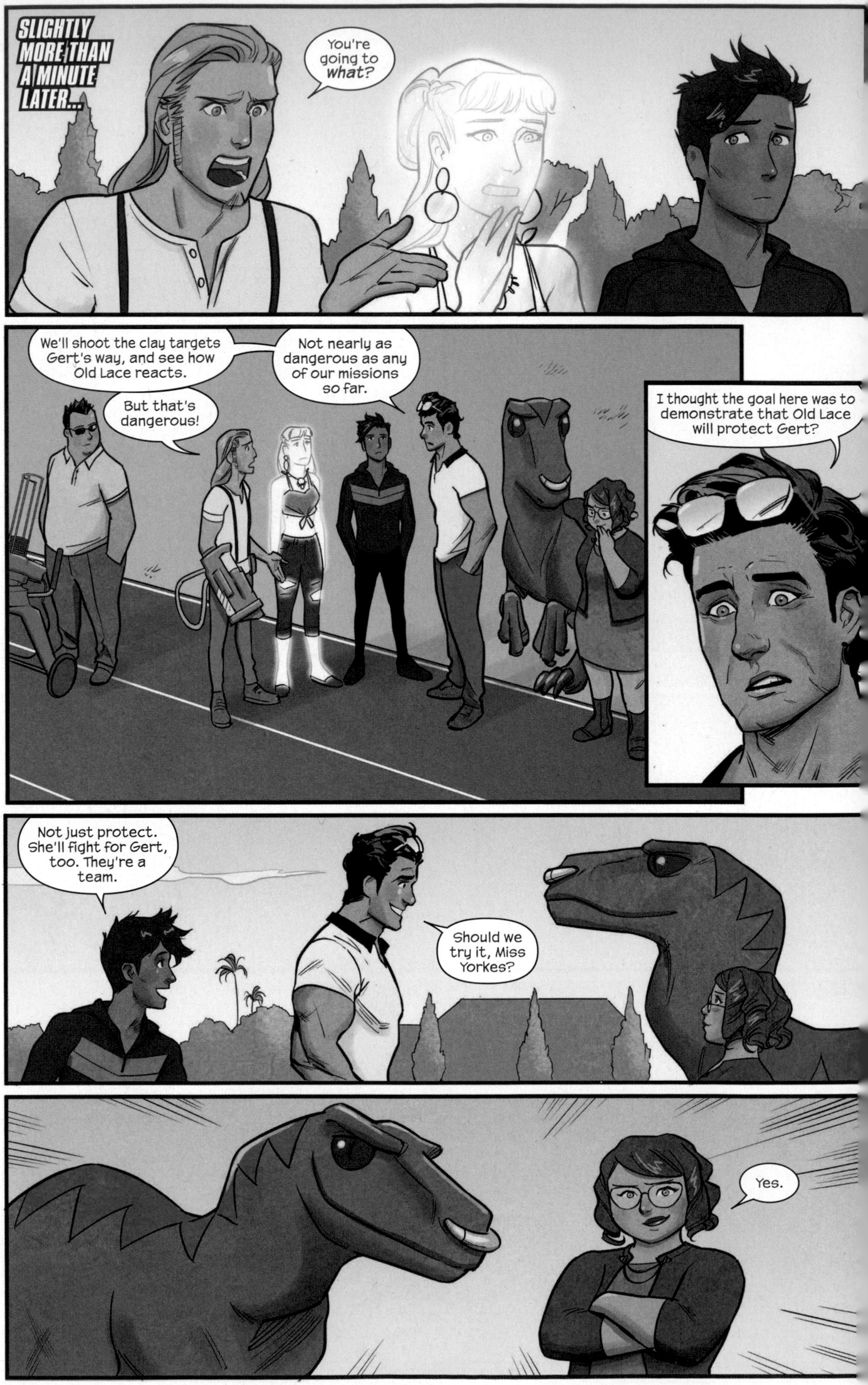
SLIGHTLY MORE THAN A MINUTE LATER...
You're going to what?
We'll shoot the clay targets Gert's way, and see how Old Lace reacts.
But that's dangerous!
Not nearly as dangerous as any of our missions so far.
I thought the goal here was to demonstrate that Old Lace will protect Gert?
Not just protect. She'll fight for Gert, too. They're a team.
Should we try it, Miss Yorkes?
Yes.

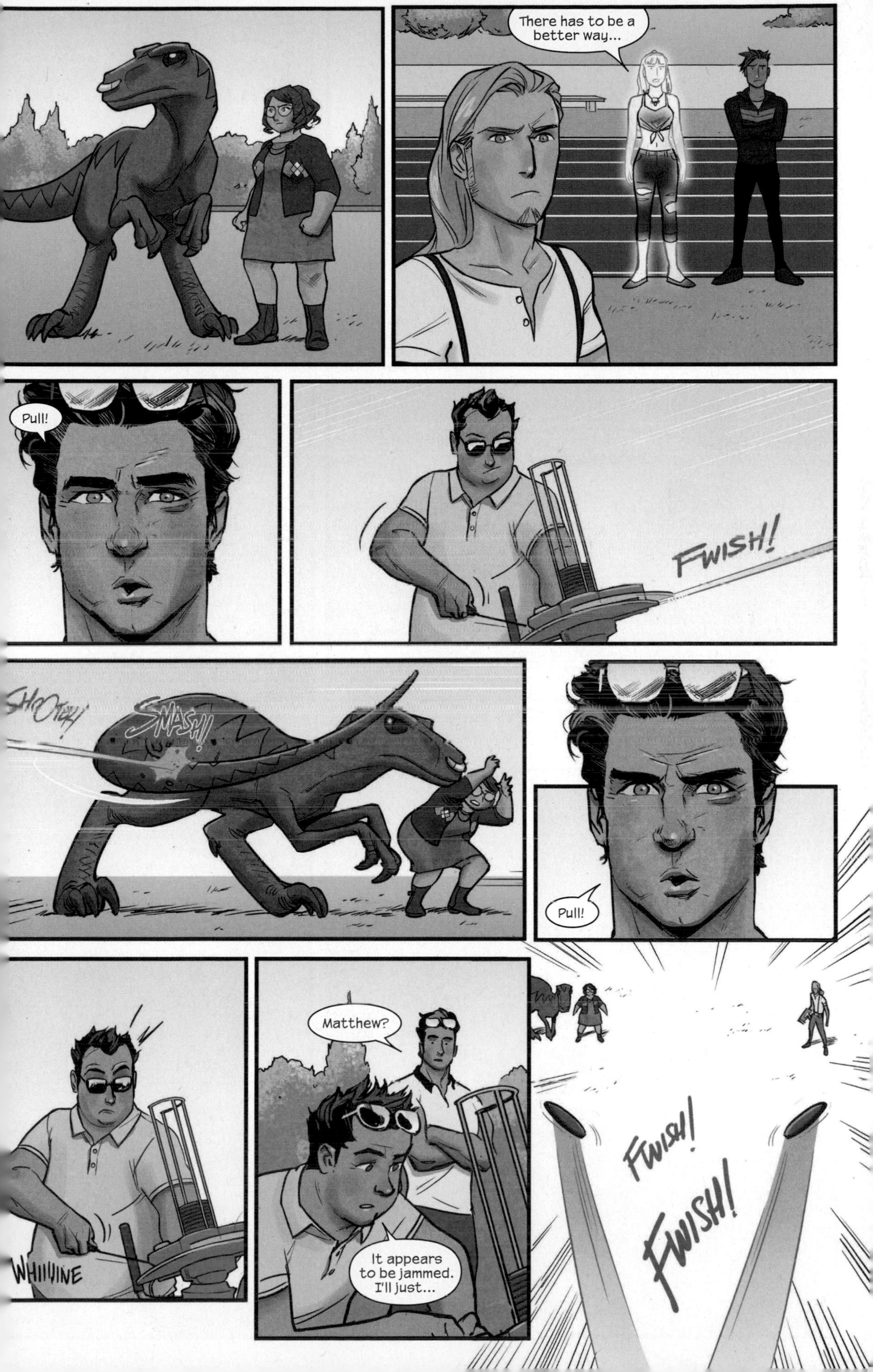
There has to be a better way...
Pull!
FWISH!
SMASH!
Pull!
Matthew?
It appears to be jammed. I'll just...
WHIIIIINE
FWISH!
FWISH!

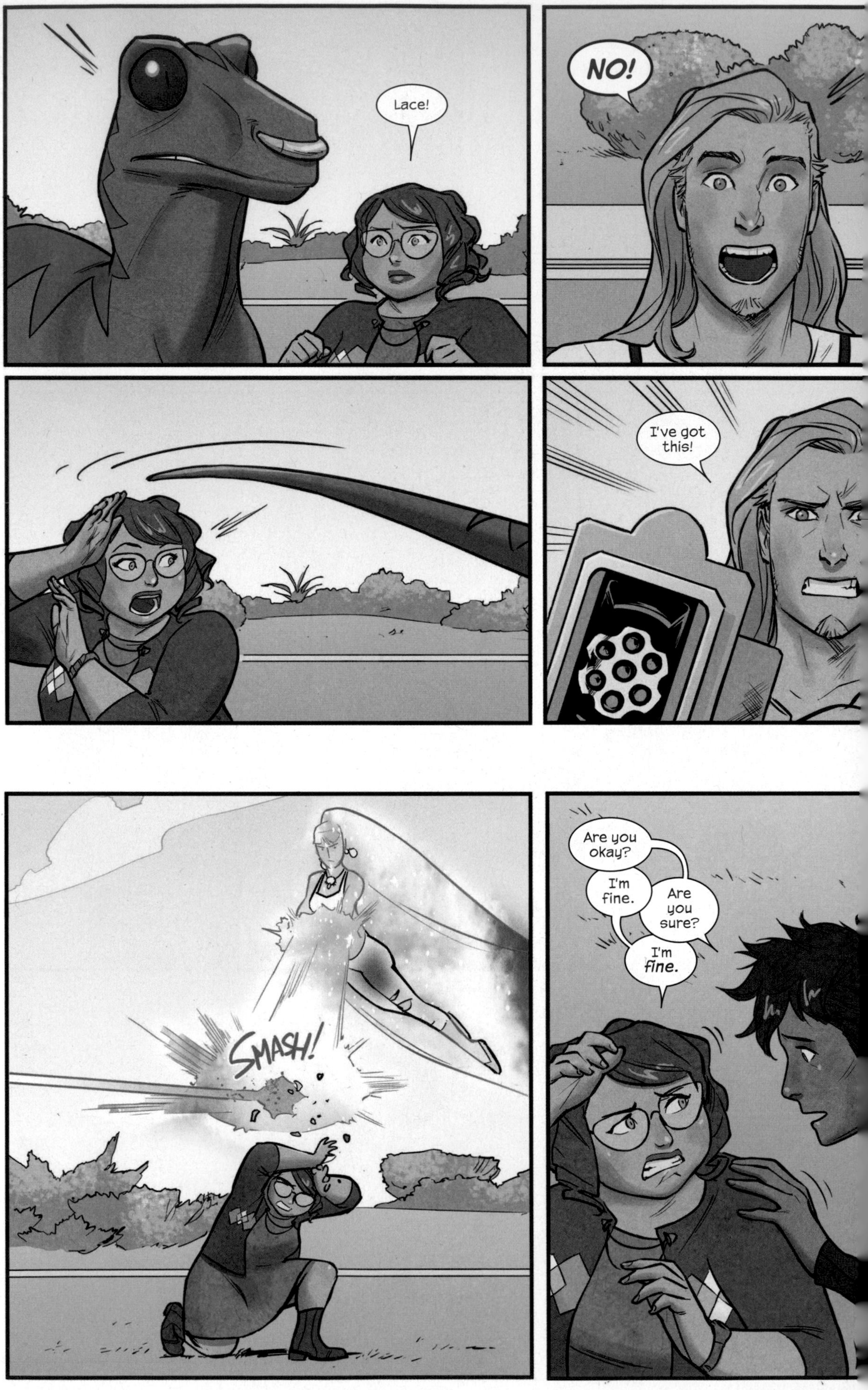
Lace!
NO!
I've got this!
SMASH!
Are you okay?
I'm fine.
Are you sure?
I'm *fine.*

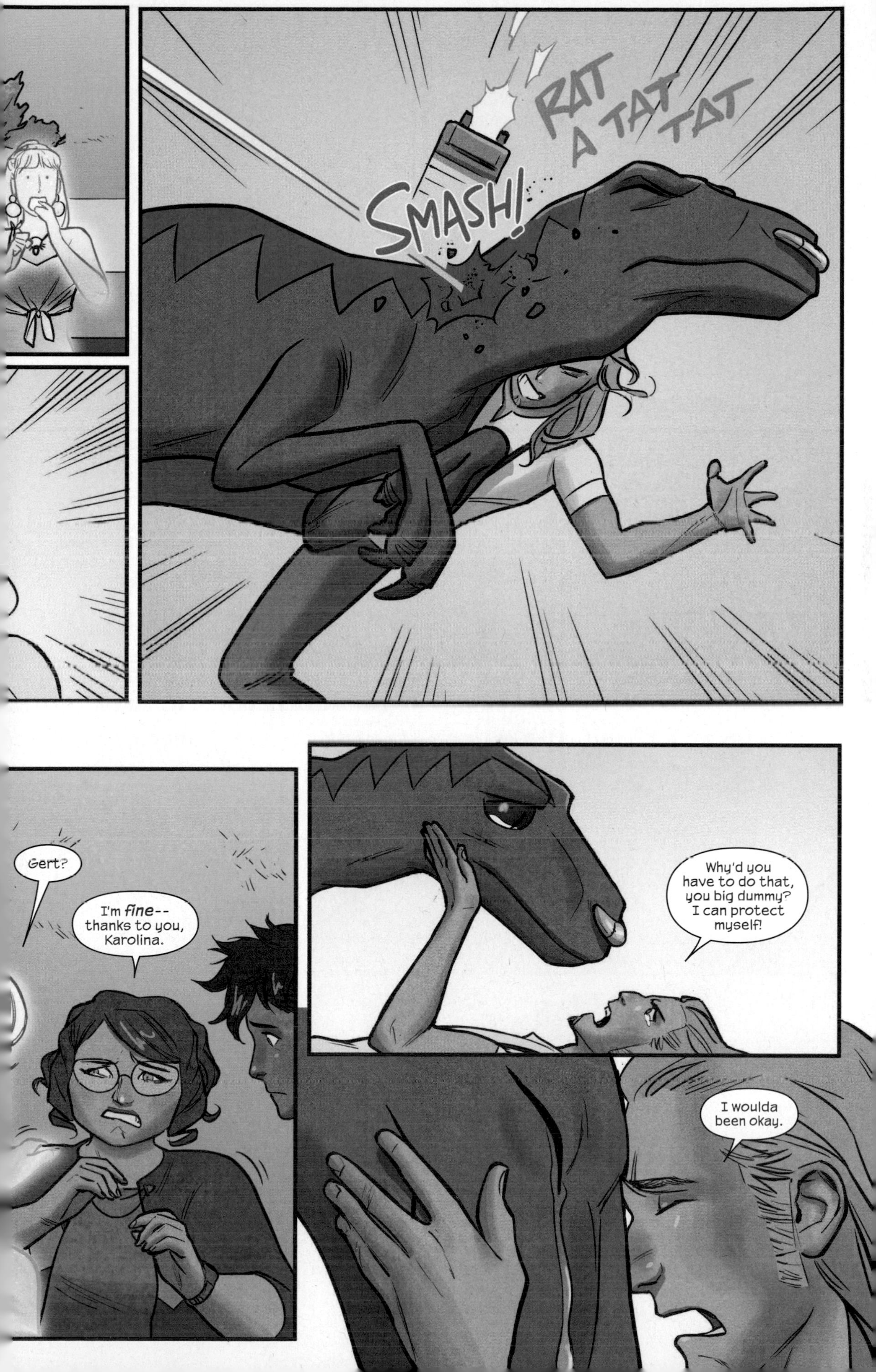
RAT A TAT TAT
SMASH!
Gert?
I'm *fine*-- thanks to you, Karolina.
Why'd you have to do that, you big dummy? I can protect myself!
I woulda been okay.

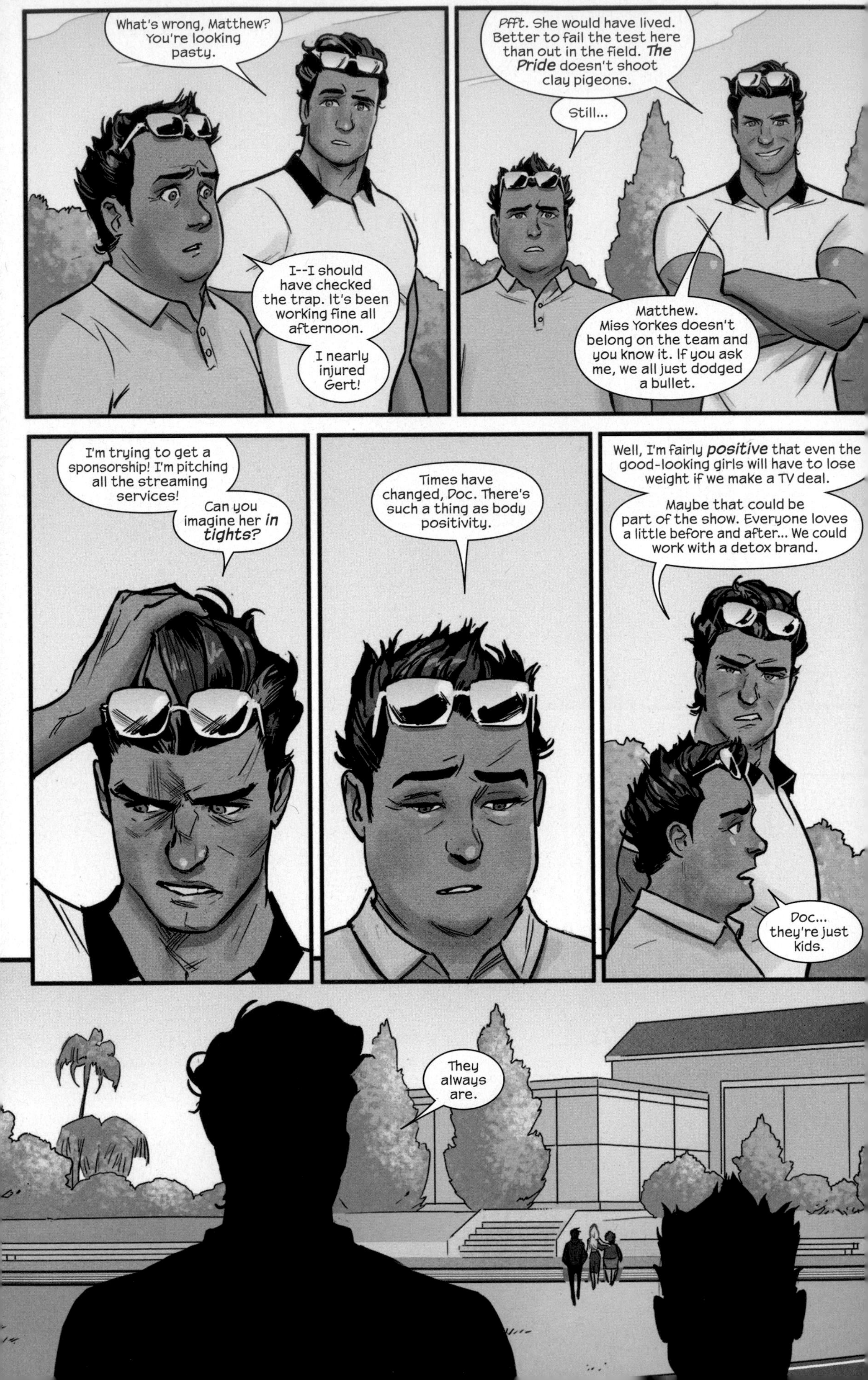
What's wrong, Matthew? You're looking pasty.
I--I should have checked the trap. It's been working fine all afternoon.
I nearly injured Gert!
Pfft. She would have lived. Better to fail the test here than out in the field. The Pride doesn't shoot clay pigeons.
Still...
Matthew. Miss Yorkes doesn't belong on the team and you know it. If you ask me, we all just dodged a bullet.
I'm trying to get a sponsorship! I'm pitching all the streaming services!
Can you imagine her in tights?
Times have changed, Doc. There's such a thing as body positivity.
Well, I'm fairly positive that even the good-looking girls will have to lose weight if we make a TV deal.
Maybe that could be part of the show. Everyone loves a little before and after... We could work with a detox brand.
Doc... they're just kids.
They always are.

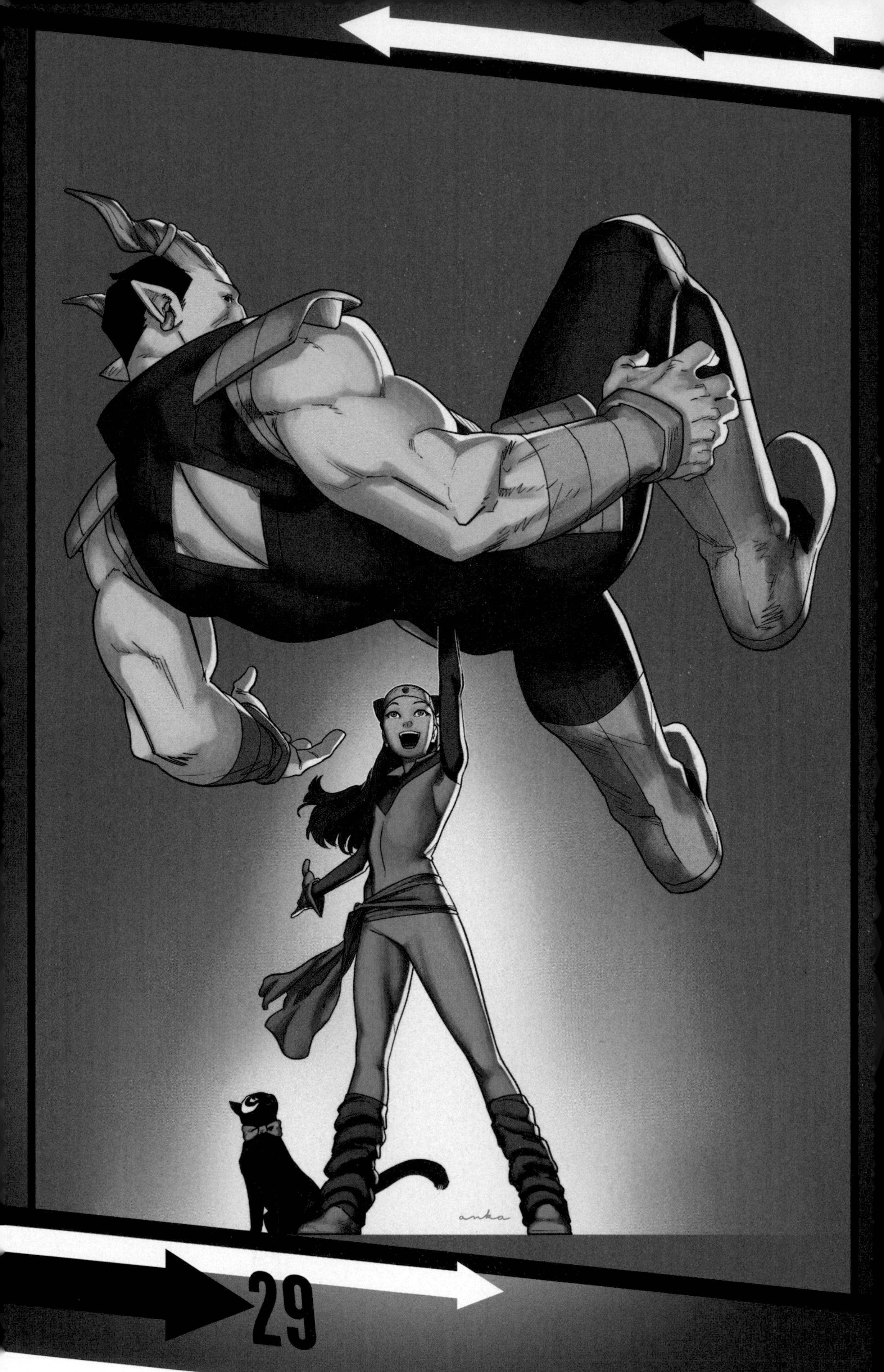
anka
29

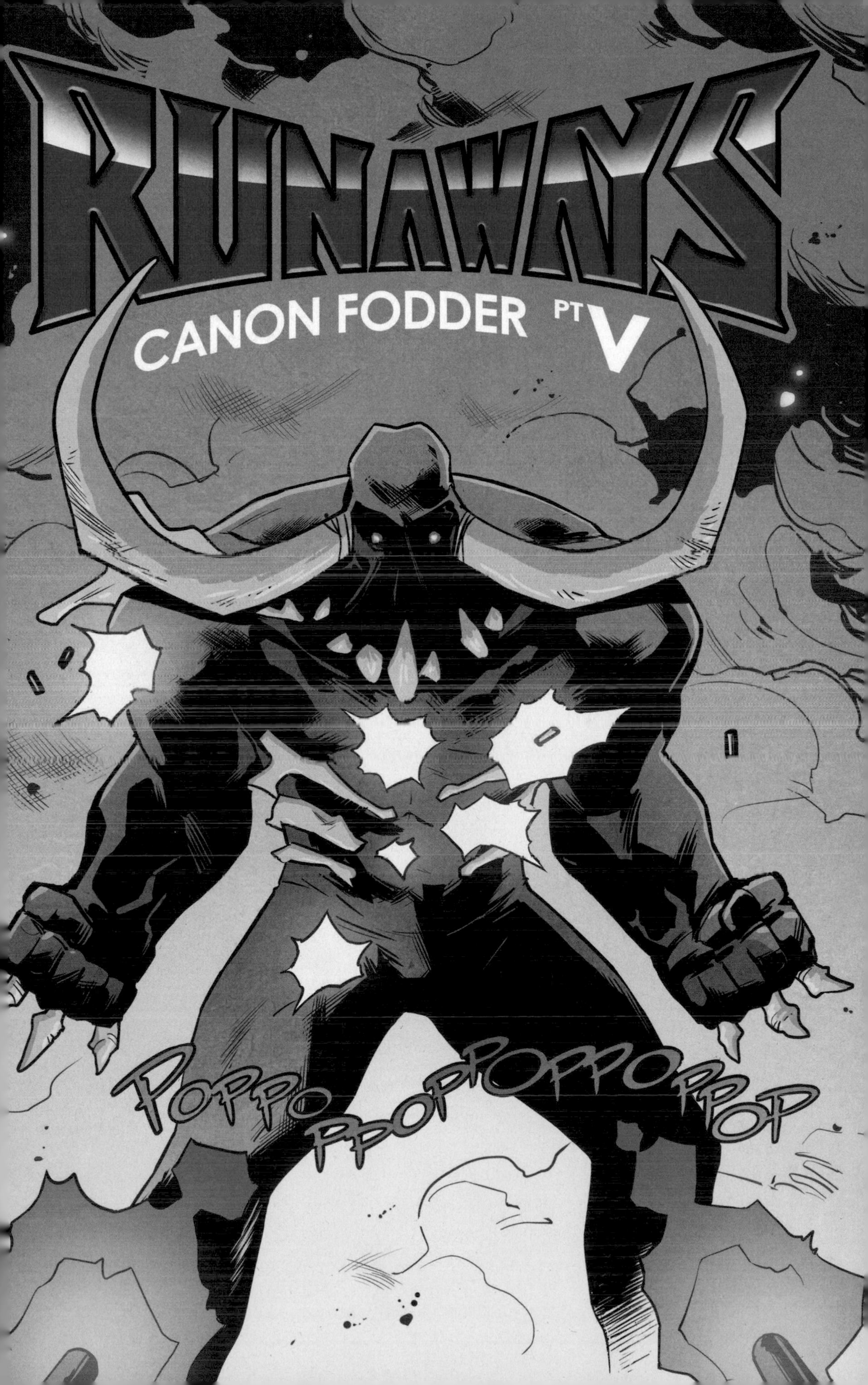
RUNAWAYS
CANON FODDER PT V
POPPOPPOPPOPPOPPOPPOP

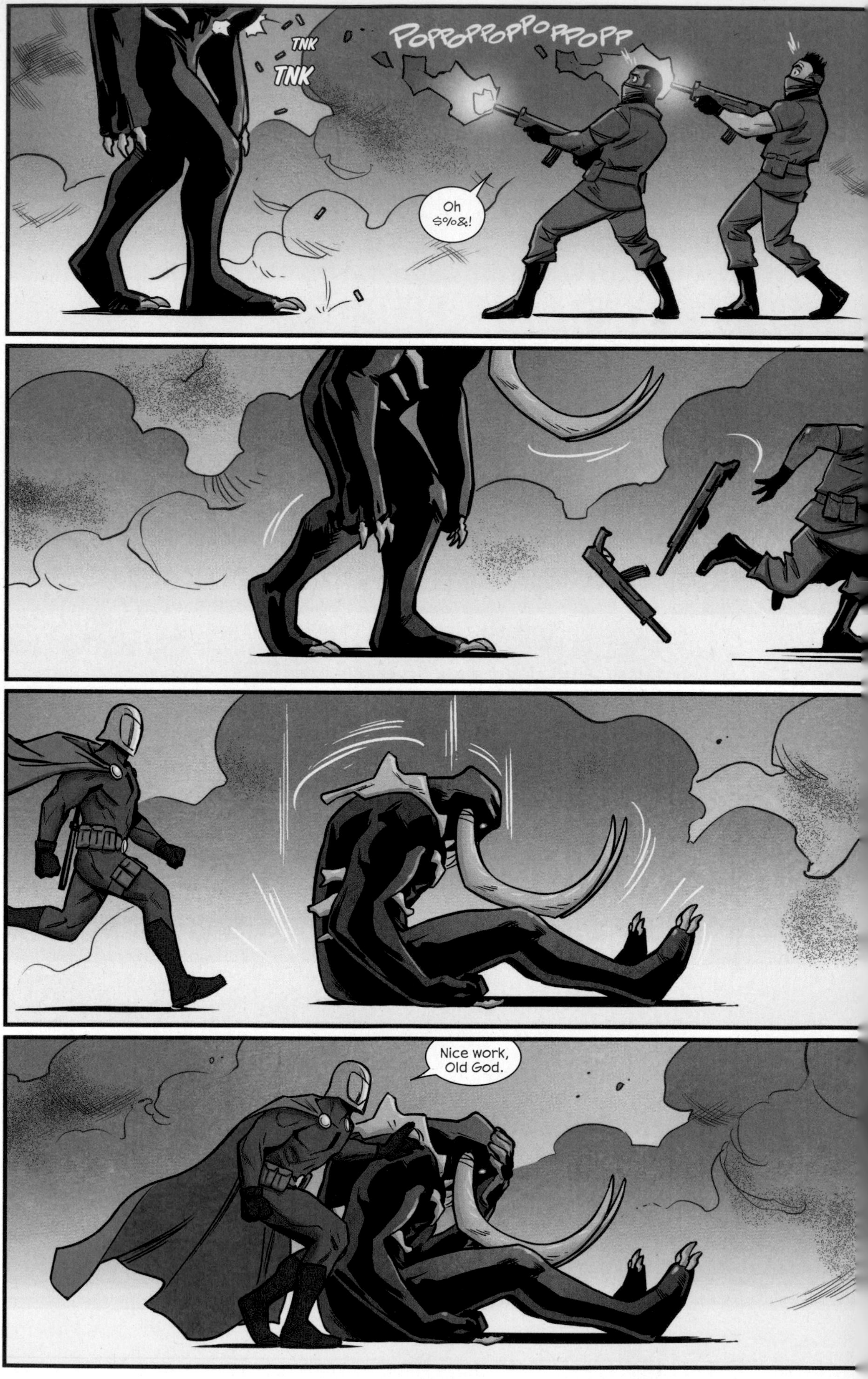
TNK
TNK
POPPOPPOPPOPPOPP
Oh $%&!
Nice work, Old God.

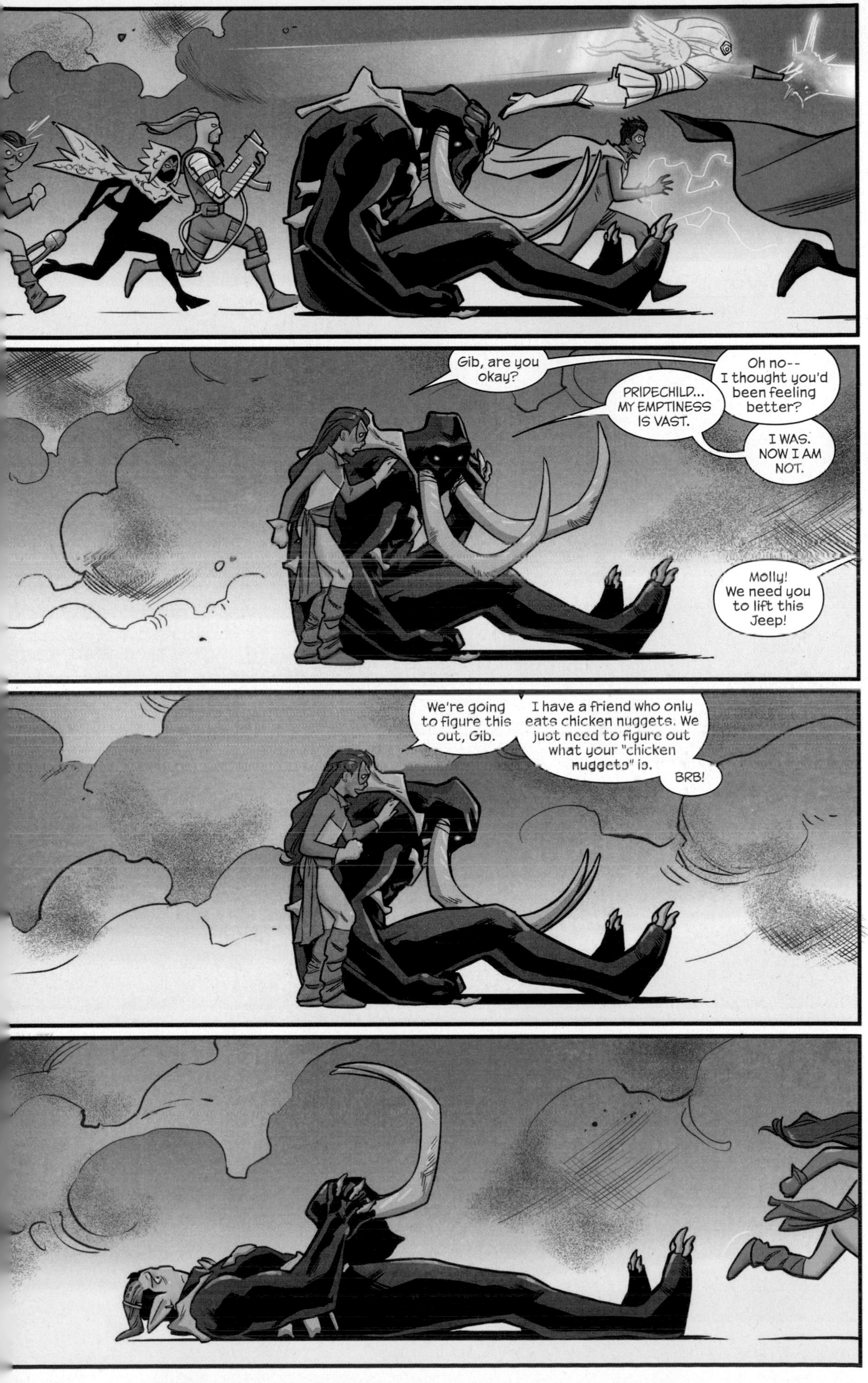
Gib, are you okay?
Oh no-- I thought you'd been feeling better?
PRIDECHILD... MY EMPTINESS IS VAST.
I WAS. NOW I AM NOT.
Molly! We need you to lift this Jeep!
We're going to figure this out, Gib.
I have a friend who only eats chicken nuggets. We just need to figure out what your "chicken nuggets" is.
BRB!

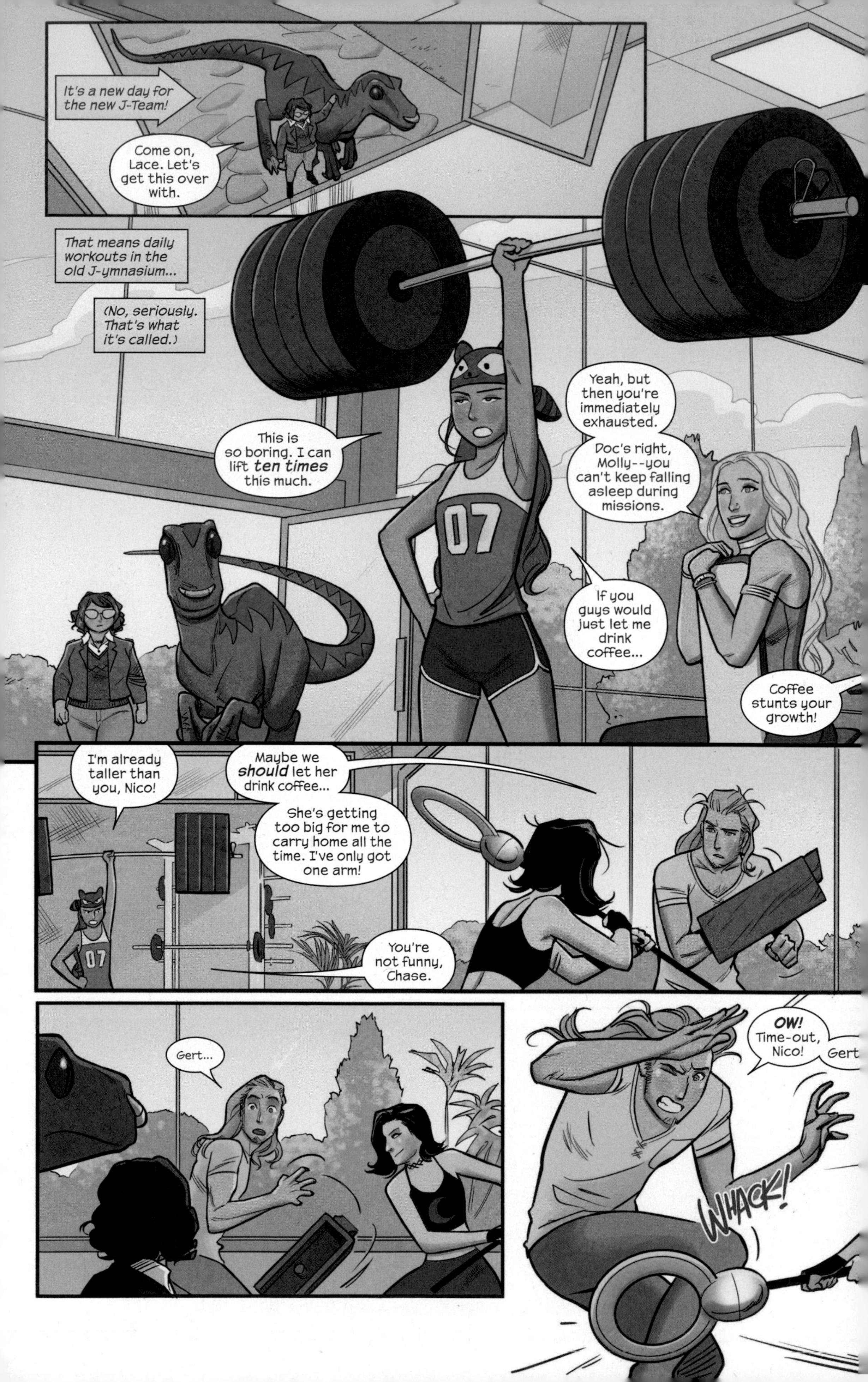
It's a new day for the new J-Team!
Come on, Lace. Let's get this over with.
That means daily workouts in the old J-ymnasium...
(No, seriously. That's what it's called.)
This is so boring. I can lift ten times this much.
Yeah, but then you're immediately exhausted.
Doc's right, Molly--you can't keep falling asleep during missions.
If you guys would just let me drink coffee...
Coffee stunts your growth!
I'm already taller than you, Nico!
Maybe we should let her drink coffee...
She's getting too big for me to carry home all the time. I've only got one arm!
You're not funny, Chase.
Gert...
OW! Time-out, Nico!
Gert
WHACK!

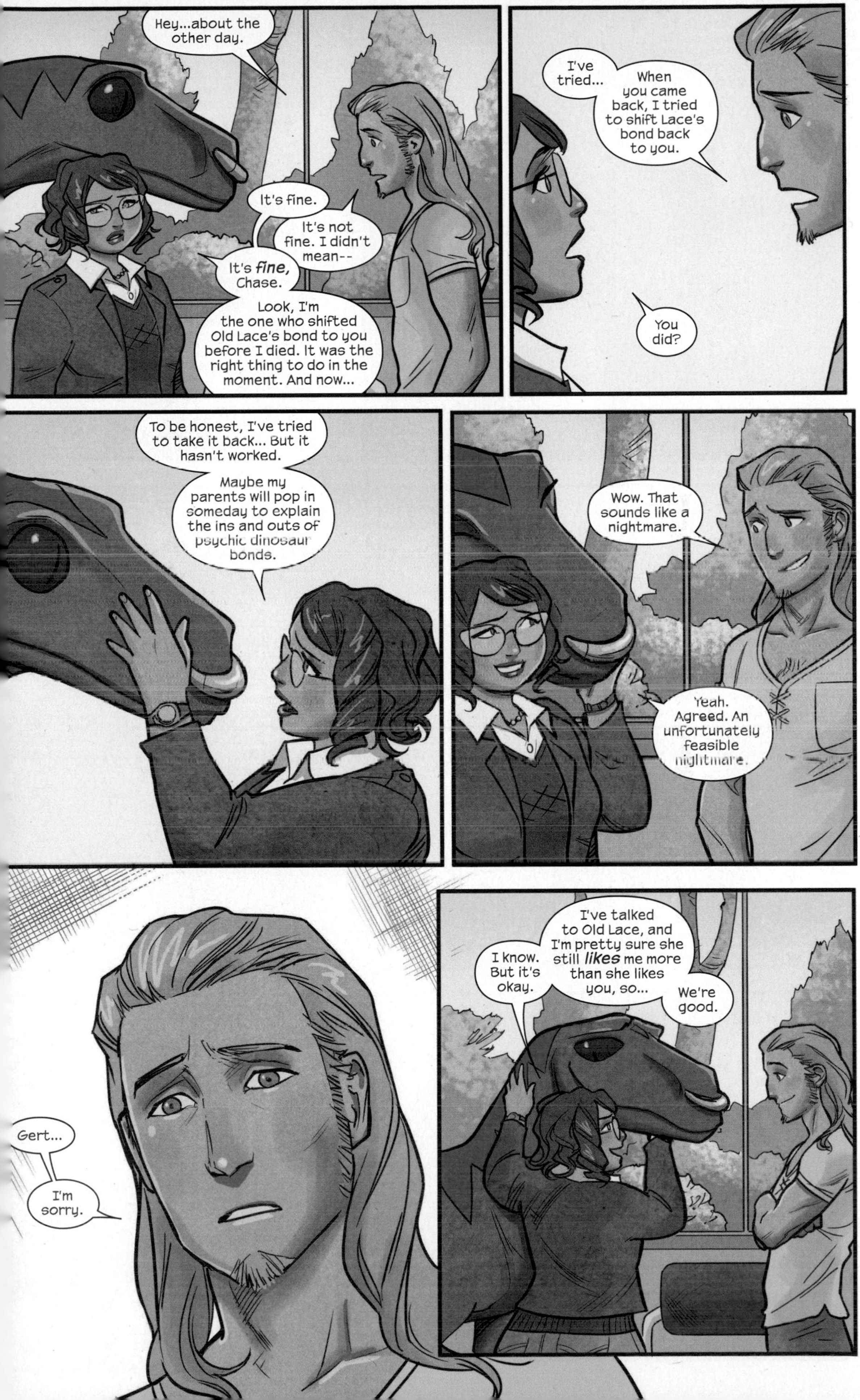
Hey...about the other day.
It's fine.
It's not fine. I didn't mean--
It's *fine,* Chase.
Look, I'm the one who shifted Old Lace's bond to you before I died. It was the right thing to do in the moment. And now...
I've tried...
When you came back, I tried to shift Lace's bond back to you.
You did?
To be honest, I've tried to take it back... But it hasn't worked.
Maybe my parents will pop in someday to explain the ins and outs of psychic dinosaur bonds.
Wow. That sounds like a nightmare.
Yeah. Agreed. An unfortunately feasible nightmare.
Gert...
I'm sorry.
I know. But it's okay.
I've talked to Old Lace, and I'm pretty sure she still *likes* me more than she likes you, so...
We're good.

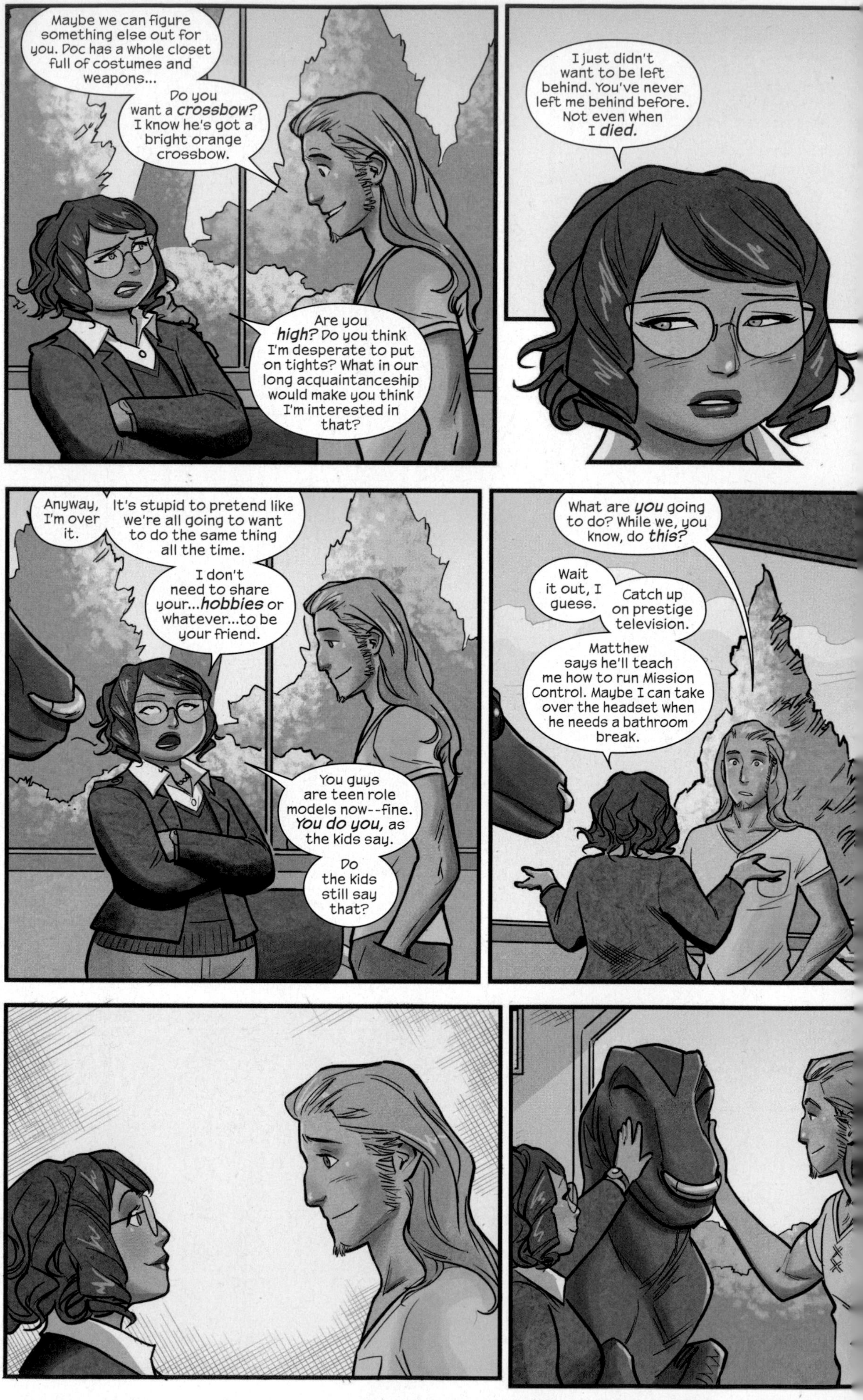
Maybe we can figure something else out for you. Doc has a whole closet full of costumes and weapons...
Do you want a crossbow? I know he's got a bright orange crossbow.
Are you high? Do you think I'm desperate to put on tights? What in our long acquaintanceship would make you think I'm interested in that?
I just didn't want to be left behind. You've never left me behind before. Not even when I died.
Anyway, I'm over it.
It's stupid to pretend like we're all going to want to do the same thing all the time.
I don't need to share your...hobbies or whatever...to be your friend.
You guys are teen role models now--fine. You do you, as the kids say.
Do the kids still say that?
What are you going to do? While we, you know, do this?
Wait it out, I guess.
Catch up on prestige television.
Matthew says he'll teach me how to run Mission Control. Maybe I can take over the headset when he needs a bathroom break.

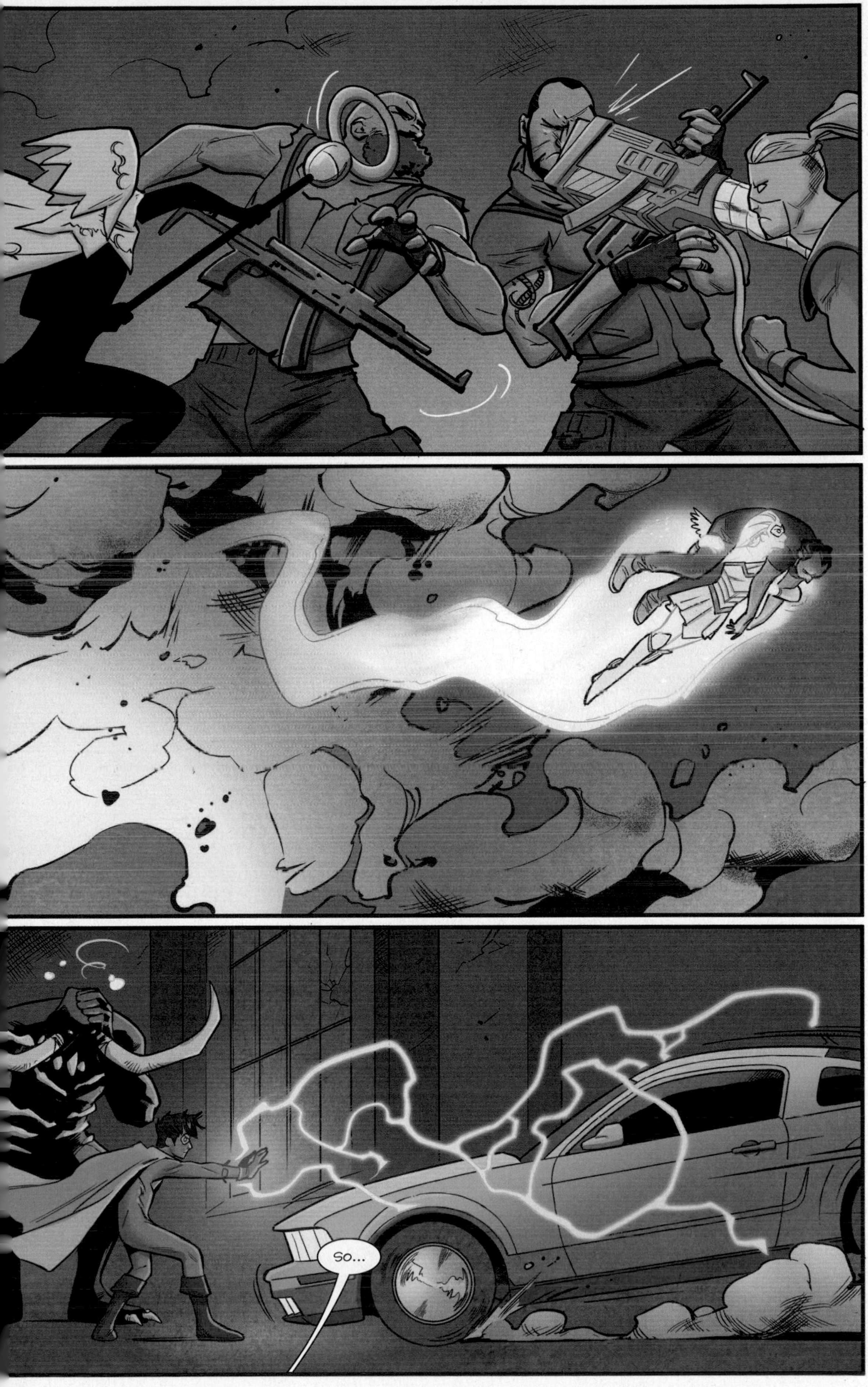
SO...

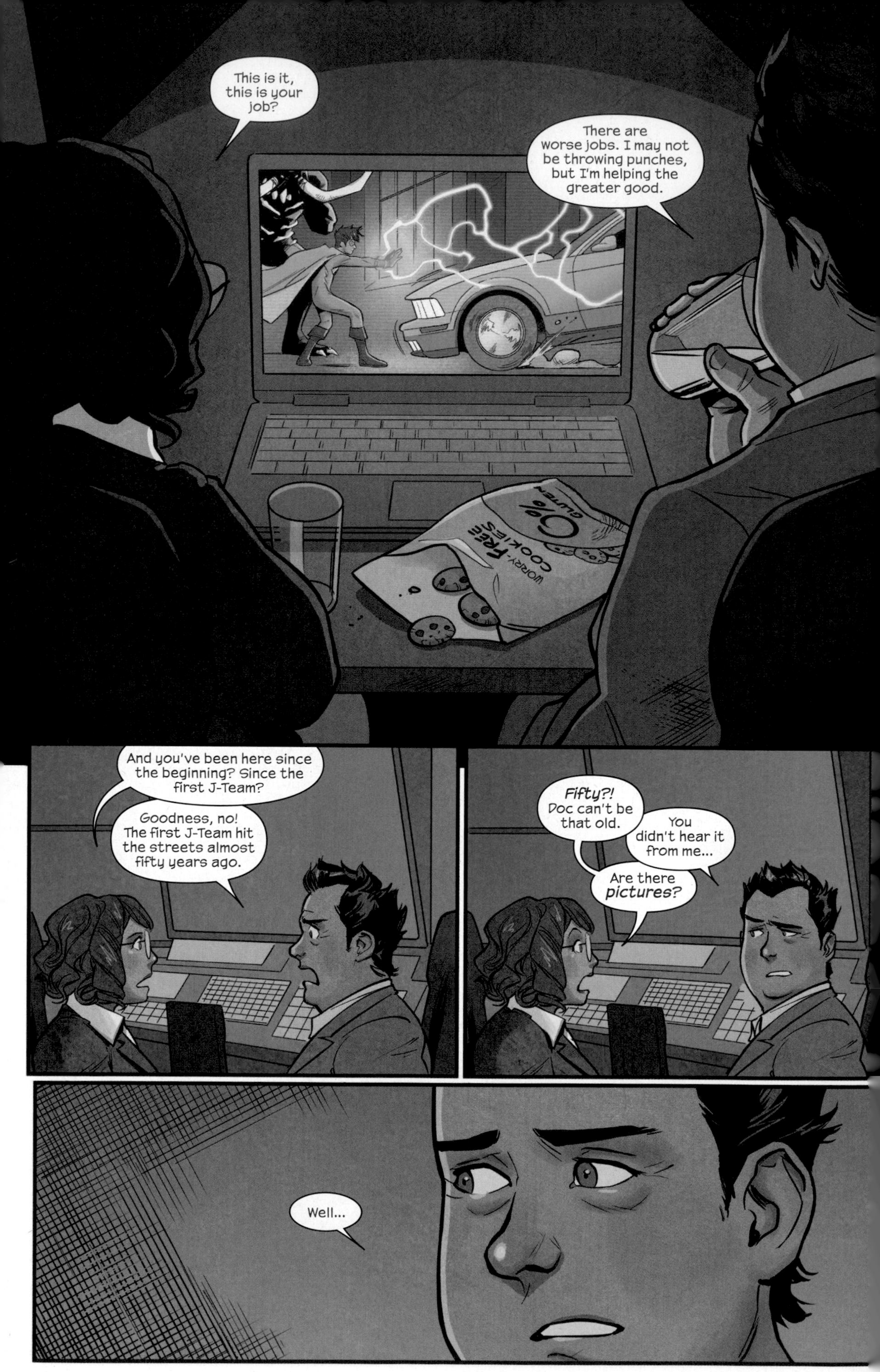
This is it, this is your job?
There are worse jobs. I may not be throwing punches, but I'm helping the greater good.
WORRY-FREE COOKIES 0% GLUTEN
And you've been here since the beginning? Since the first J-Team?
Goodness, no! The first J-Team hit the streets almost fifty years ago.
Fifty?! Doc can't be that old.
You didn't hear it from me...
Are there pictures?
Well...

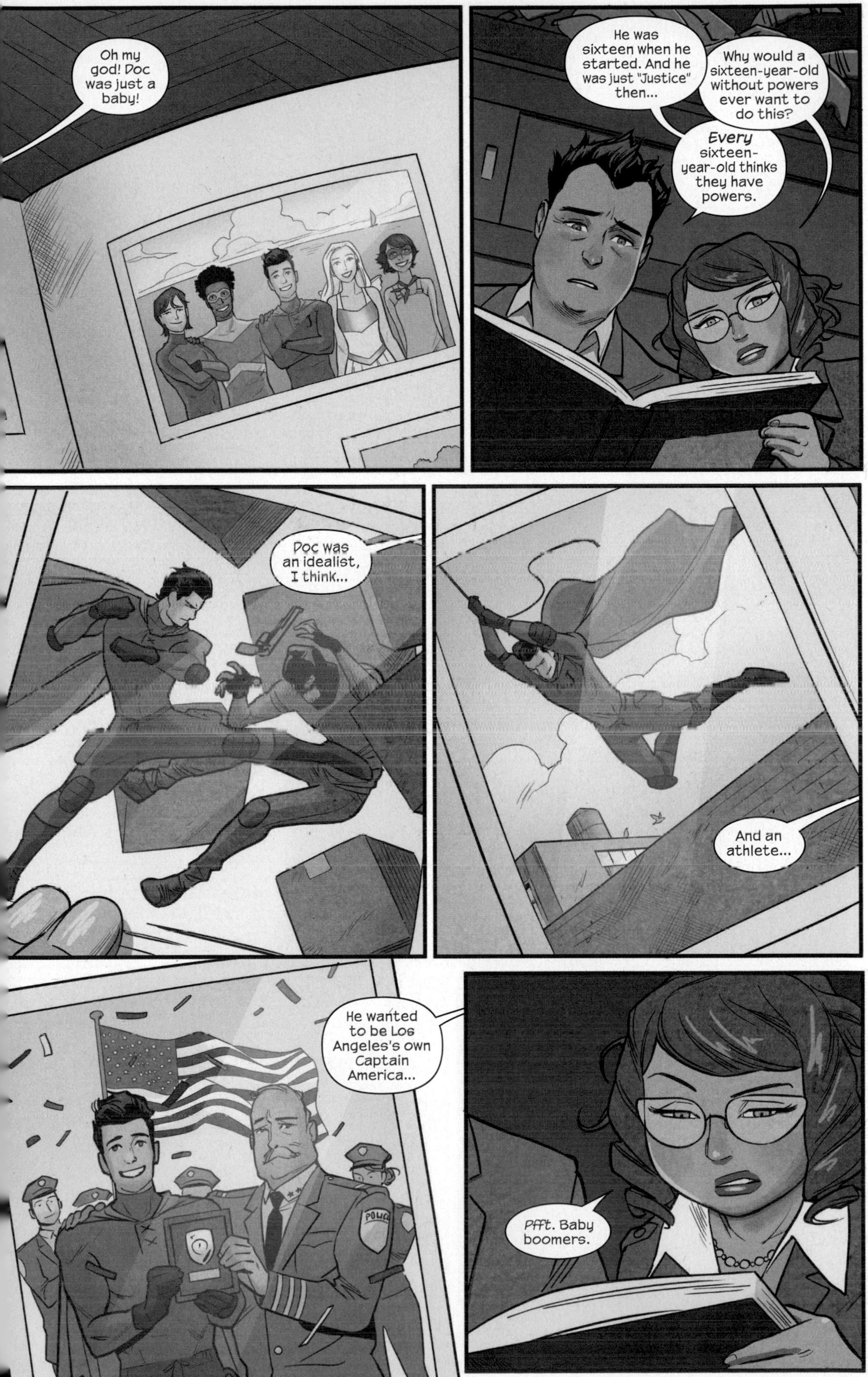

Oh my god! Doc was just a baby!
He was sixteen when he started. And he was just "Justice" then...
Why would a sixteen-year-old without powers ever want to do this?
Every sixteen-year-old thinks they have powers.
Doc was an idealist, I think...
And an athlete...
He wanted to be Los Angeles's own Captain America...
POLICE
Pfft. Baby boomers.

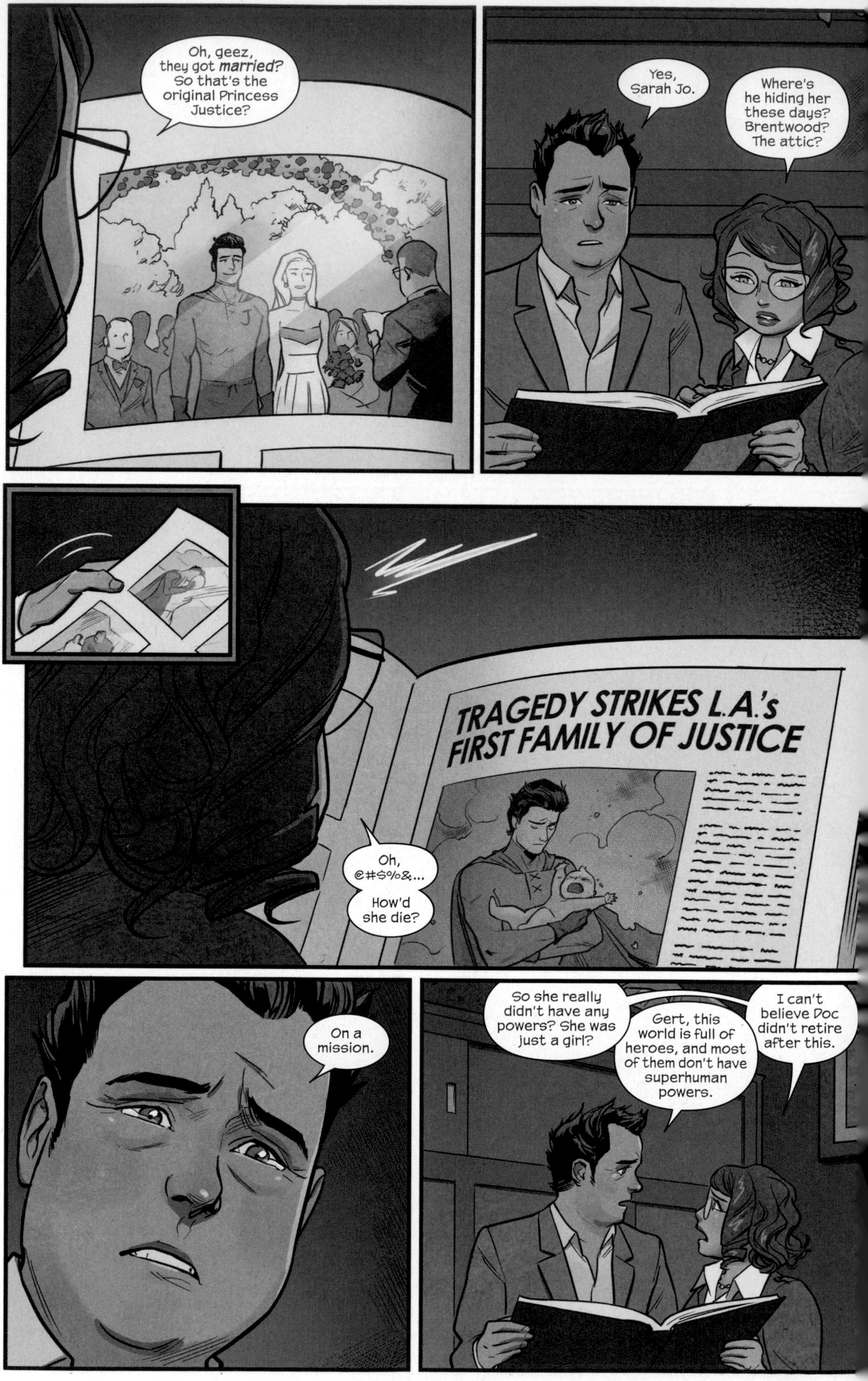
Oh, geez, they got *married*? So that's the original Princess Justice?
Yes, Sarah Jo.
Where's he hiding her these days? Brentwood? The attic?
TRAGEDY STRIKES L.A.'s FIRST FAMILY OF JUSTICE
Oh, @#$%&...
How'd she die?
On a mission.
So she really didn't have any powers? She was just a girl?
Gert, this world is full of heroes, and most of them don't have superhuman powers.
I can't believe Doc didn't retire after this.

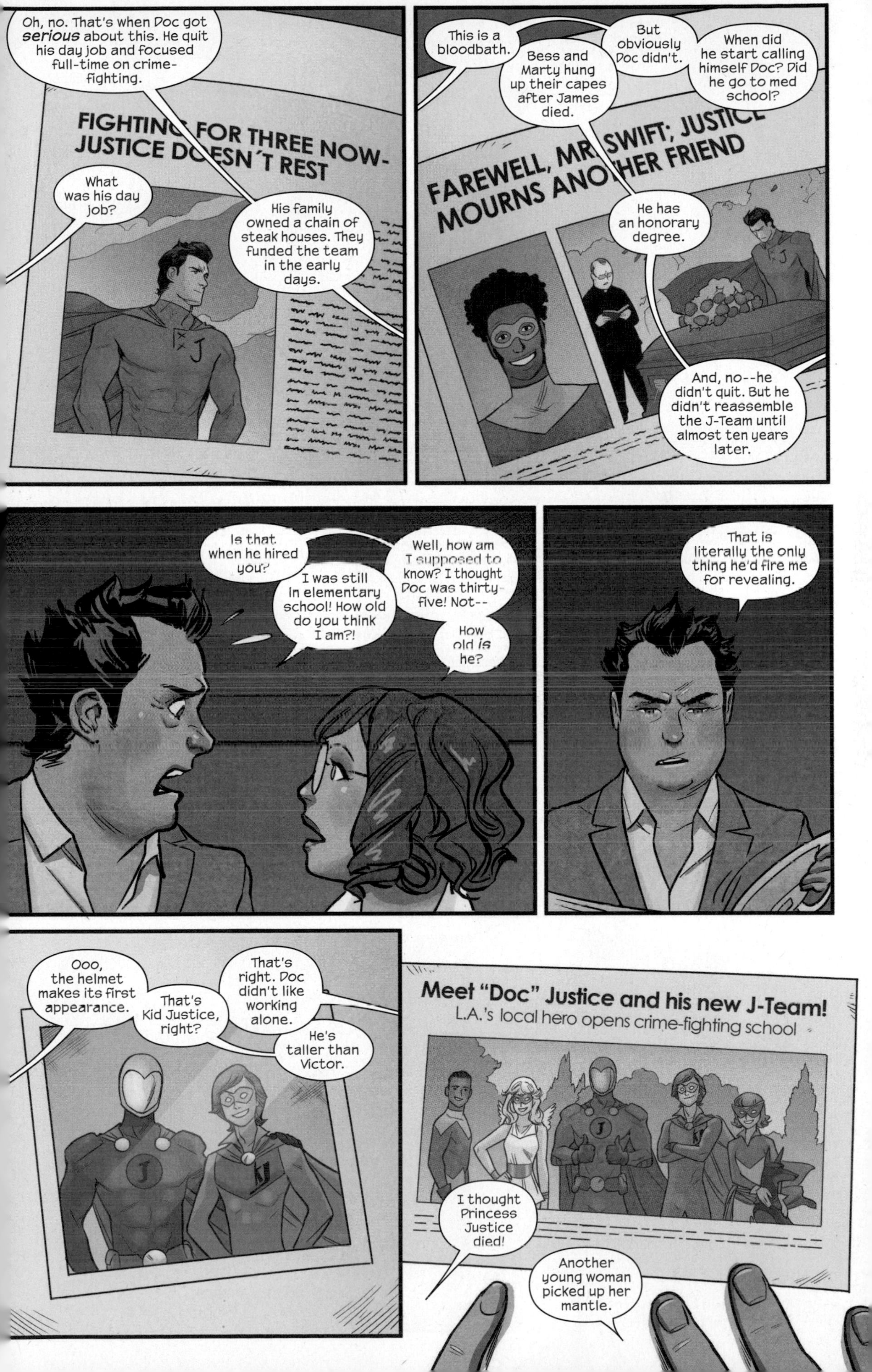
Oh, no. That's when Doc got serious about this. He quit his day job and focused full-time on crime-fighting.
FIGHTING FOR THREE NOW-JUSTICE DOESN'T REST
What was his day job?
His family owned a chain of steak houses. They funded the team in the early days.
This is a bloodbath.
Bess and Marty hung up their capes after James died.
But obviously Doc didn't.
When did he start calling himself Doc? Did he go to med school?
FAREWELL, MR. SWIFT; JUSTICE MOURNS ANOTHER FRIEND
He has an honorary degree.
And, no--he didn't quit. But he didn't reassemble the J-Team until almost ten years later.
Is that when he hired you?
I was still in elementary school! How old do you think I am?!
Well, how am I supposed to know? I thought Doc was thirty-five! Not--
How old is he?
That is literally the only thing he'd fire me for revealing.
Ooo, the helmet makes its first appearance.
That's Kid Justice, right?
That's right. Doc didn't like working alone.
He's taller than Victor.
Meet "Doc" Justice and his new J-Team!
L.A.'s local hero opens crime-fighting school
I thought Princess Justice died!
Another young woman picked up her mantle.

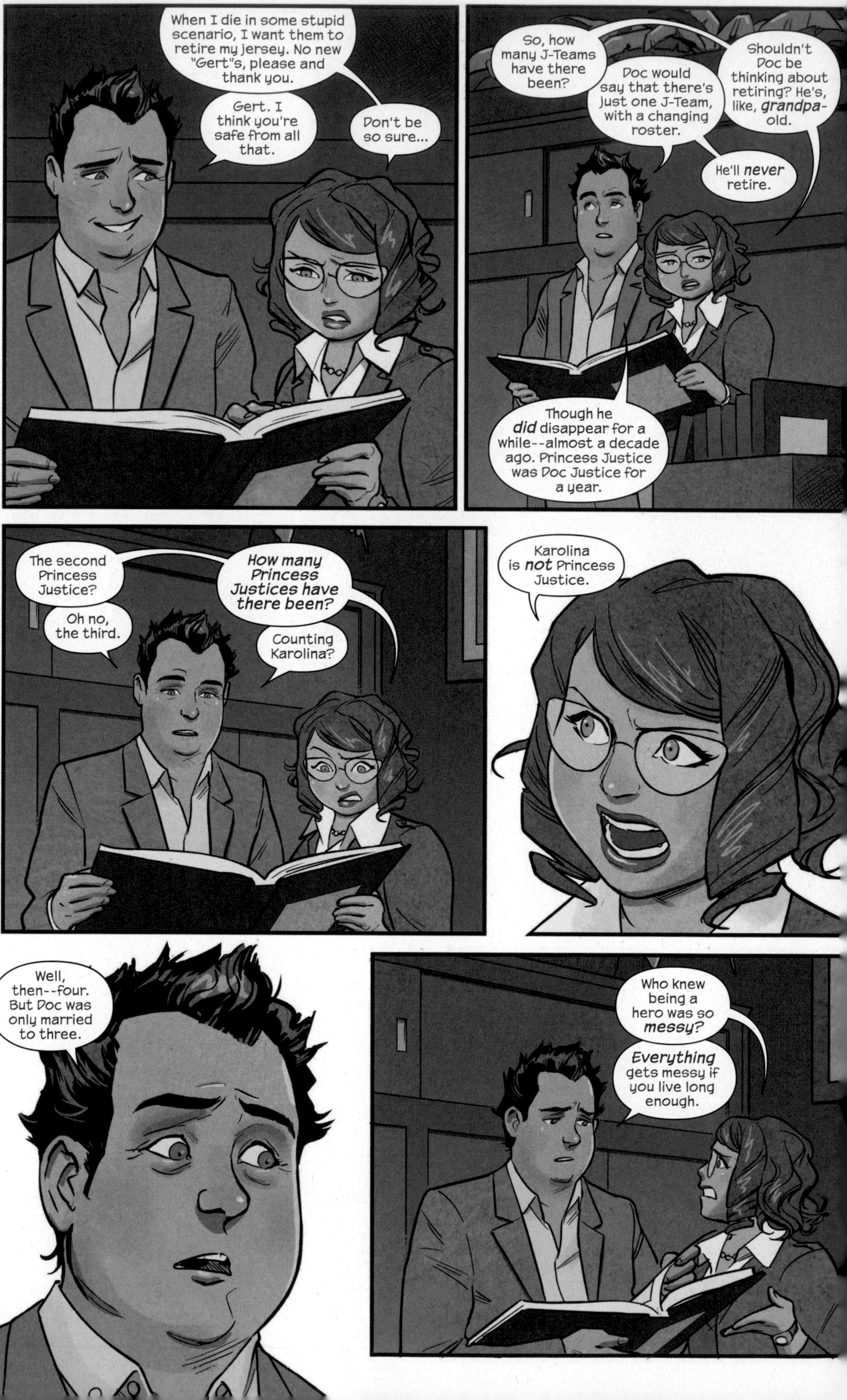
When I die in some stupid scenario, I want them to retire my jersey. No new "Gert"s, please and thank you.
Gert. I think you're safe from all that.
Don't be so sure...
So, how many J-Teams have there been?
Doc would say that there's just one J-Team, with a changing roster.
Shouldn't Doc be thinking about retiring? He's, like, *grandpa*-old.
He'll *never* retire.
Though he *did* disappear for a while--almost a decade ago. Princess Justice was Doc Justice for a year.
The second Princess Justice?
Oh no, the third.
How many Princess Justices have there been?
Counting Karolina?
Karolina is *not* Princess Justice.
Well, then--four. But Doc was only married to three.
Who knew being a hero was so *messy?*
Everything gets messy if you live long enough.

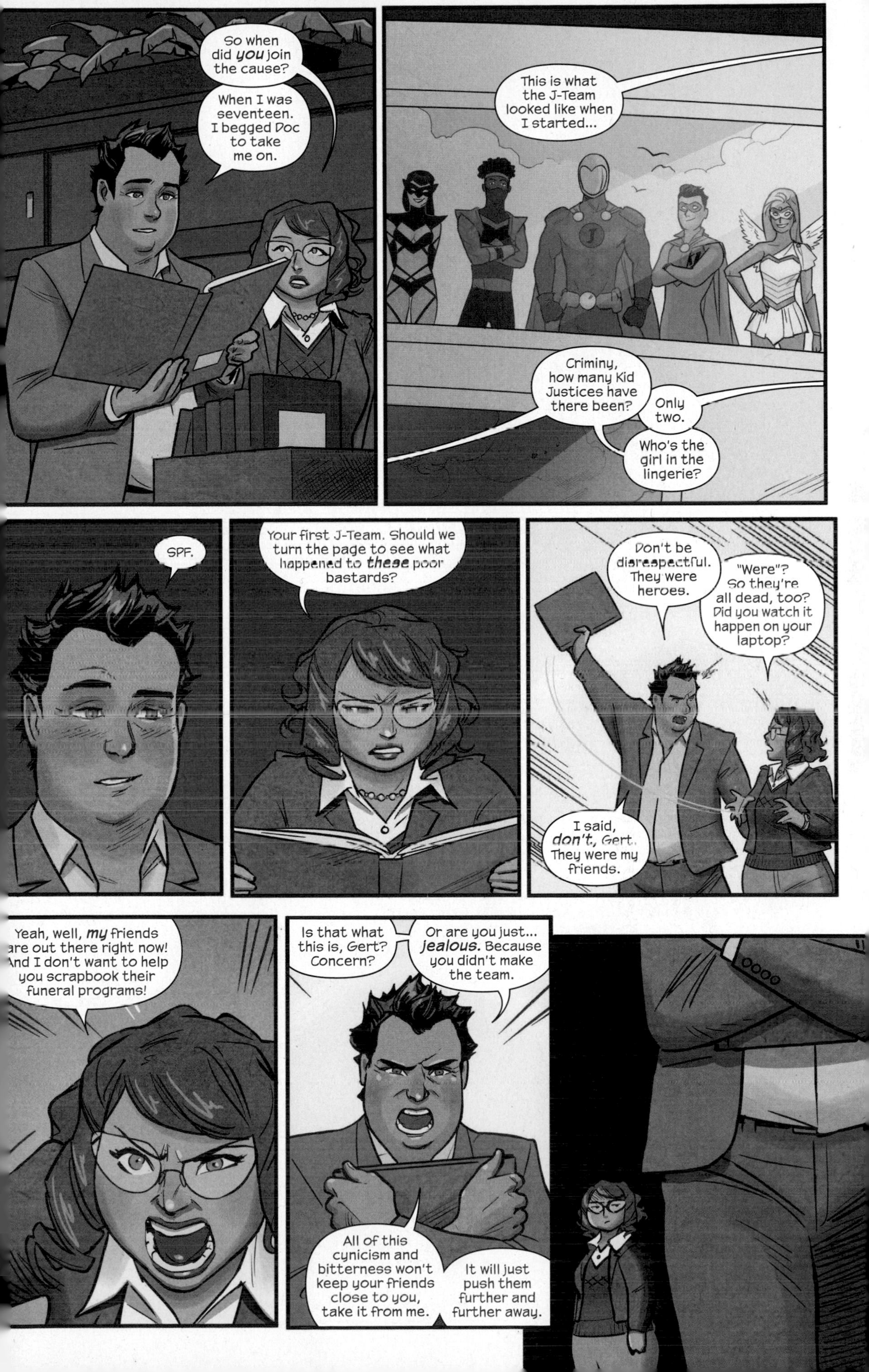
So when did *you* join the cause?
When I was seventeen. I begged Doc to take me on.
This is what the J-Team looked like when I started...
Criminy, how many Kid Justices have there been?
Only two.
Who's the girl in the lingerie?
SPF.
Your first J-Team. Should we turn the page to see what happened to *these* poor bastards?
Don't be disrespectful. They were heroes.
"Were"? So they're all dead, too? Did you watch it happen on your laptop?
I said, *don't,* Gert. They were my friends.
Yeah, well, *my* friends are out there right now! And I don't want to help you scrapbook their funeral programs!
Is that what this is, Gert? Concern?
Or are you just... *jealous.* Because you didn't make the team.
All of this cynicism and bitterness won't keep your friends close to you, take it from me.
It will just push them further and further away.

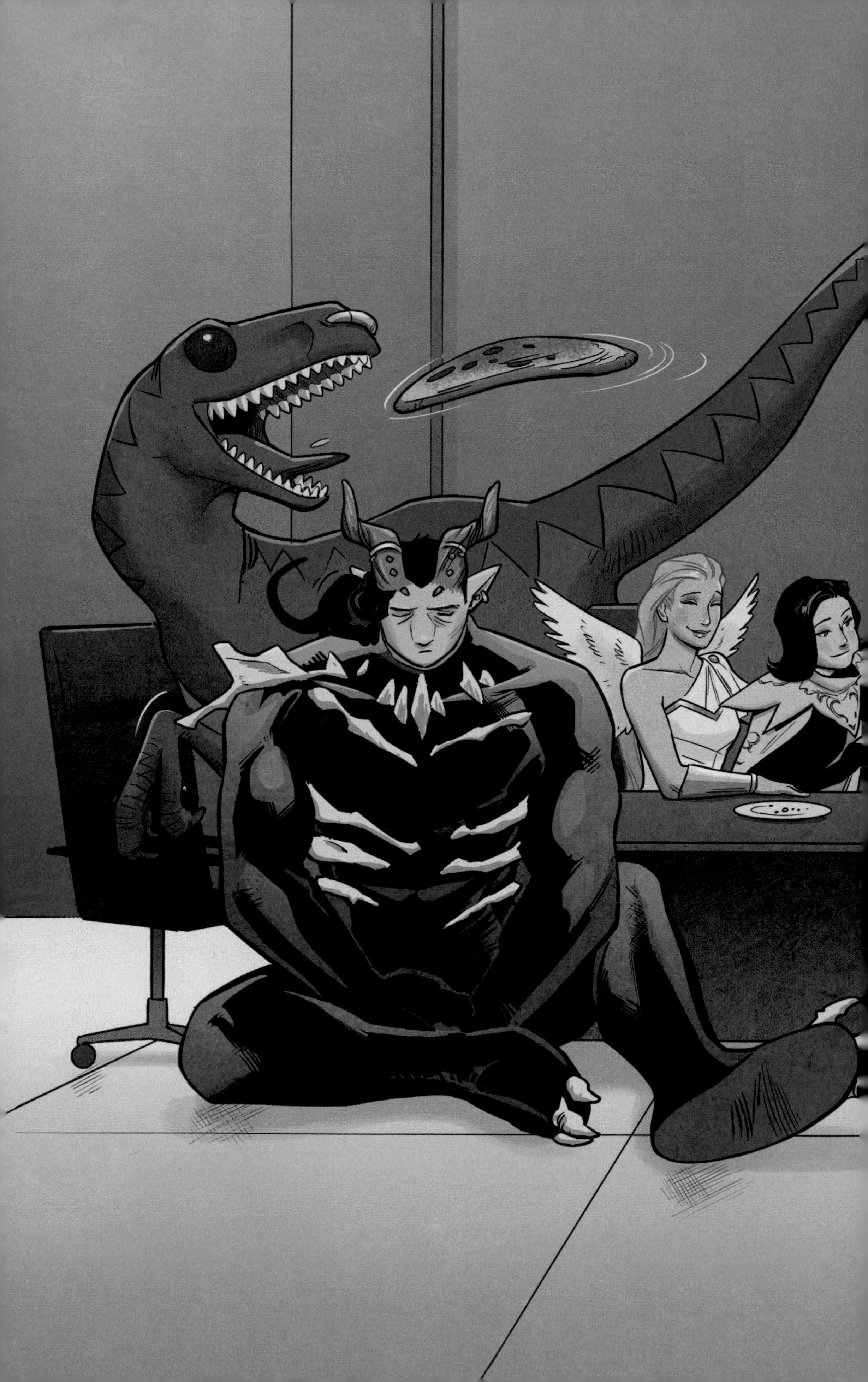

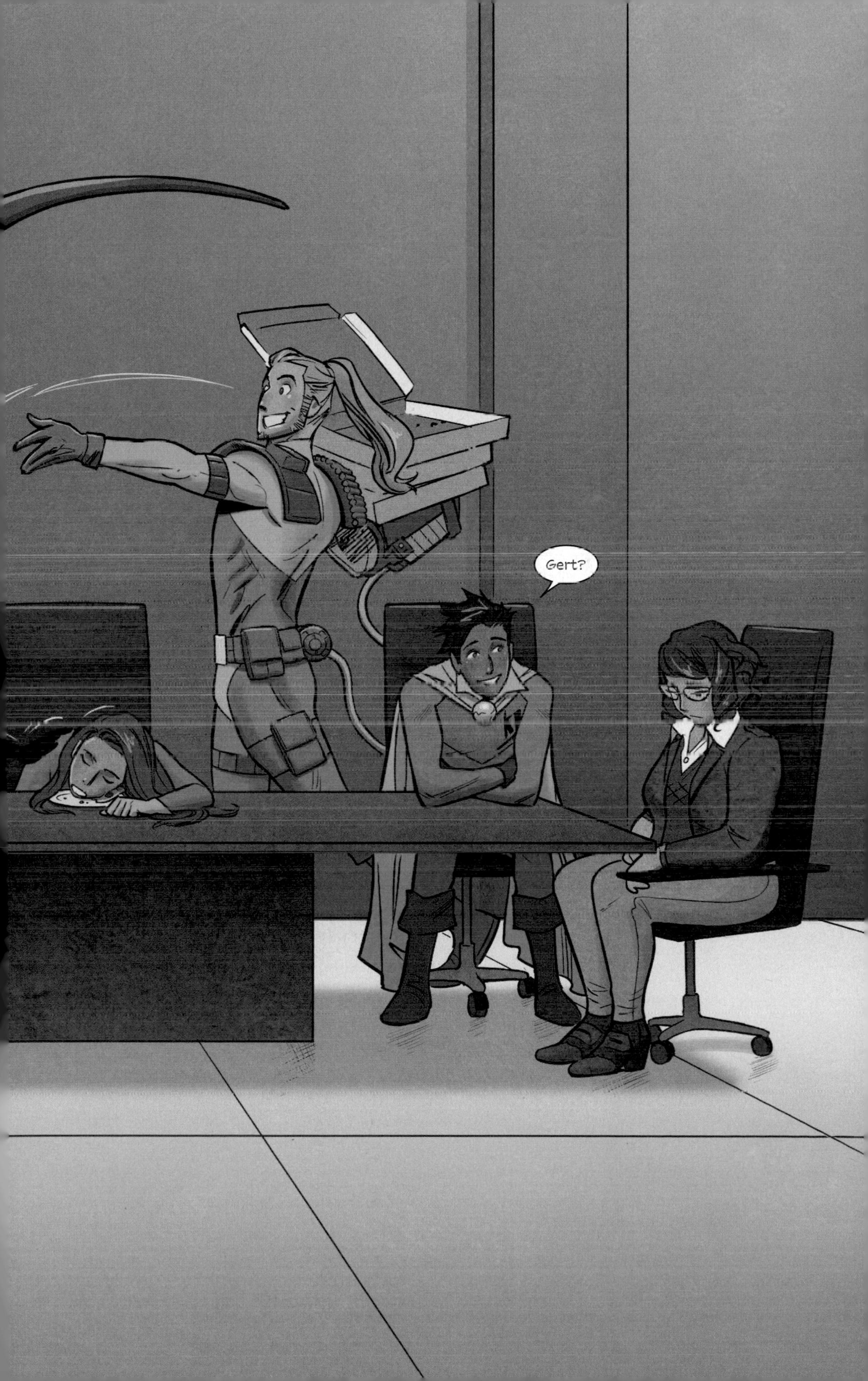
Gert?

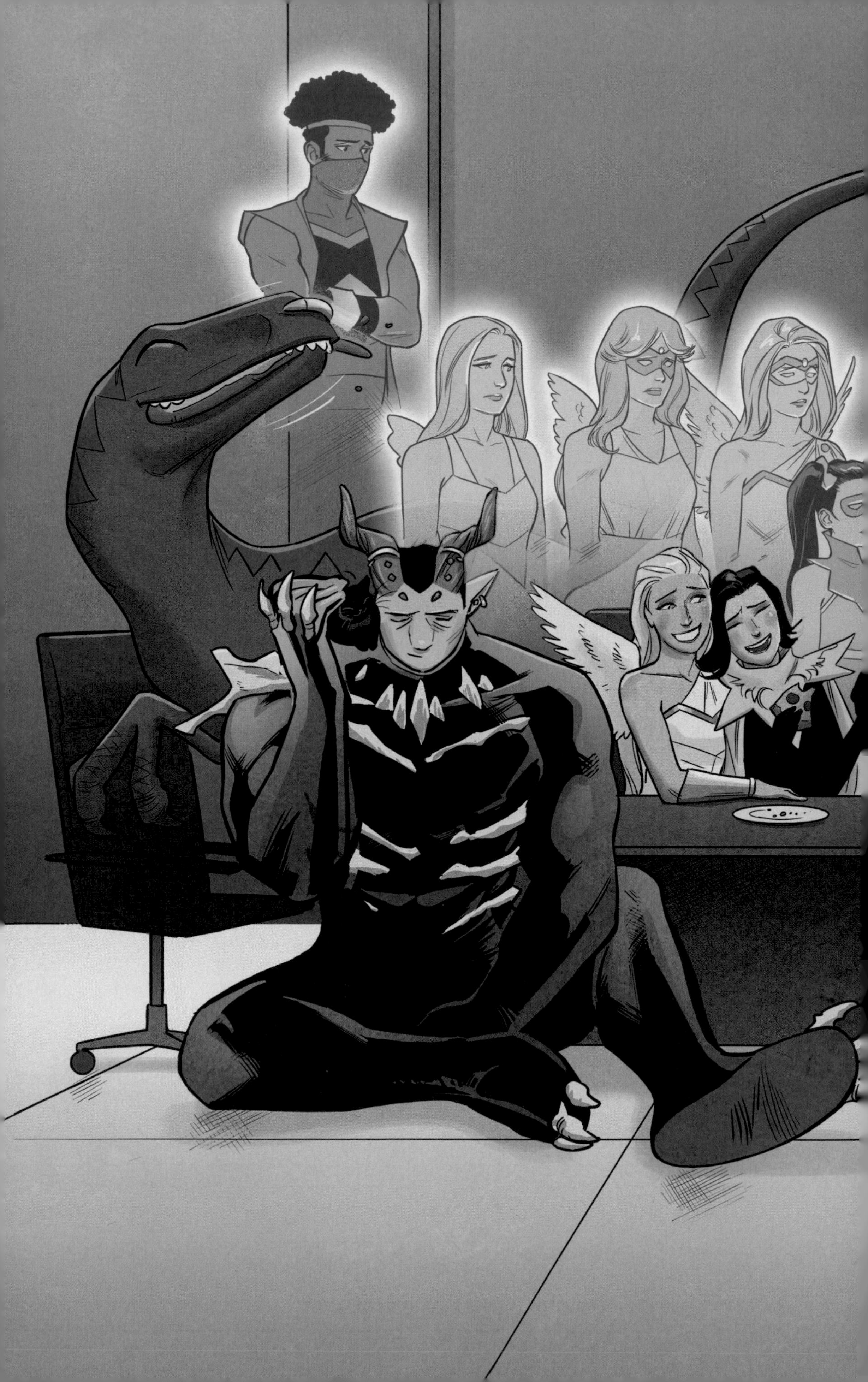

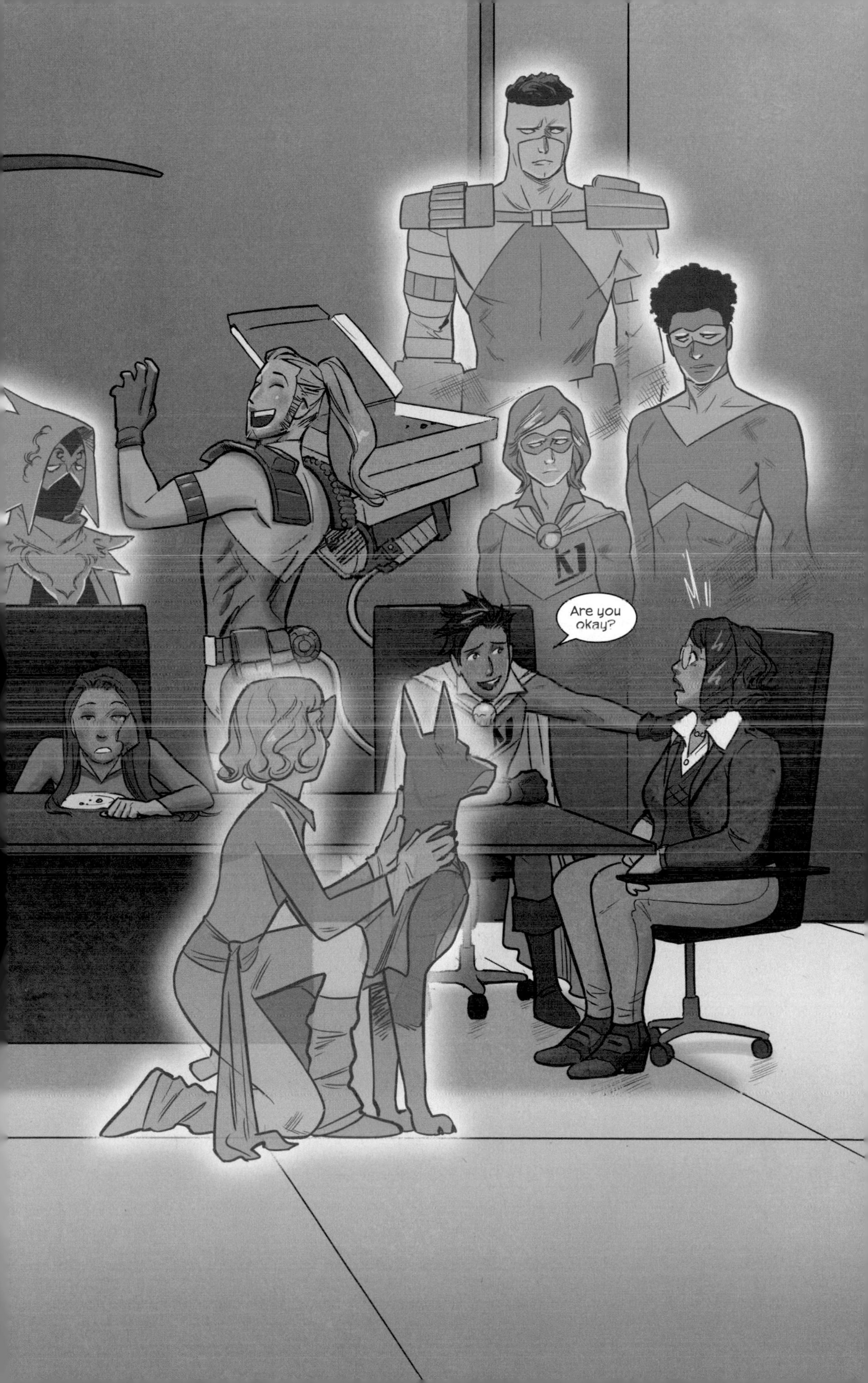
Are you okay?

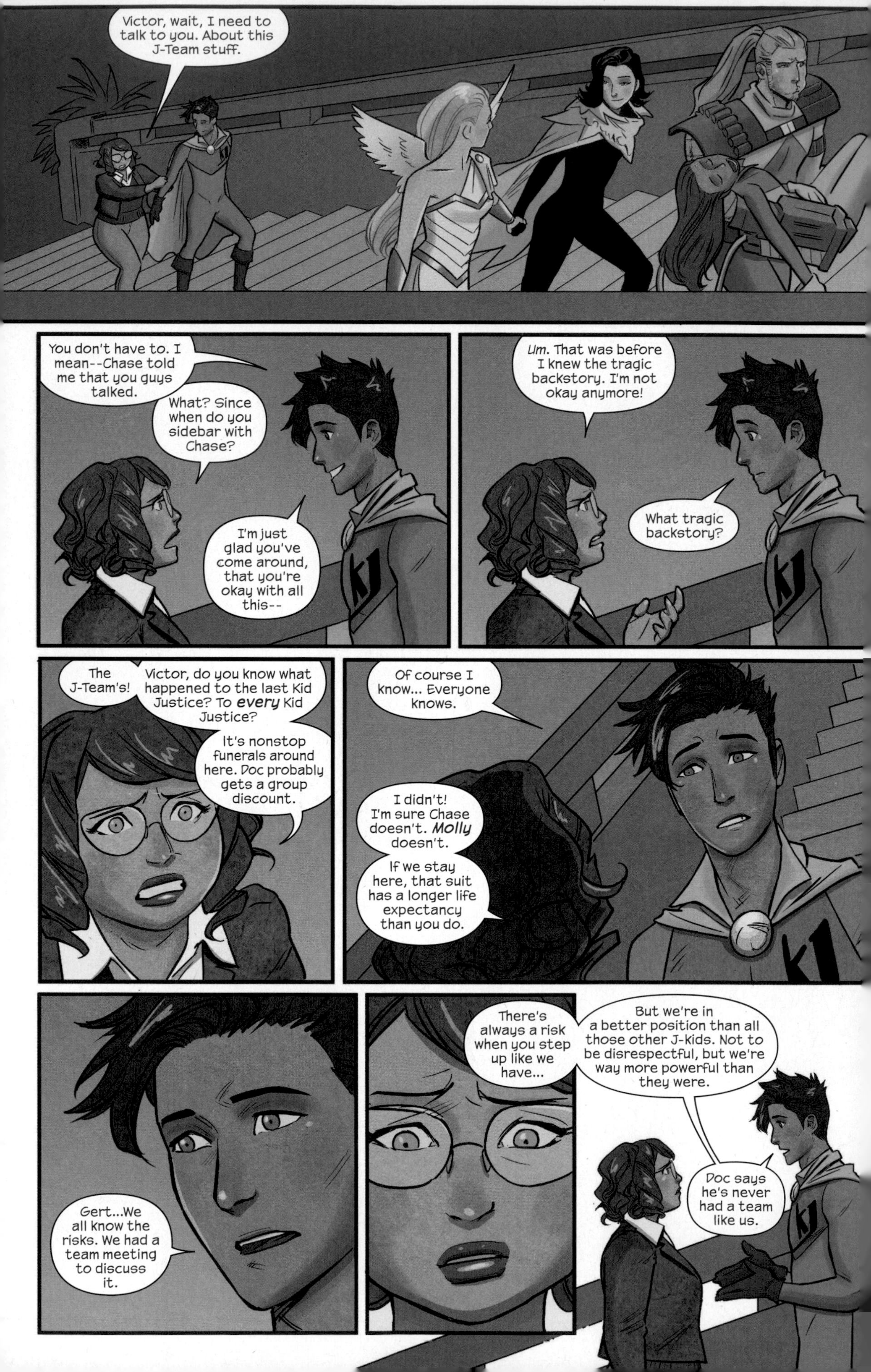
Victor, wait, I need to talk to you. About this J-Team stuff.
You don't have to. I mean--Chase told me that you guys talked.
What? Since when do you sidebar with Chase?
I'm just glad you've come around, that you're okay with all this--
Um. That was before I knew the tragic backstory. I'm not okay anymore!
What tragic backstory?
The J-Team's!
Victor, do you know what happened to the last Kid Justice? To ***every*** Kid Justice?
It's nonstop funerals around here. Doc probably gets a group discount.
Of course I know... Everyone knows.
I didn't! I'm sure Chase doesn't. ***Molly*** doesn't.
If we stay here, that suit has a longer life expectancy than you do.
Gert...We all know the risks. We had a team meeting to discuss it.
There's always a risk when you step up like we have...
But we're in a better position than all those other J-kids. Not to be disrespectful, but we're way more powerful than they were.
Doc says he's never had a team like us.

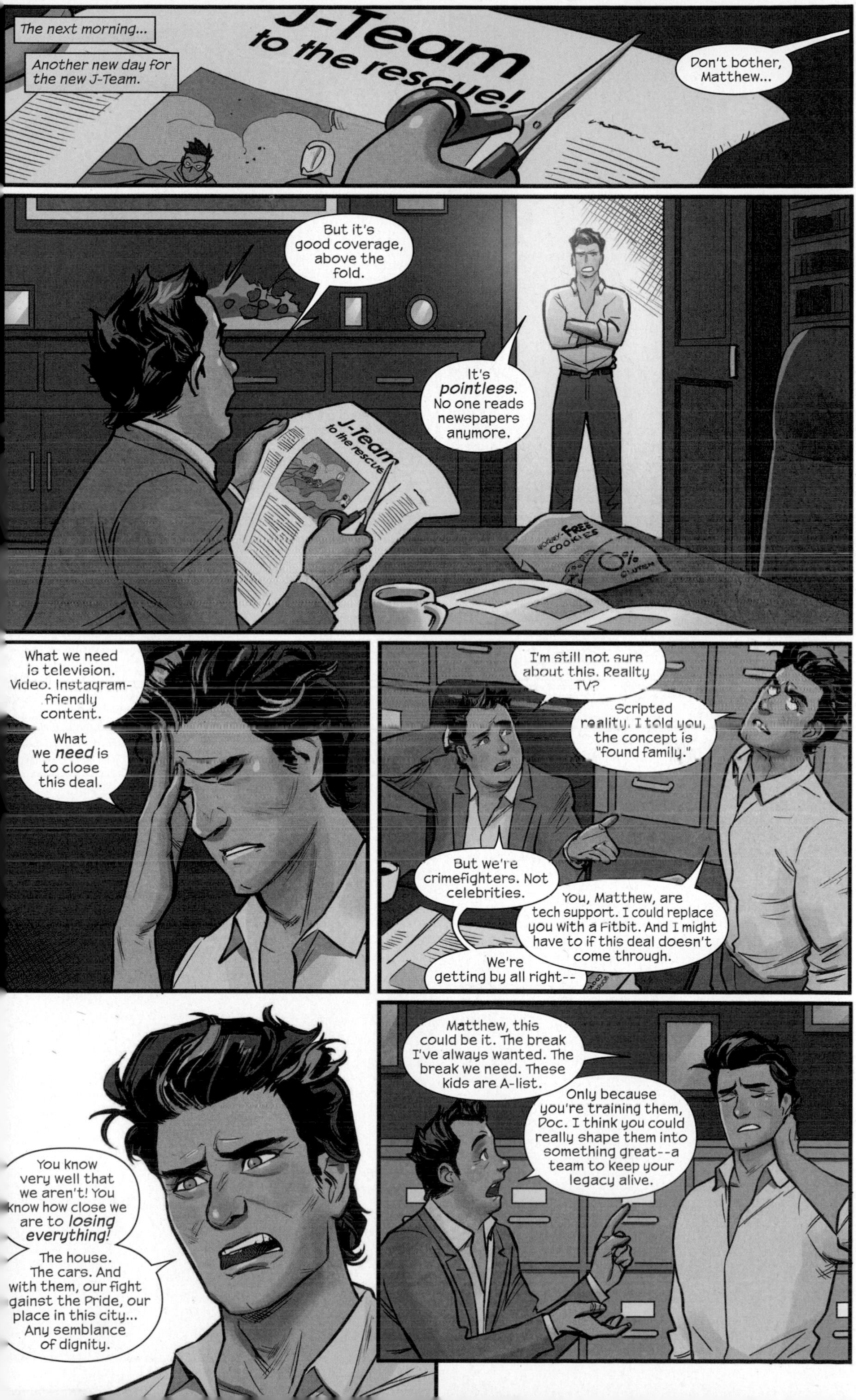
The next morning...
Another new day for the new J-Team.
J-Team to the rescue!
Don't bother, Matthew...
But it's good coverage, above the fold.
It's pointless. No one reads newspapers anymore.
J-Team to the rescue
FREE COOKIES
What we need is television. Video. Instagram-friendly content.
What we need is to close this deal.
I'm still not sure about this. Reality TV?
Scripted reality. I told you, the concept is "found family."
But we're crimefighters. Not celebrities.
You, Matthew, are tech support. I could replace you with a Fitbit. And I might have to if this deal doesn't come through.
We're getting by all right--
You know very well that we aren't! You know how close we are to losing everything!
The house. The cars. And with them, our fight gainst the Pride, our place in this city... Any semblance of dignity.
Matthew, this could be it. The break I've always wanted. The break we need. These kids are A-list.
Only because you're training them, Doc. I think you could really shape them into something great--a team to keep your legacy alive.

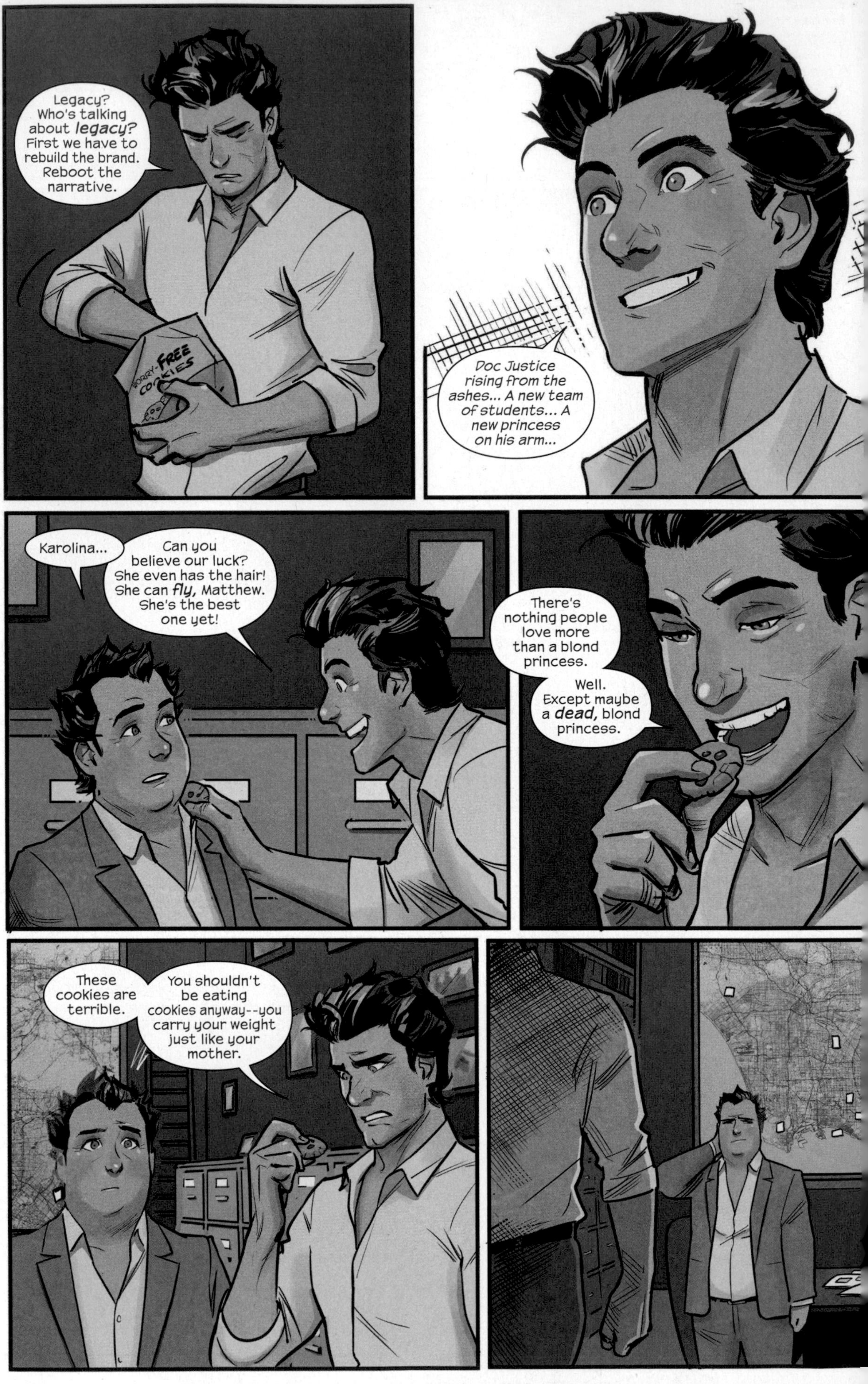

Legacy? Who's talking about *legacy?* First we have to rebuild the brand. Reboot the narrative.
WORRY-FREE COOKIES
Doc Justice rising from the ashes... A new team of students... A new princess on his arm...
Karolina...
Can you believe our luck? She even has the hair! She can *fly,* Matthew. She's the best one yet!
There's nothing people love more than a blond princess.
Well. Except maybe a *dead,* blond princess.
These cookies are terrible.
You shouldn't be eating cookies anyway--you carry your weight just like your mother.

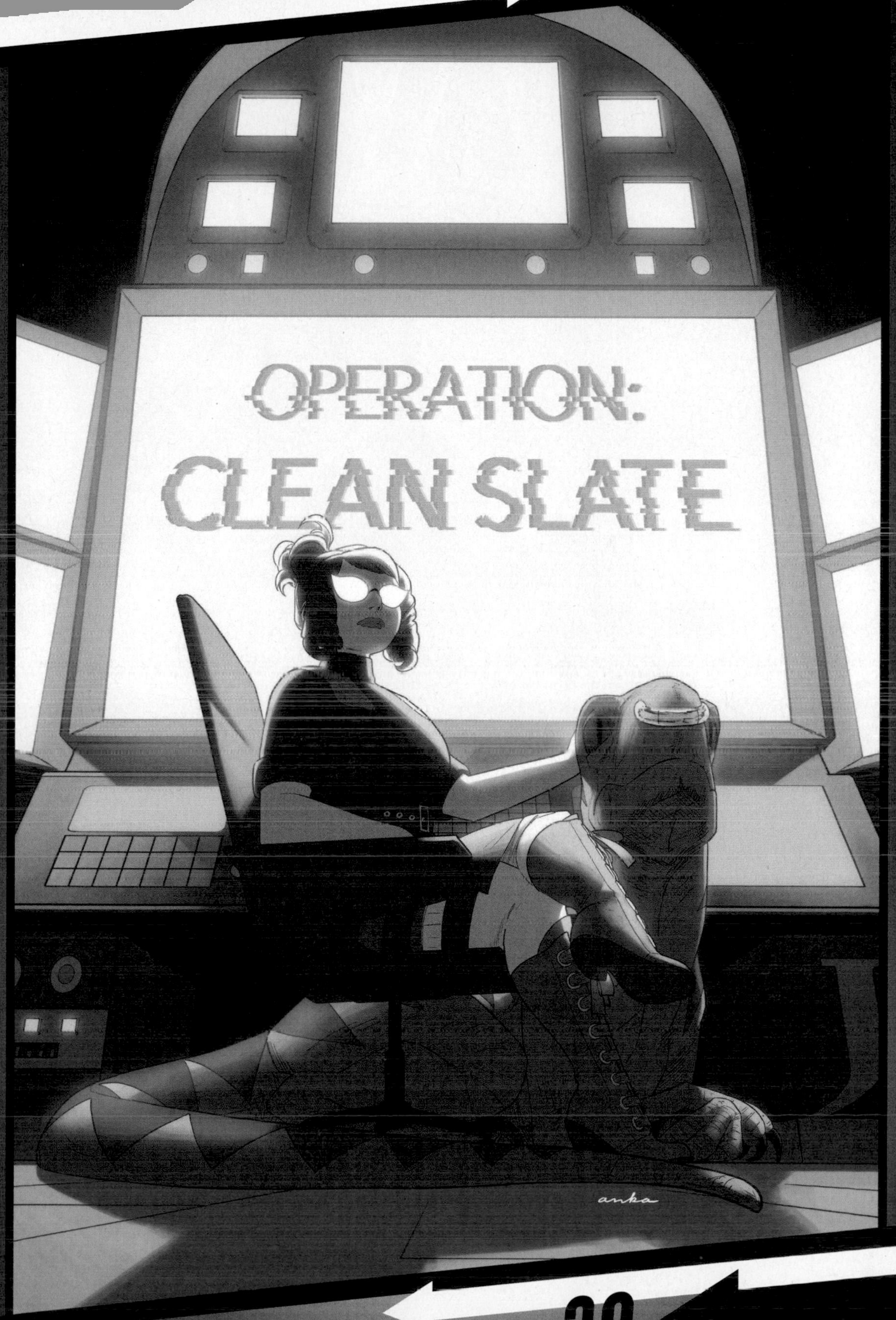
OPERATION:
CLEAN SLATE
anka

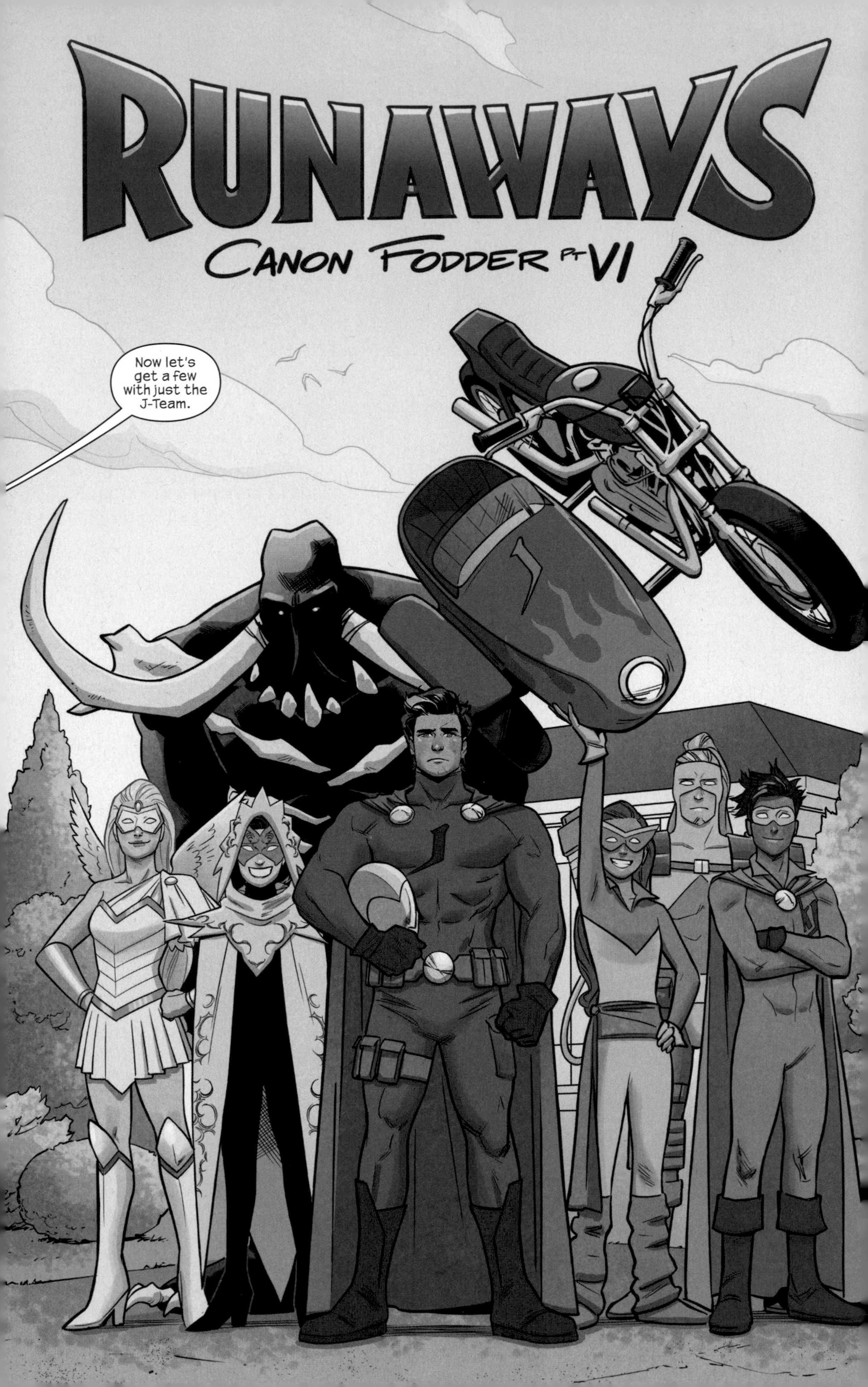
RUNAWAYS
CANON FODDER PT VI
Now let's get a few with just the J-Team.

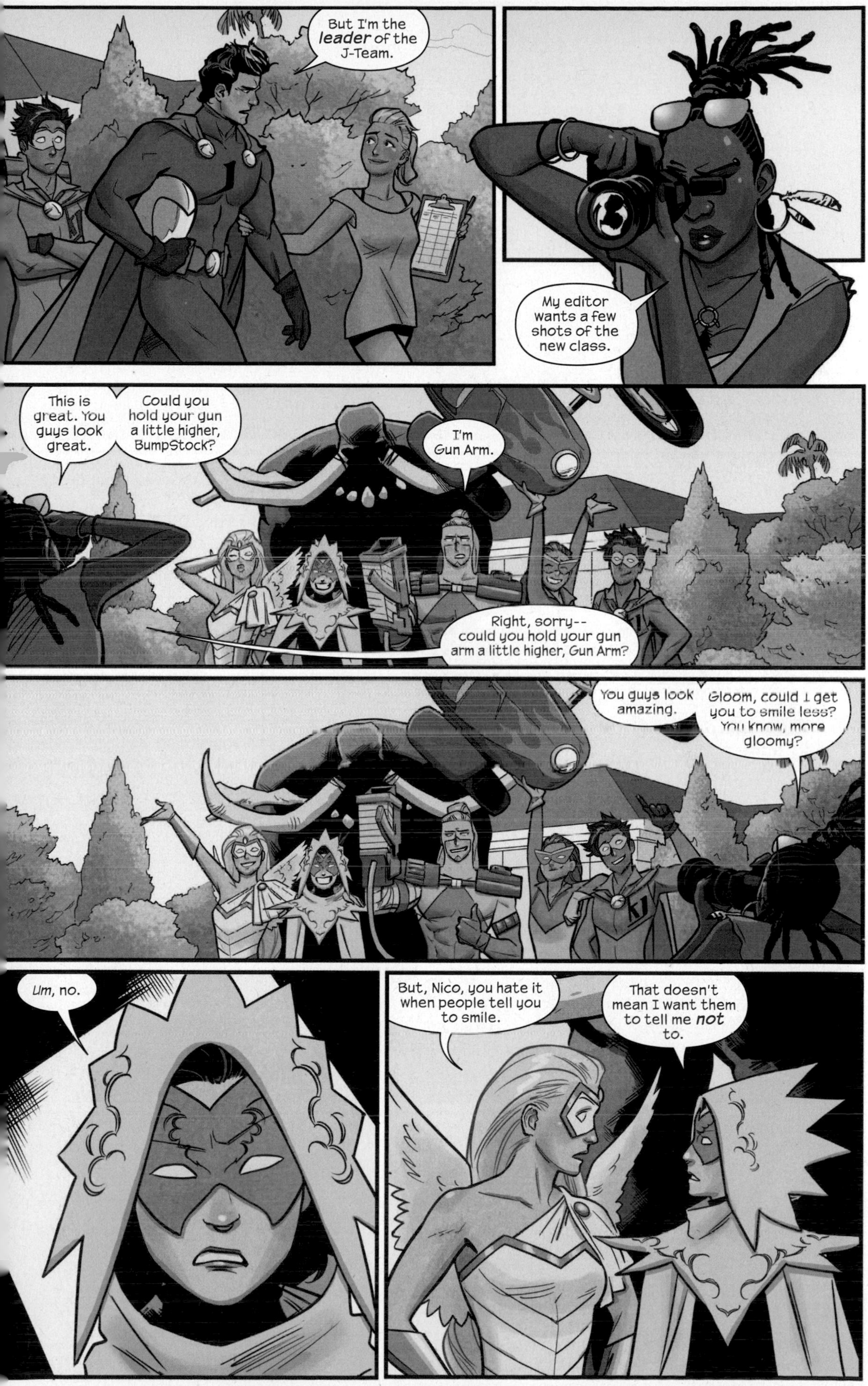
But I'm the *leader* of the J-Team.
My editor wants a few shots of the new class.
This is great. You guys look great.
Could you hold your gun a little higher, BumpStock?
I'm Gun Arm.
Right, sorry-- could you hold your gun arm a little higher, Gun Arm?
You guys look amazing.
Gloom, could I get you to smile less? You know, more gloomy?
Um, no.
But, Nico, you hate it when people tell you to smile.
That doesn't mean I want them to tell me *not* to.

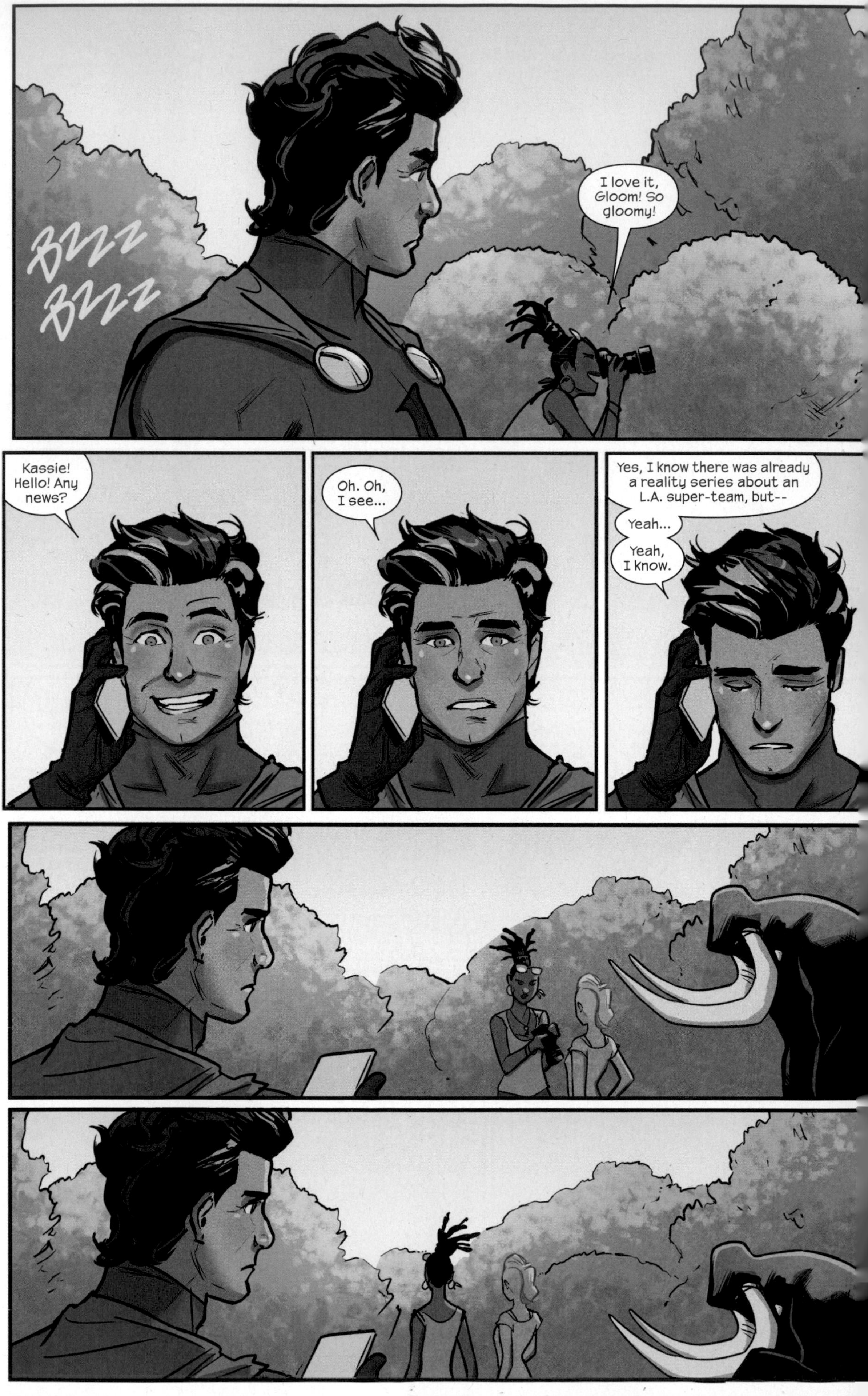
BZZZ BZZZ
I love it, Gloom! So gloomy!
Kassie! Hello! Any news?
Oh. Oh, I see...
Yes, I know there was already a reality series about an L.A. super-team, but--
Yeah...
Yeah, I know.

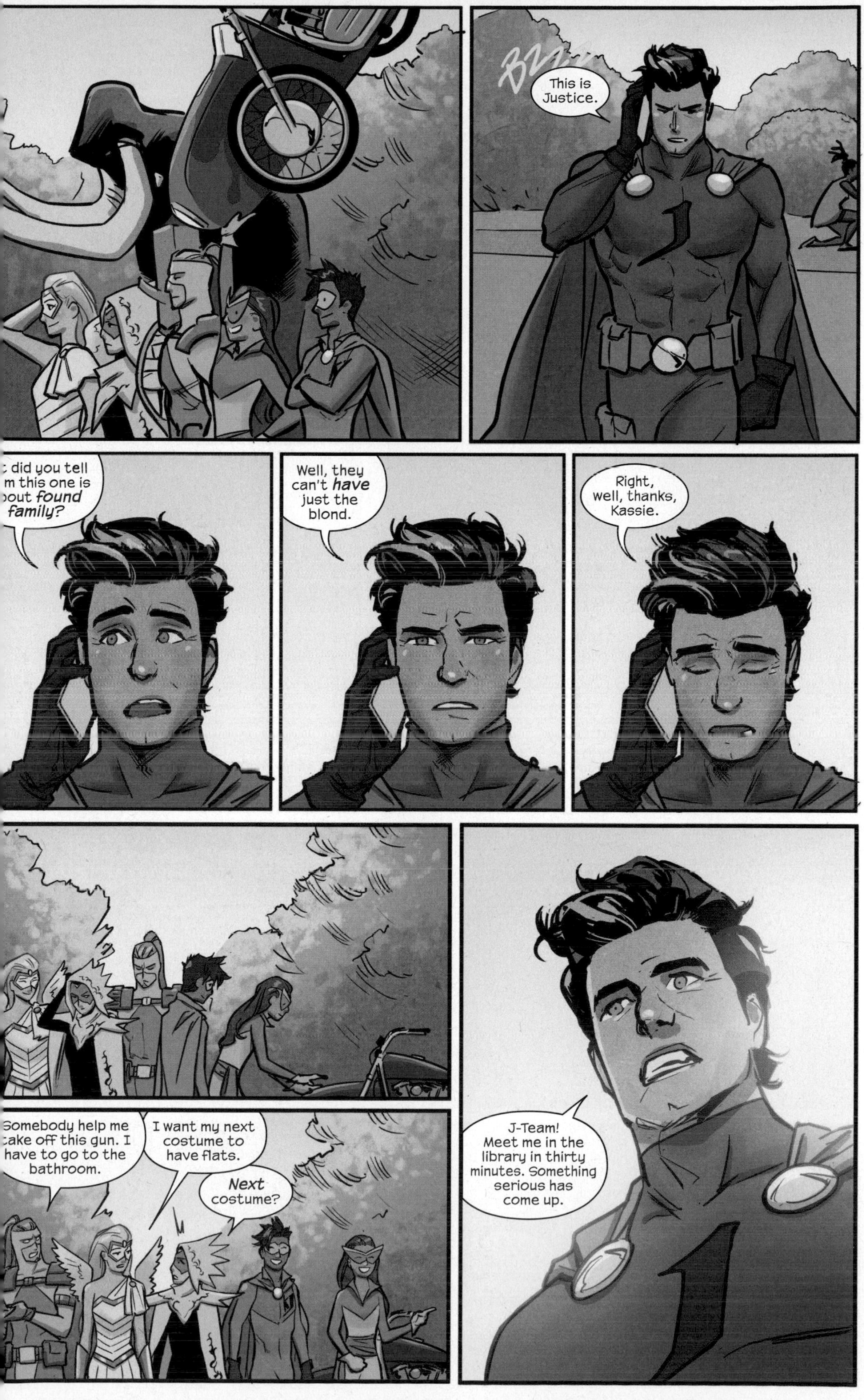
BZZZ
This is Justice.
...did you tell ...m this one is ...bout *found family?*
Well, they can't *have* just the blond.
Right, well, thanks, Kassie.
Somebody help me take off this gun. I have to go to the bathroom.
I want my next costume to have flats.
Next costume?
J-Team! Meet me in the library in thirty minutes. Something serious has come up.

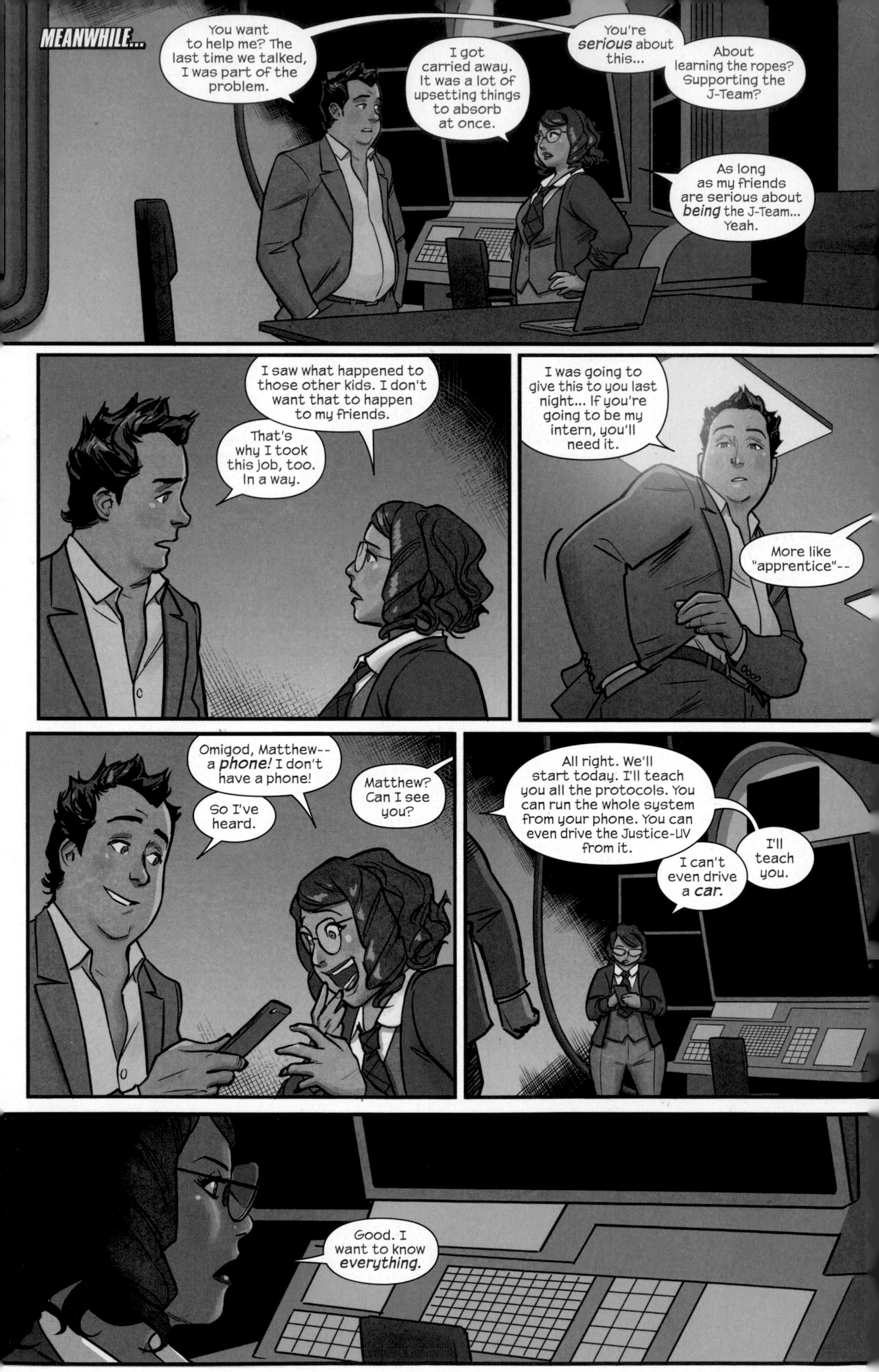
MEANWHILE...
You want to help me? The last time we talked, I was part of the problem.
I got carried away. It was a lot of upsetting things to absorb at once.
You're *serious* about this...
About learning the ropes? Supporting the J-Team?
As long as my friends are serious about *being* the J-Team... Yeah.
I saw what happened to those other kids. I don't want that to happen to my friends.
That's why I took this job, too. In a way.
I was going to give this to you last night... If you're going to be my intern, you'll need it.
More like "apprentice"--
Omigod, Matthew--a *phone!* I don't have a phone!
So I've heard.
Matthew? Can I see you?
All right. We'll start today. I'll teach you all the protocols. You can run the whole system from your phone. You can even drive the Justice-UV from it.
I can't even drive a *car.*
I'll teach you.
Good. I want to know *everything.*

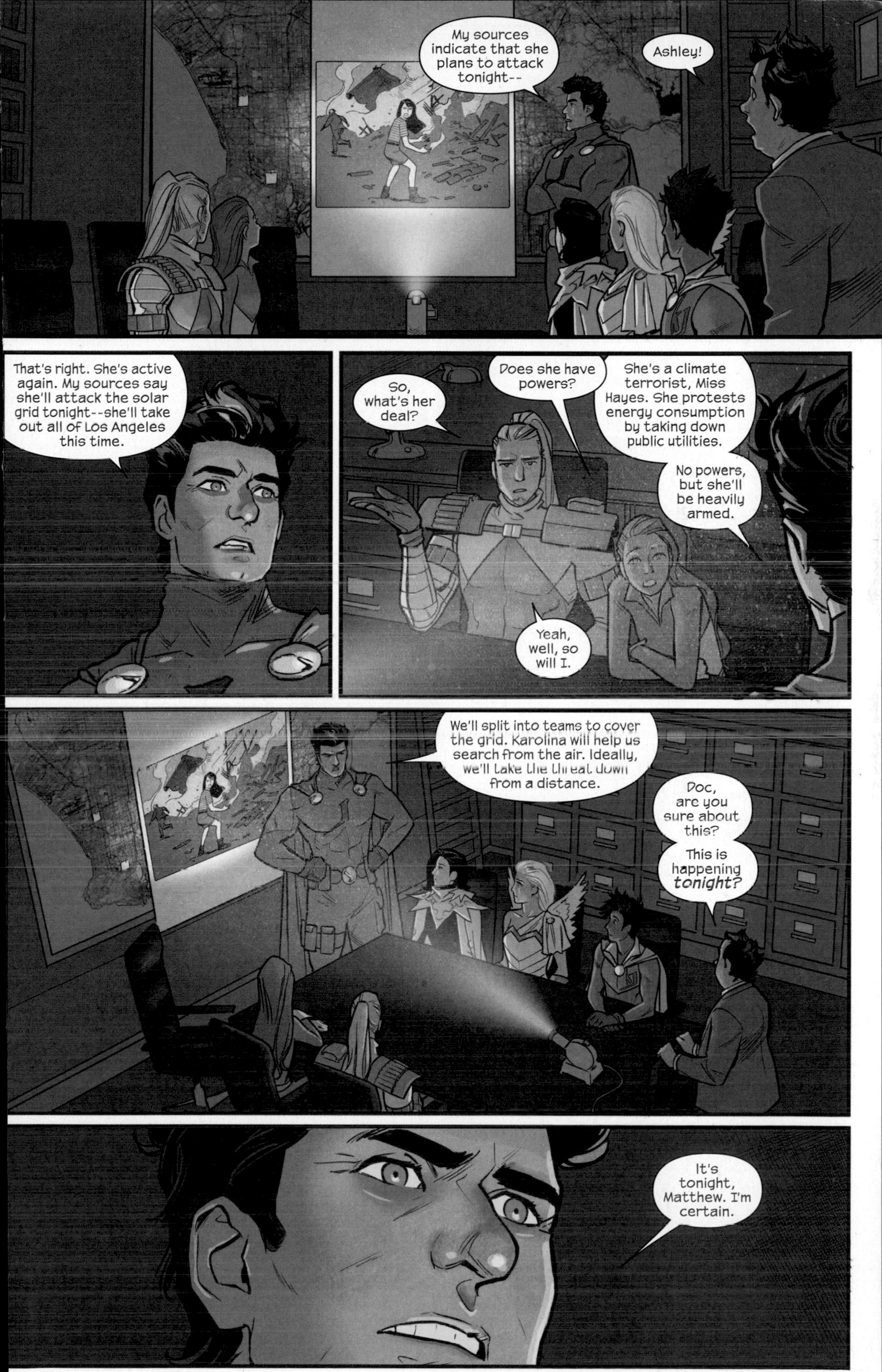

My sources indicate that she plans to attack tonight--
Ashley!
That's right. She's active again. My sources say she'll attack the solar grid tonight--she'll take out all of Los Angeles this time.
So, what's her deal?
Does she have powers?
She's a climate terrorist, Miss Hayes. She protests energy consumption by taking down public utilities.
No powers, but she'll be heavily armed.
Yeah, well, so will I.
We'll split into teams to cover the grid. Karolina will help us search from the air. Ideally, we'll take the threat down from a distance.
Doc, are you sure about this?
This is happening *tonight?*
It's tonight, Matthew. I'm certain.

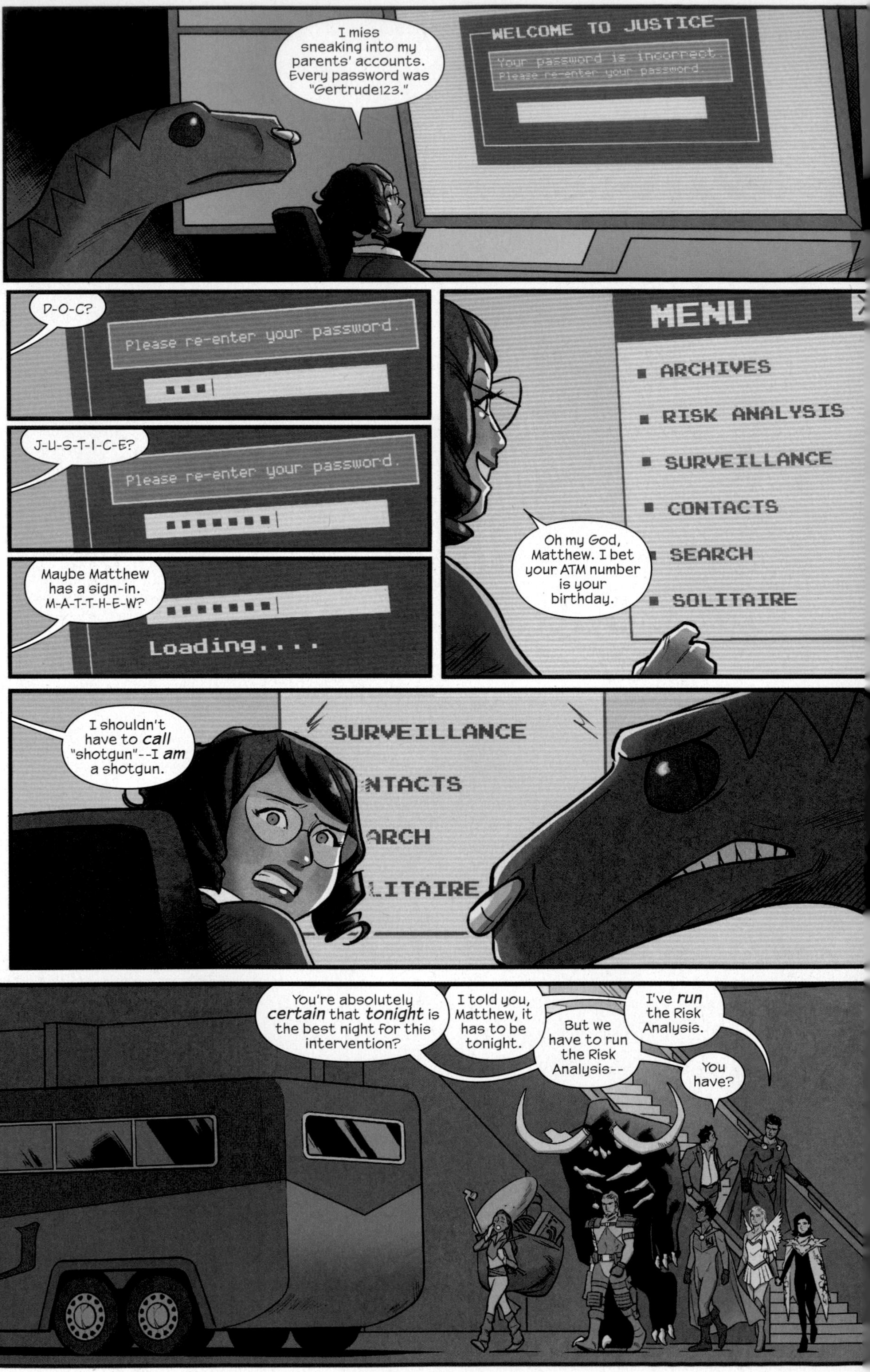
WELCOME TO JUSTICE
Your password is incorrect.
Please re-enter your password.
I miss sneaking into my parents' accounts. Every password was "Gertrude123."
D-O-C?
Please re-enter your password.
J-U-S-T-I-C-E?
Please re-enter your password.
Maybe Matthew has a sign-in. M-A-T-T-H-E-W?
Loading....
MENU
ARCHIVES
RISK ANALYSIS
SURVEILLANCE
CONTACTS
SEARCH
SOLITAIRE
Oh my God, Matthew. I bet your ATM number is your birthday.
I shouldn't have to *call* "shotgun"--I *am* a shotgun.
You're absolutely *certain* that *tonight* is the best night for this intervention?
I told you, Matthew, it has to be tonight.
But we have to run the Risk Analysis--
I've *run* the Risk Analysis.
You have?

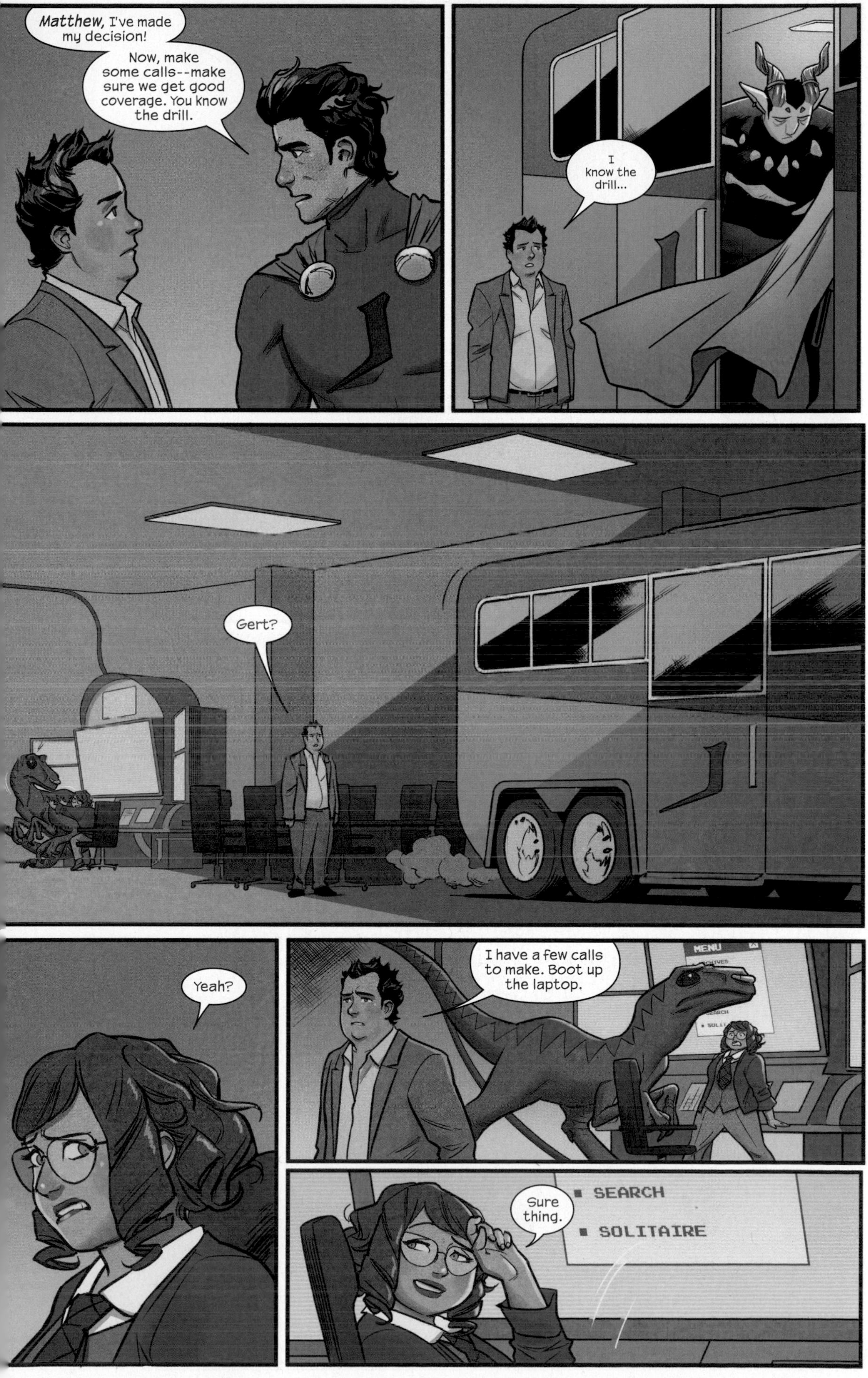

Matthew, I've made my decision!
Now, make some calls--make sure we get good coverage. You know the drill.
I know the drill...
Gert?
Yeah?
I have a few calls to make. Boot up the laptop.
MENU
SEARCH
SOLITAIRE
Sure thing.

All right, Lace, time to find some dirt on Doc Justice.

Apparently "everybody around here dies" isn't enough of a red flag for my dumb friends...

What are we looking for--tax fraud? Unfortunate pornography?

MENU

■ ARCHIVES

■ RISK ANALYSIS

■ SURVEILLANCE

■ CONTACTS

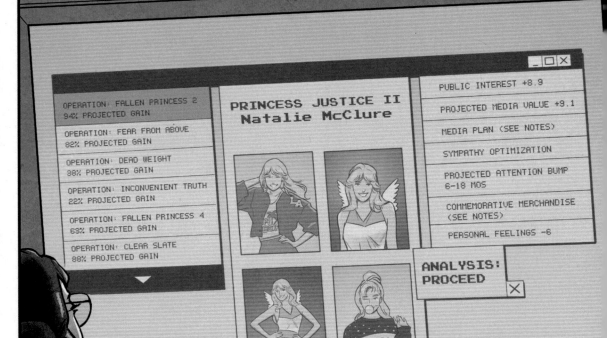

OPERATION: FALLEN PRINCESS 2
94% PROJECTED GAIN

OPERATION: FEAR FROM ABOVE
82% PROJECTED GAIN

OPERATION: DEAD WEIGHT
38% PROJECTED GAIN

OPERATION: INCONVENIENT TRUTH
22% PROJECTED GAIN

OPERATION: FALLEN PRINCESS 4
63% PROJECTED GAIN

OPERATION: CLEAR SLATE
88% PROJECTED GAIN

PRINCESS JUSTICE II
Natalie McClure

PUBLIC INTEREST +8.9

PROJECTED MEDIA VALUE +9.1

MEDIA PLAN (SEE NOTES)

SYMPATHY OPTIMIZATION

PROJECTED ATTENTION BUMP
6-18 MOS

COMMEMORATIVE MERCHANDISE
(SEE NOTES)

PERSONAL FEELINGS -6

ANALYSIS:
PROCEED

What the actual...

PERATION: DEAD WEIGHT
8% PROJECTED GAIN
PERATION: INCONVENIENT TRUTH
2% PROJECTED GAIN
OPERATION: FALLEN PRINCESS 4
3% PROJECTED GAIN
OPERATION: CLEAR SLATE
88% PROJECTED GAIN
OPERATION: FEAR FROM ABOVE
82% PROJECTED GAIN
CLICK
ATION: FEAR FROM ABOVE
PROJECTED GAIN
ATION: DEAD WEIGHT
PROJECTED GAIN
ATION: INCONVENIENT TRUTH
PROJECTED GAIN
ATION: FALLEN PRINCESS 4
PROJECTED GAIN
ATION: CLEAR SLATE
PROJECTED GAIN
ATION: FEAR FROM ABOVE
PROJECTED GAIN
BLUE-J
Jennifer Moore
PUBLIC
PROJEC
MEDIA
SYMPAT
PROJEC
6-18 M
COMME
(SEE N
PERSON
ANALYSI
PROCEED
BUMPSTOCK
Todd Robb
PUBLIC INT
PROJECTED
MEDIA PLAN
SYMPATHY
PROJECTED
COMMEMORA
(SEE NOTE
PERSONAL
ANALYSIS:
PROCEED
SPF
Ashley Pearson
PUBLIC INT
PROJECTED
MEDIA PLAN
SYMPATHY
PROJECTED
COMMEMORA
(SEE NOTE
PERSONAL
ANALYSIS:
DO NOT PRO
RINCESS JUSTICE IV
Melinda Cass
PUBLIC INT
PROJECTED
MEDIA PLAN
SYMPATHY
PROJECTED
COMMEMORA
(SEE NOTE
PERSONAL
ANALYSIS:
PROCEED
OPERATION: CLEAR SLATE
88% PROJECTED GAIN
FEAR FROM ABOVE
CTED GAIN
PRINCESS
JUSTICE III
Jen Gaines
SPF
Ashley Pearson
*MISSING IN ACTION
ANALYSIS:
PROCEED*
KID JUSTICE
Matthew Caniglia
*MISSING IN ACTION
TRENCH
James McClintock
Matthew?

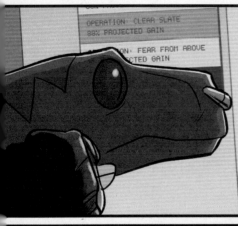

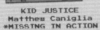

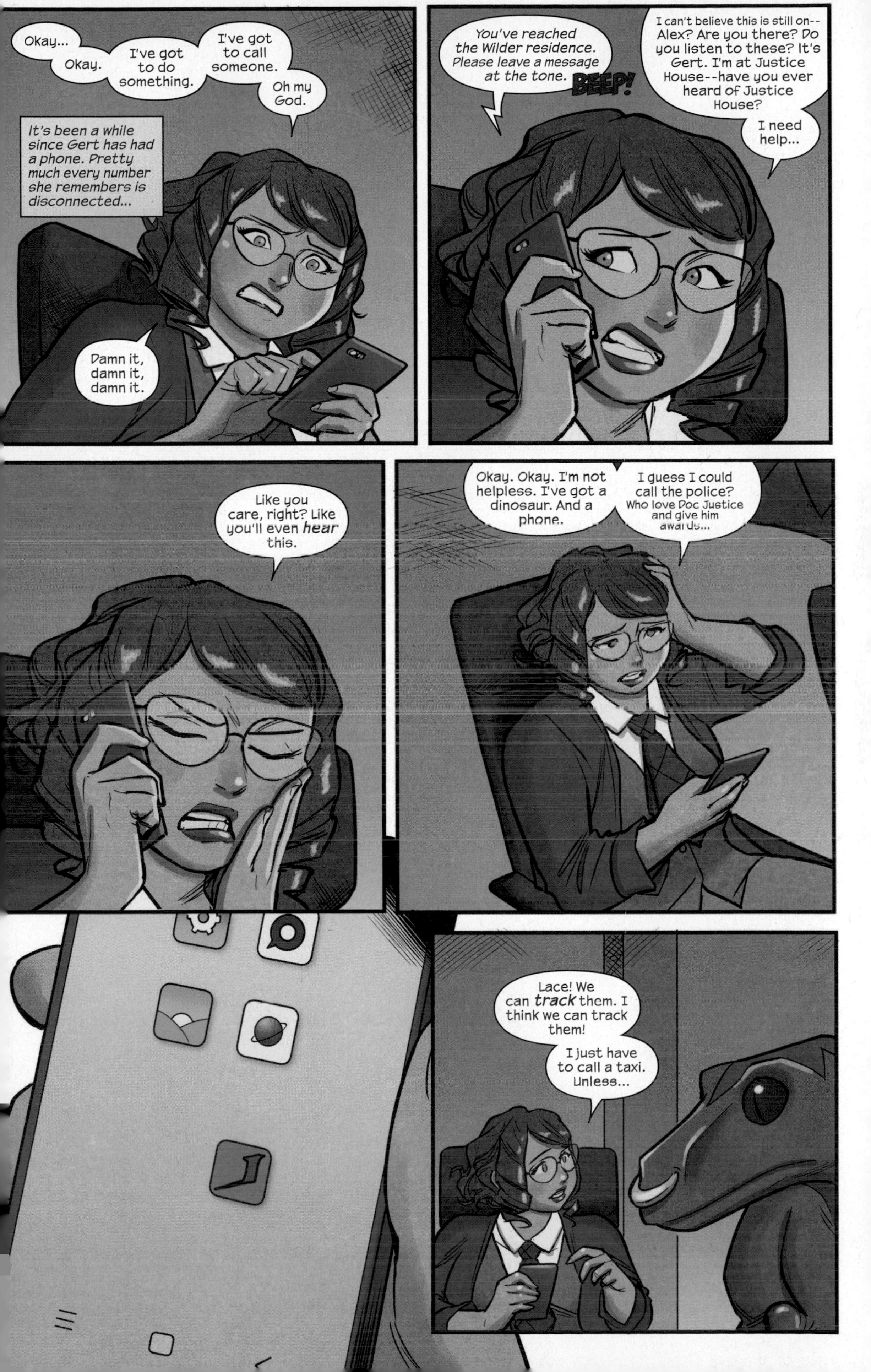

Okay...
Okay.
I've got to do something.
I've got to call someone.
Oh my God.
It's been a while since Gert has had a phone. Pretty much every number she remembers is disconnected...
Damn it, damn it, damn it.
You've reached the Wilder residence. Please leave a message at the tone.
BEEP!
I can't believe this is still on-- Alex? Are you there? Do you listen to these? It's Gert. I'm at Justice House--have you ever heard of Justice House?
I need help...
Like you care, right? Like you'll even hear this.
Okay. Okay. I'm not helpless. I've got a dinosaur. And a phone.
I guess I could call the police? Who love Doc Justice and give him awards...
Lace! We can track them. I think we can track them!
I just have to call a taxi. Unless...

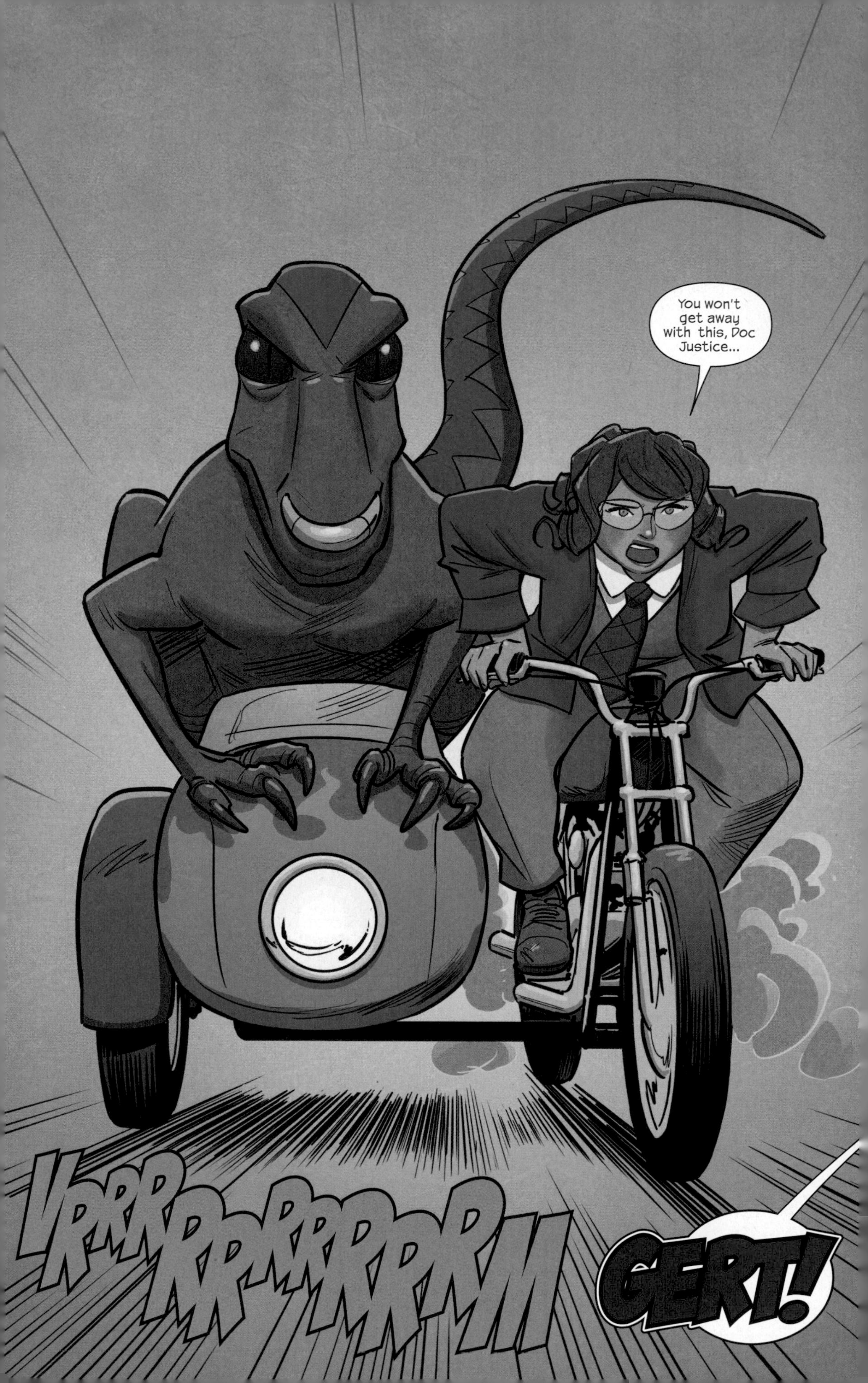
You won't get away with this, Doc Justice...
VRRRRRRRRRRRRRM
GERT!

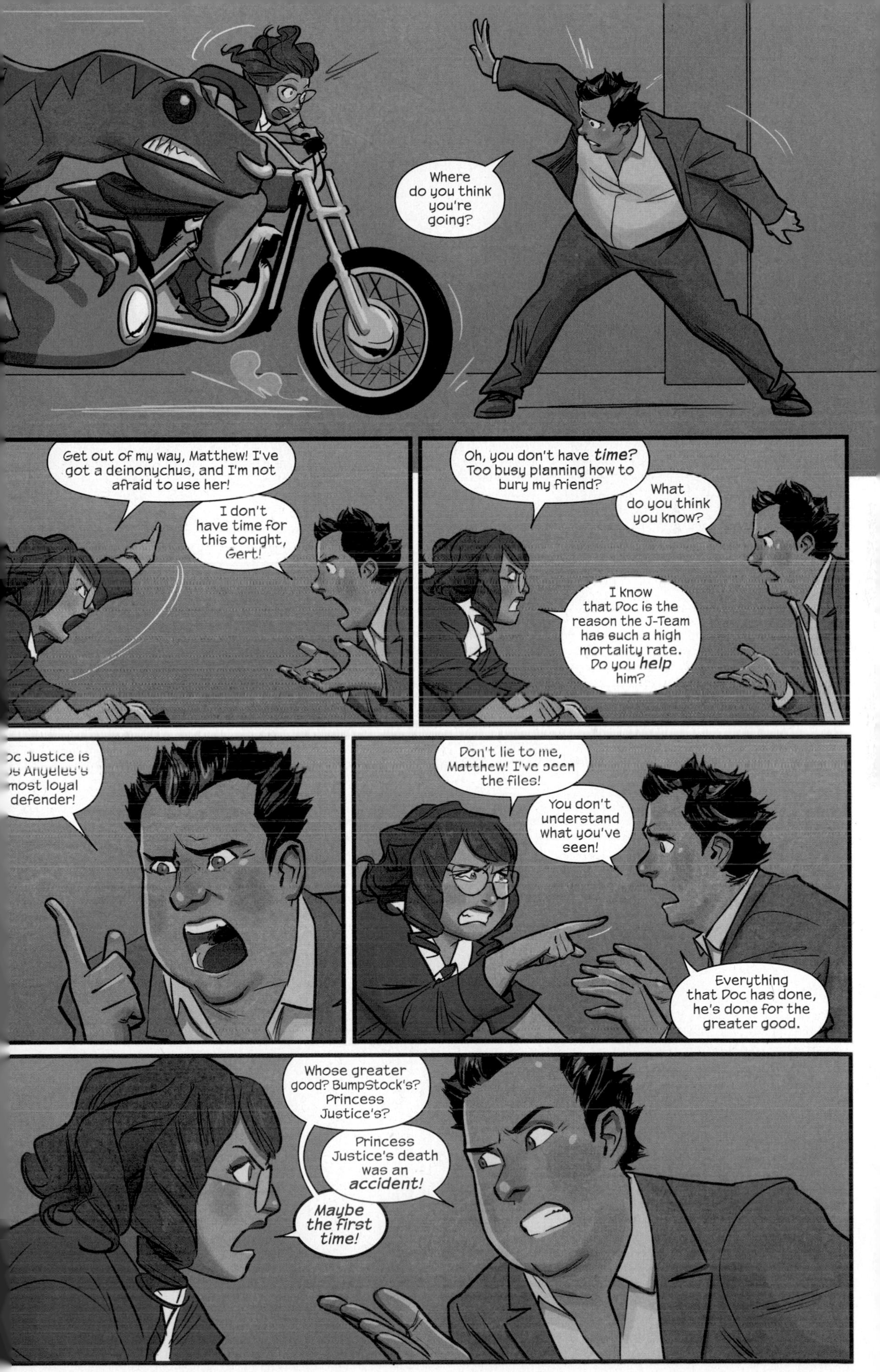
Where do you think you're going?
Get out of my way, Matthew! I've got a deinonychus, and I'm not afraid to use her!
I don't have time for this tonight, Gert!
Oh, you don't have *time?* Too busy planning how to bury my friend?
What do you think you know?
I know that Doc is the reason the J-Team has such a high mortality rate. Do you *help* him?
oc Justice is os Angeles's most loyal defender!
Don't lie to me, Matthew! I've seen the files!
You don't understand what you've seen!
Everything that Doc has done, he's done for the greater good.
Whose greater good? BumpStock's? Princess Justice's?
Princess Justice's death was an *accident!*
Maybe the first time!

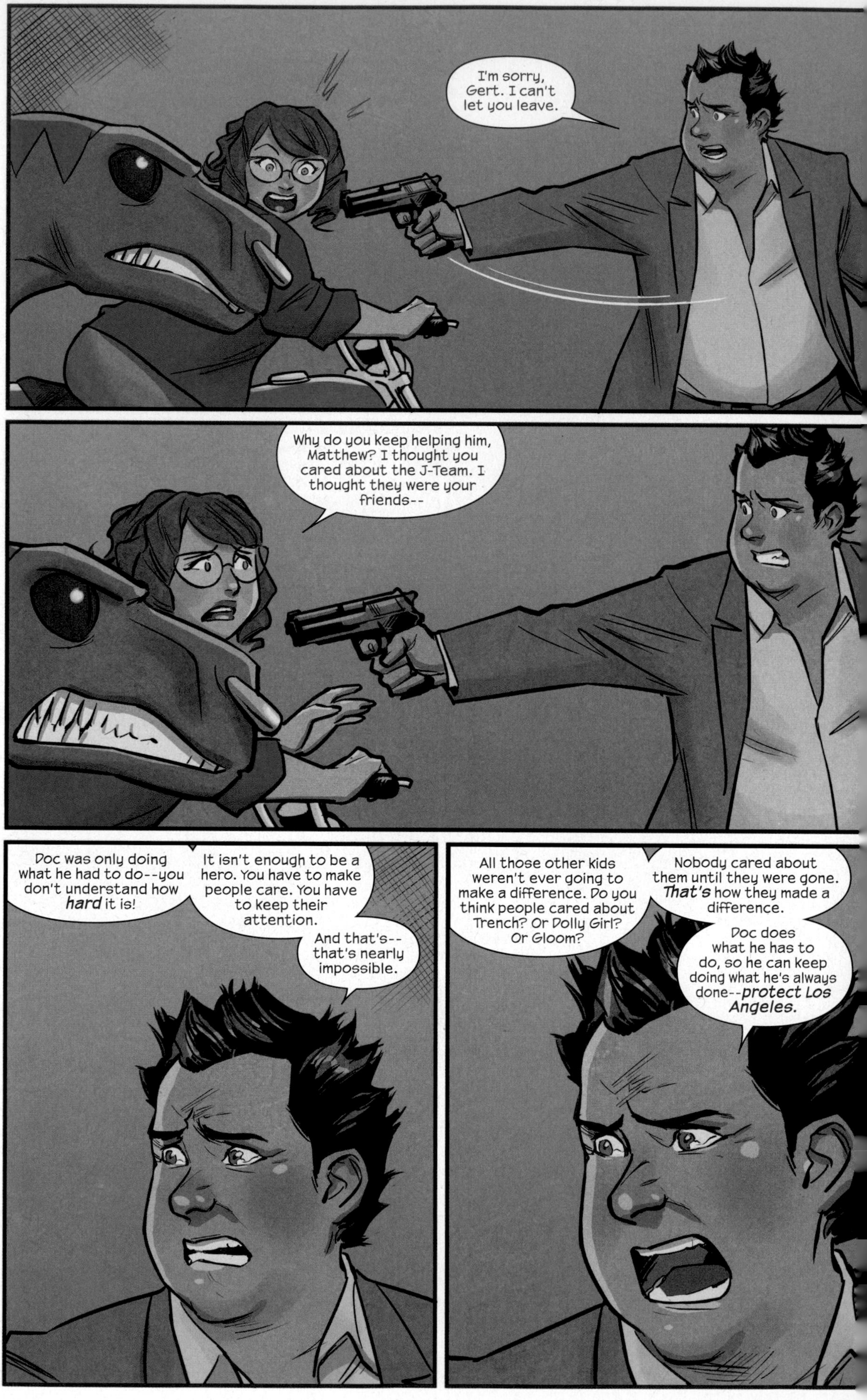
I'm sorry, Gert. I can't let you leave.
Why do you keep helping him, Matthew? I thought you cared about the J-Team. I thought they were your friends--
Doc was only doing what he had to do--you don't understand how *hard* it is!
It isn't enough to be a hero. You have to make people care. You have to keep their attention.
And that's--that's nearly impossible.
All those other kids weren't ever going to make a difference. Do you think people cared about Trench? Or Dolly Girl? Or Gloom?
Nobody cared about them until they were gone. *That's* how they made a difference.
Doc does what he has to do, so he can keep doing what he's always done--*protect Los Angeles.*

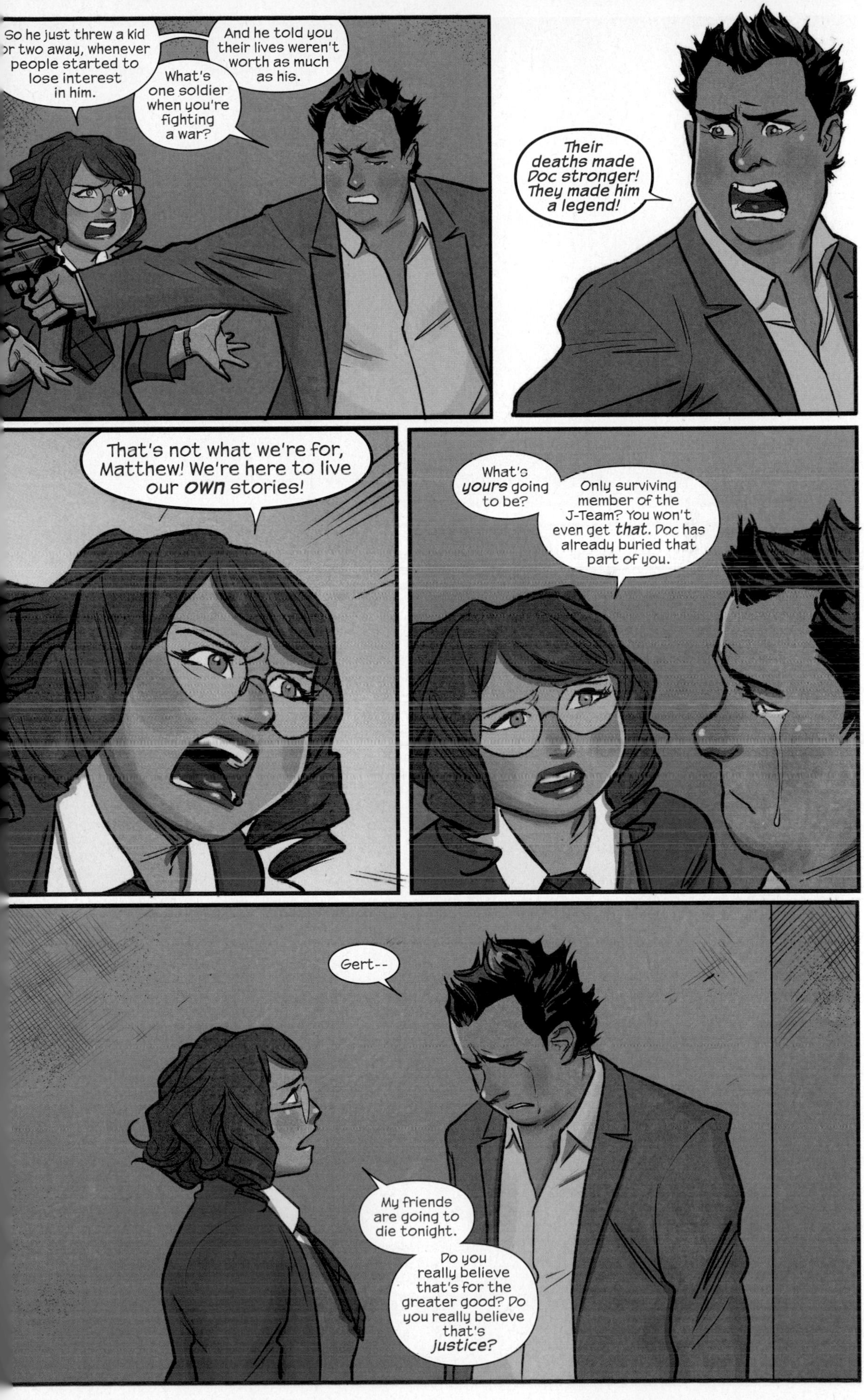
So he just threw a kid or two away, whenever people started to lose interest in him.
What's one soldier when you're fighting a war?
And he told you their lives weren't worth as much as his.
Their deaths made Doc stronger! They made him a legend!
That's not what we're for, Matthew! We're here to live our OWN stories!
What's yours going to be?
Only surviving member of the J-Team? You won't even get that. Doc has already buried that part of you.
Gert--
My friends are going to die tonight.
Do you really believe that's for the greater good? Do you really believe that's justice?

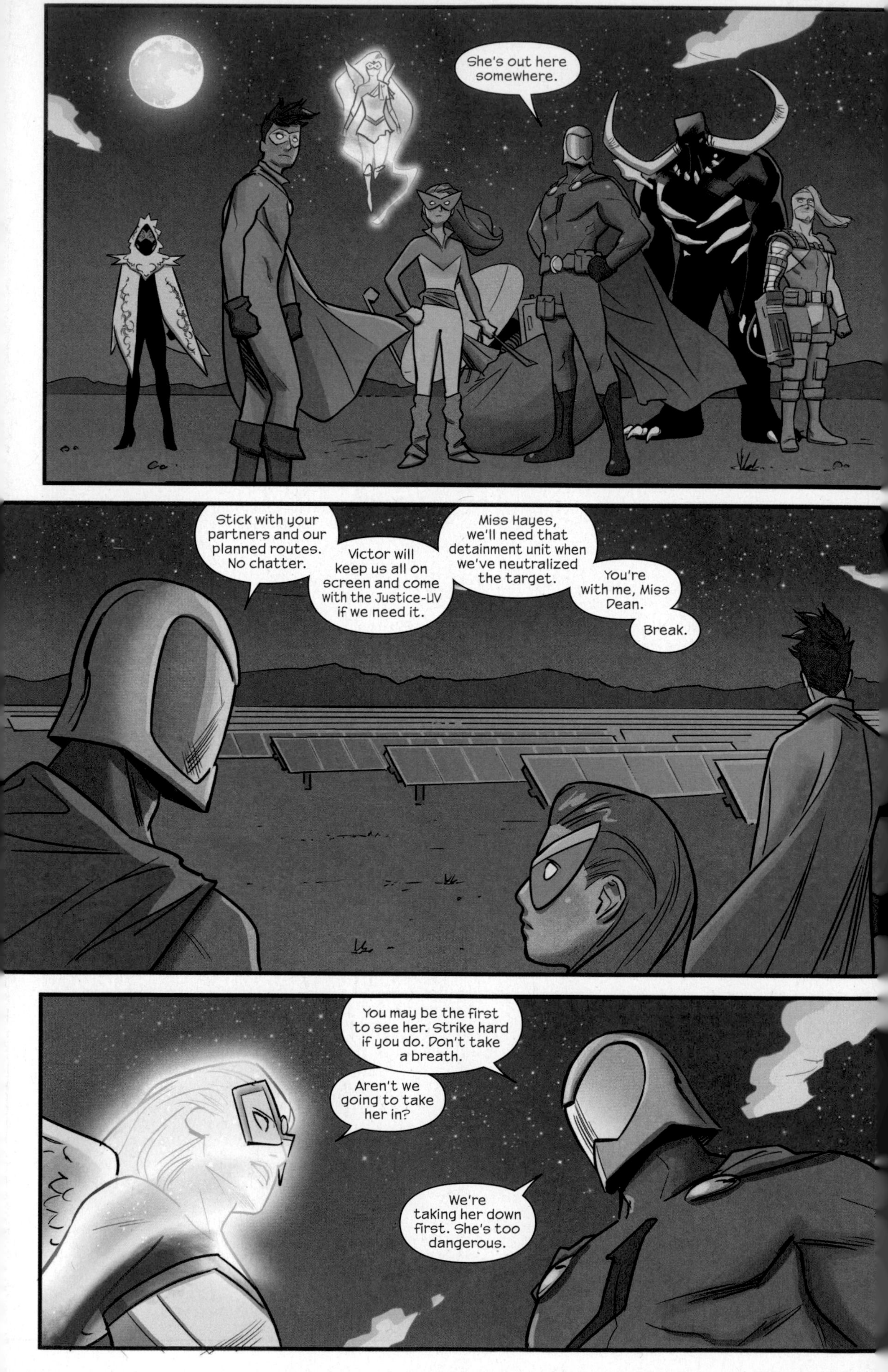
She's out here somewhere.
Stick with your partners and our planned routes. No chatter.
Victor will keep us all on screen and come with the Justice-UV if we need it.
Miss Hayes, we'll need that detainment unit when we've neutralized the target.
You're with me, Miss Dean.
Break.
You may be the first to see her. Strike hard if you do. Don't take a breath.
Aren't we going to take her in?
We're taking her down first. She's too dangerous.

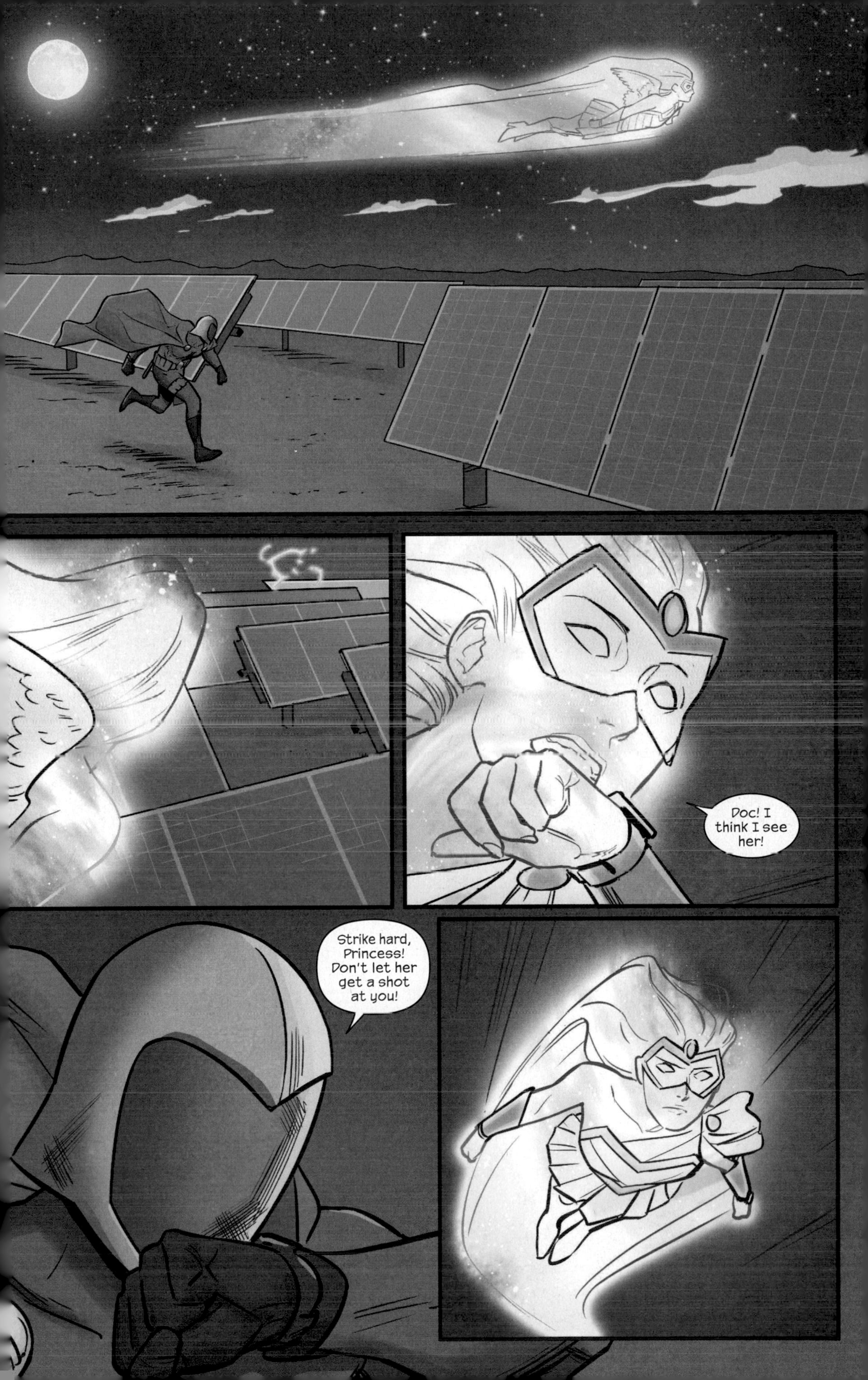
Doc! I think I see her!
Strike hard, Princess! Don't let her get a shot at you!

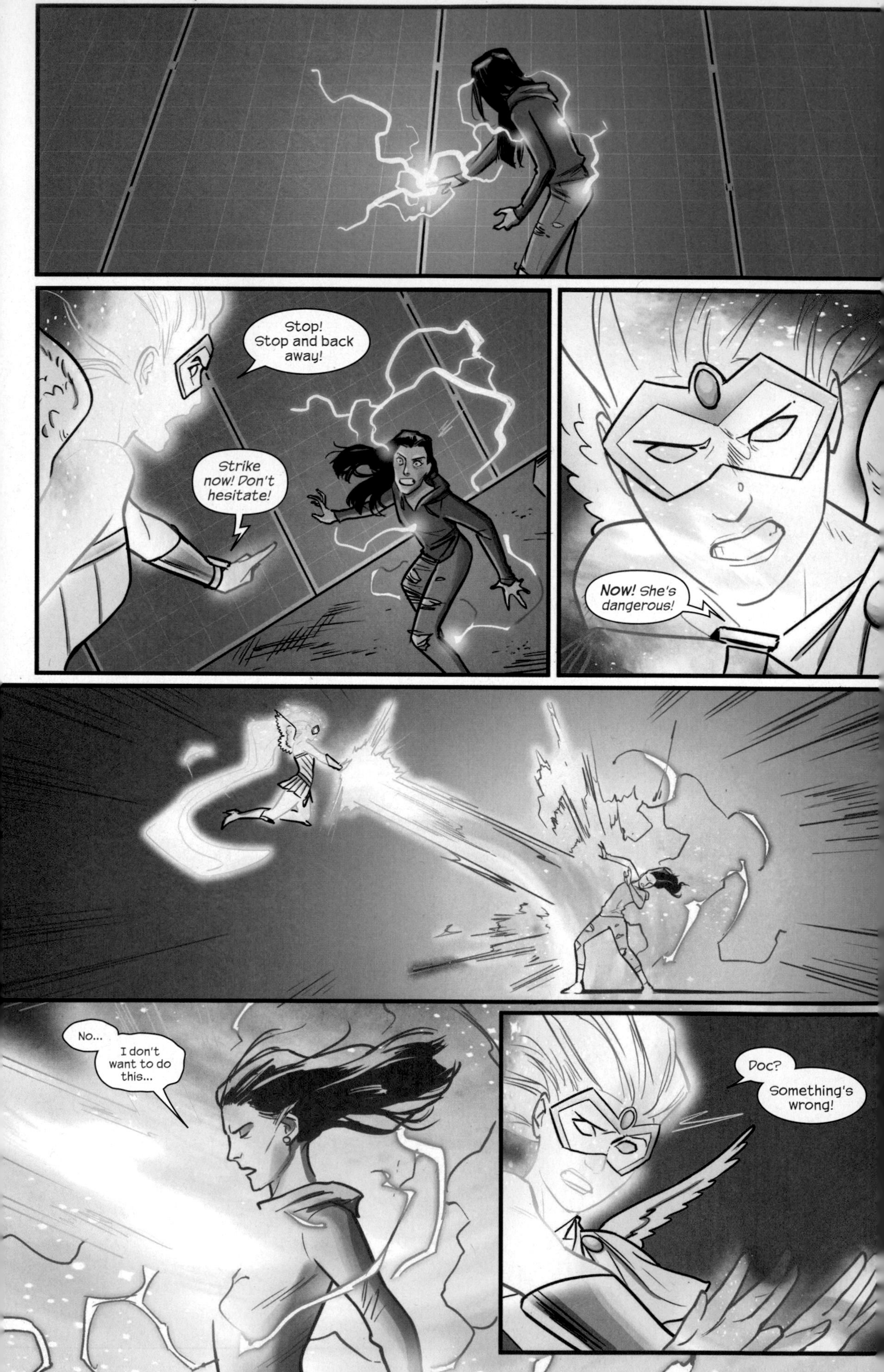

Stop! Stop and back away!
Strike now! Don't hesitate!
NOW! She's dangerous!
No...
I don't want to do this...
Doc?
Something's wrong!

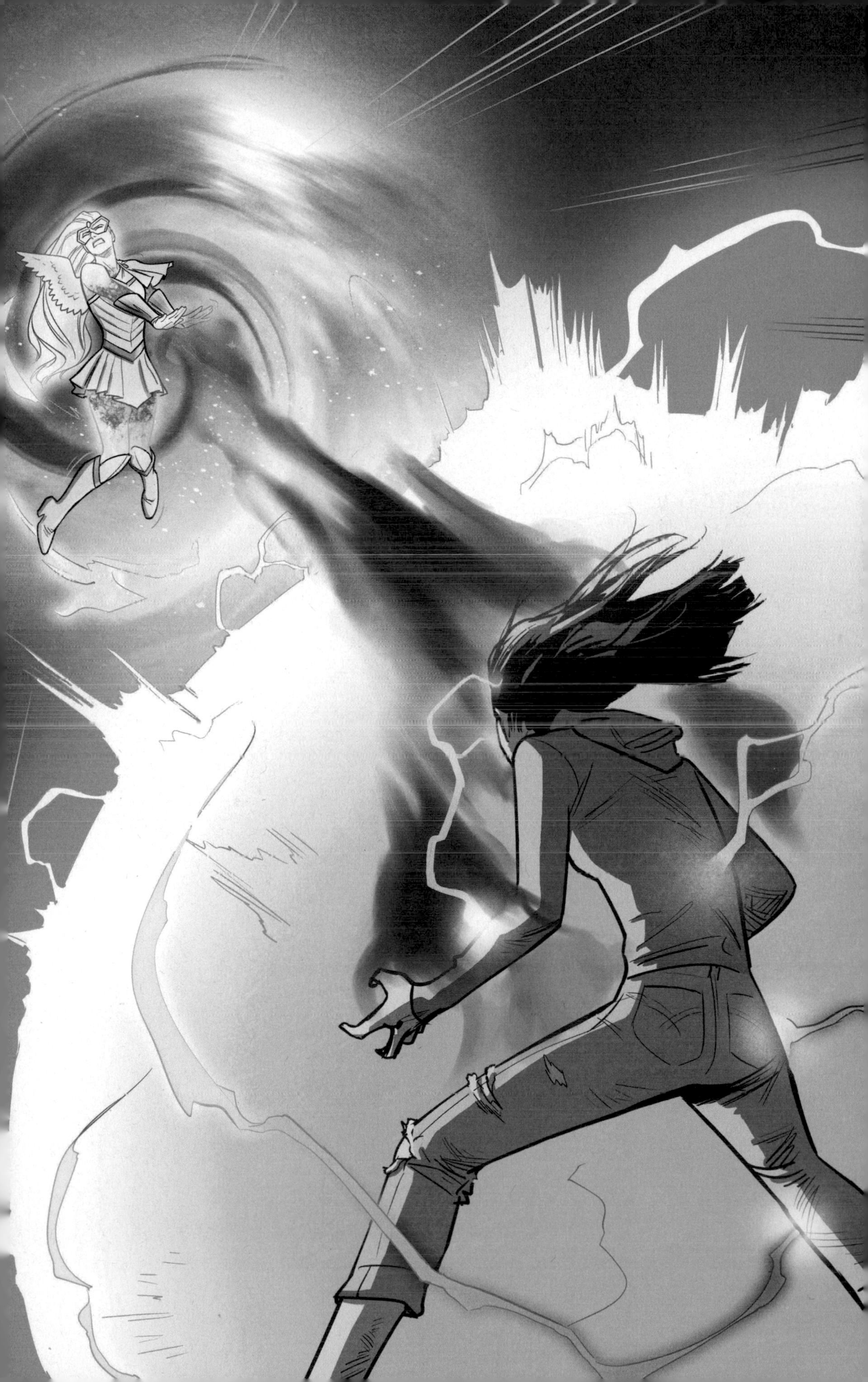

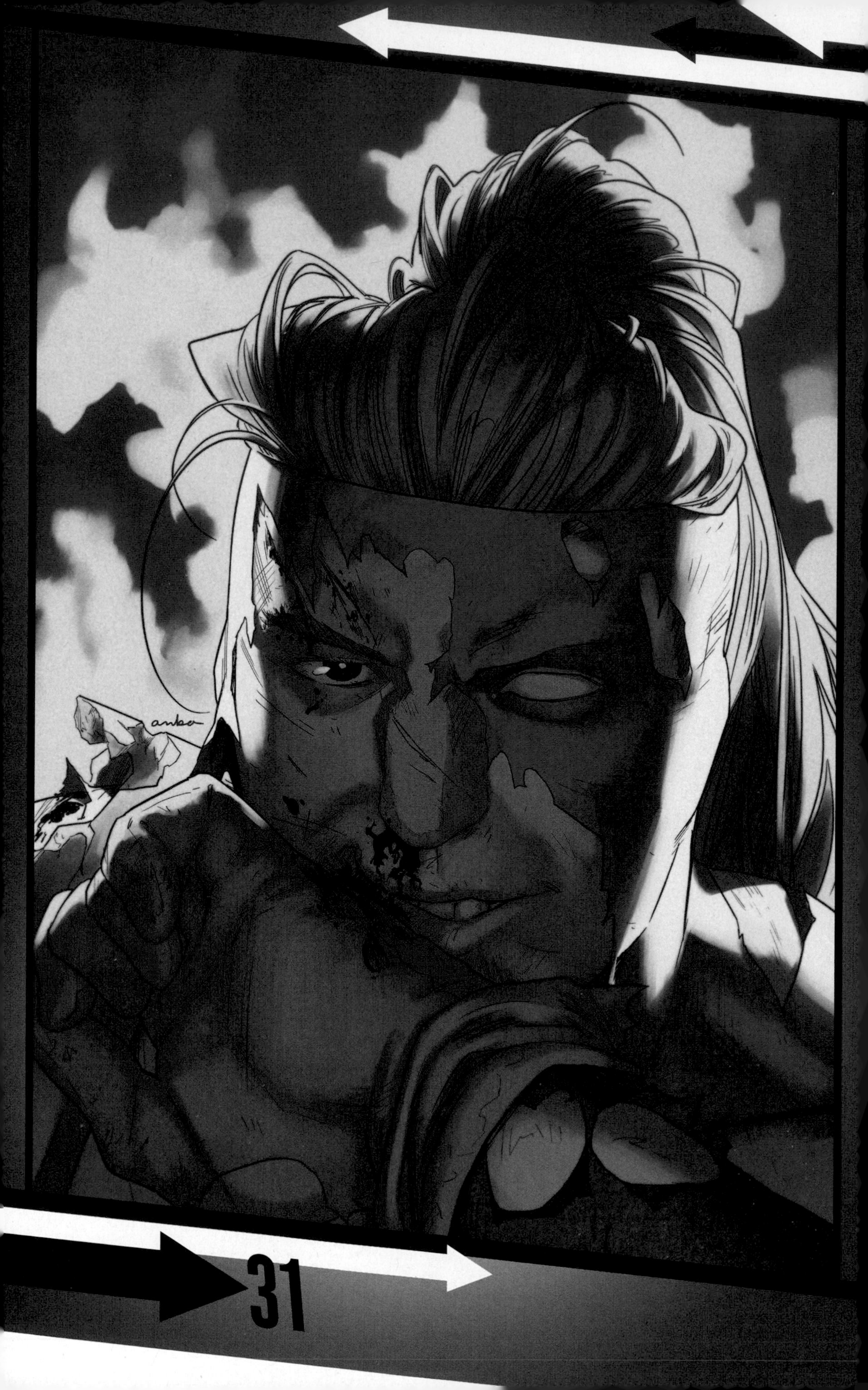
31

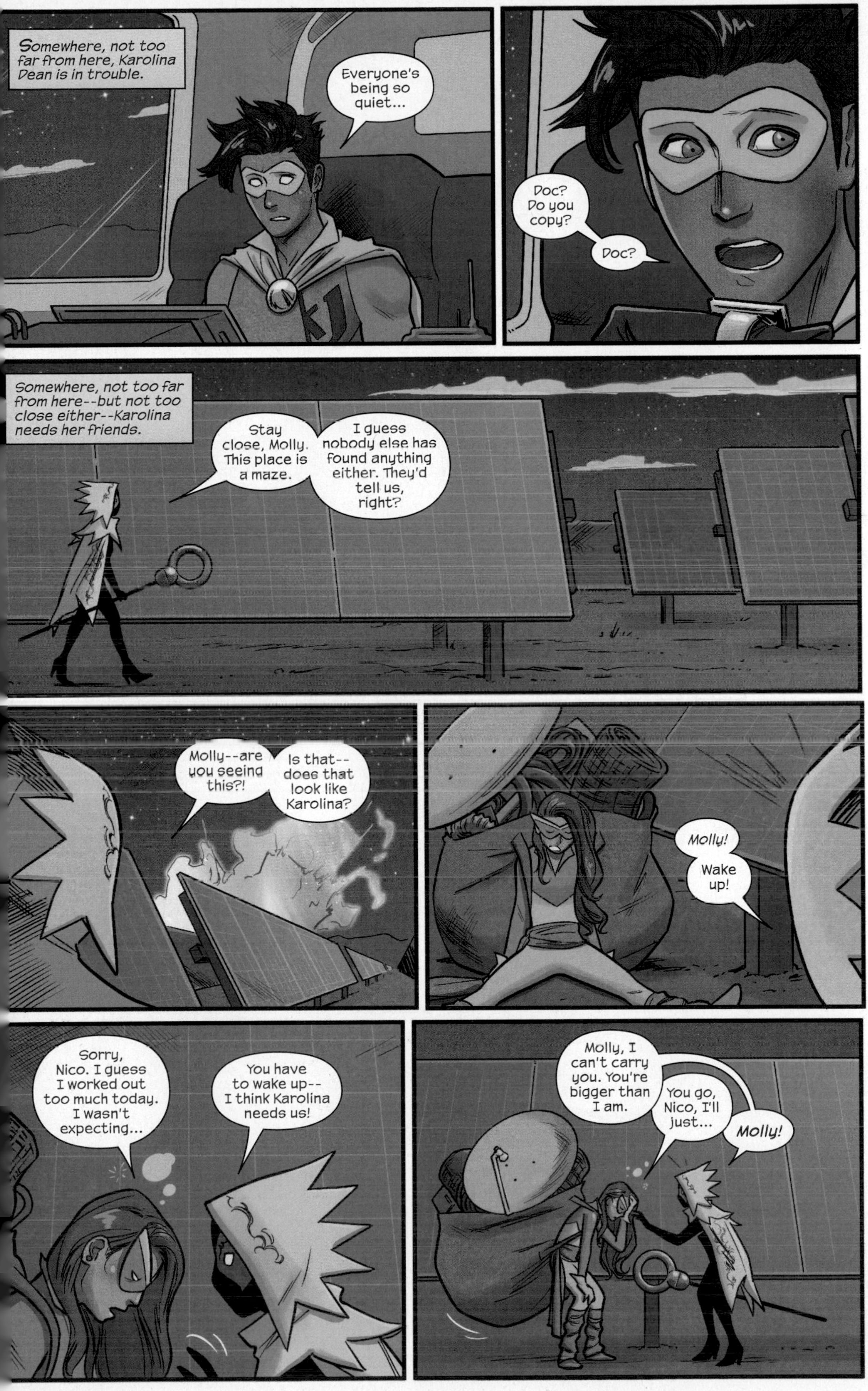
Somewhere, not too far from here, Karolina Dean is in trouble.
Everyone's being so quiet...
Doc? Do you copy?
Doc?
Somewhere, not too far from here--but not too close either--Karolina needs her friends.
Stay close, Molly. This place is a maze.
I guess nobody else has found anything either. They'd tell us, right?
Molly--are you seeing this?!
Is that--does that look like Karolina?
Molly!
Wake up!
Sorry, Nico. I guess I worked out too much today. I wasn't expecting...
You have to wake up--I think Karolina needs us!
Molly, I can't carry you. You're bigger than I am.
You go, Nico, I'll just...
Molly!

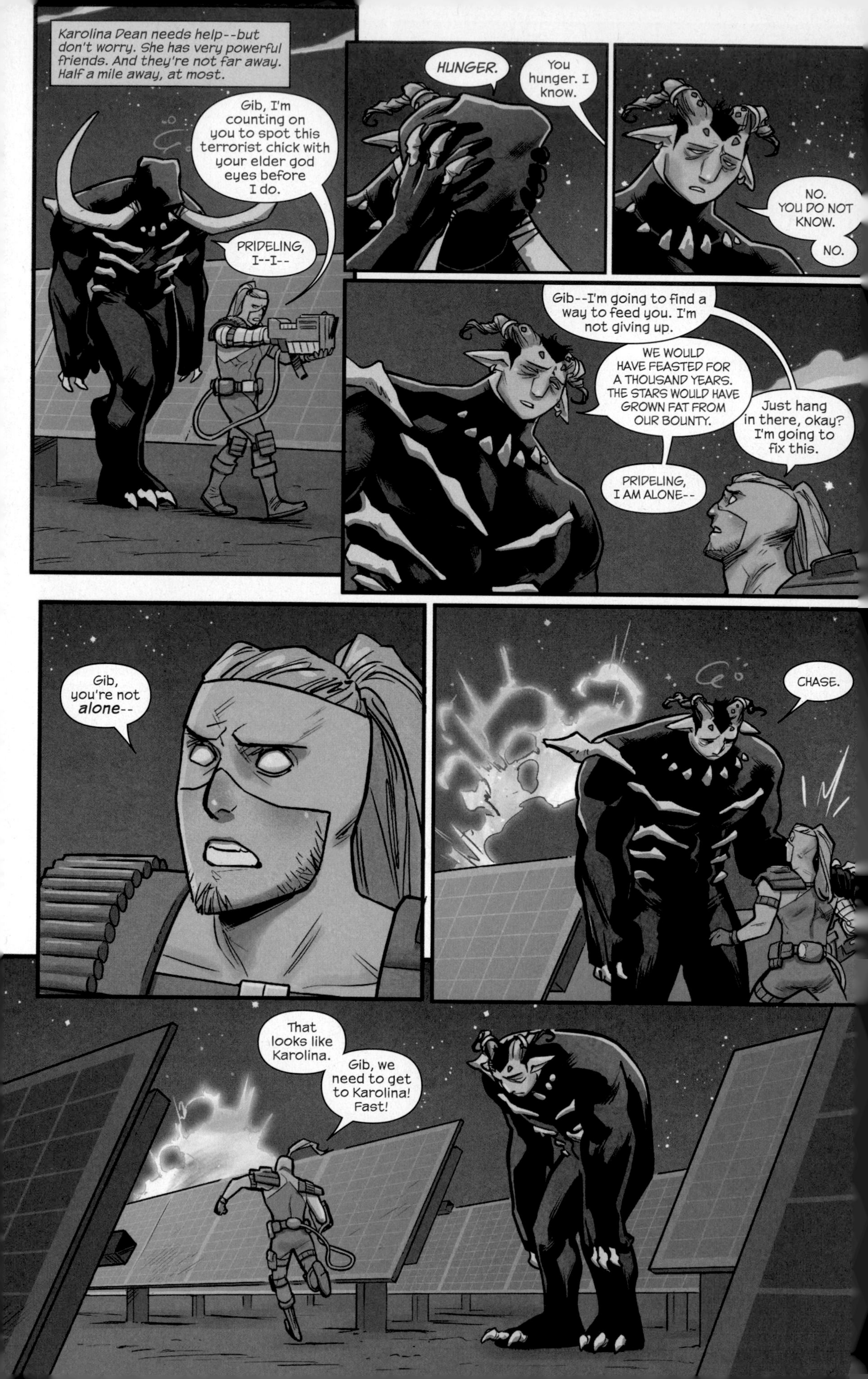
Karolina Dean needs help--but don't worry. She has very powerful friends. And they're not far away. Half a mile away, at most.
Gib, I'm counting on you to spot this terrorist chick with your elder god eyes before I do.
PRIDELING, I--I--
HUNGER.
You hunger. I know.
NO. YOU DO NOT KNOW.
NO.
Gib--I'm going to find a way to feed you. I'm not giving up.
WE WOULD HAVE FEASTED FOR A THOUSAND YEARS. THE STARS WOULD HAVE GROWN FAT FROM OUR BOUNTY.
Just hang in there, okay? I'm going to fix this.
PRIDELING, I AM ALONE--
Gib, you're not alone--
CHASE.
That looks like Karolina.
Gib, we need to get to Karolina! Fast!

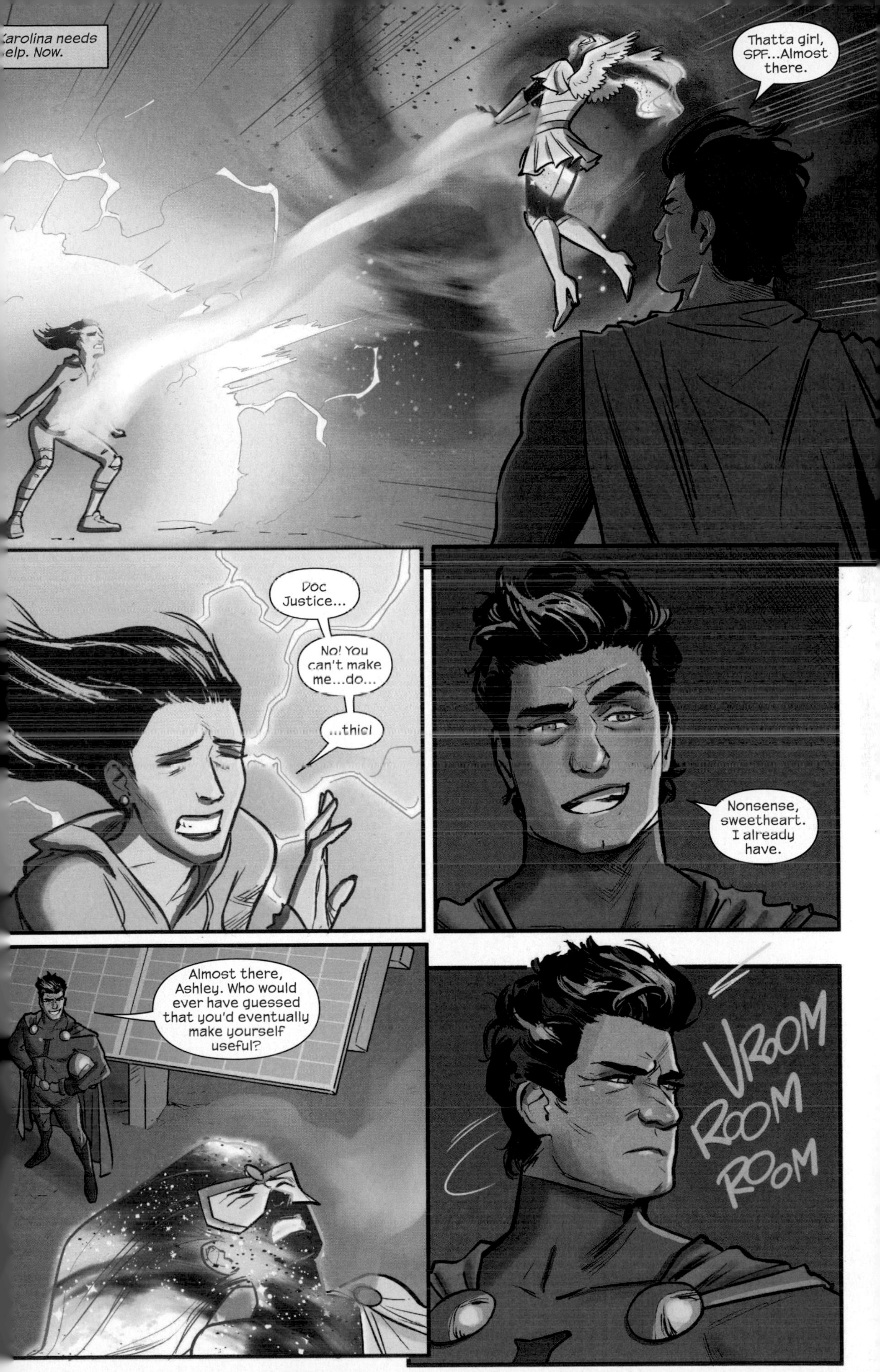

Karolina needs help. Now.
Thatta girl, SPF...Almost there.
Doc Justice...
No! You can't make me...do...
...this!
Nonsense, sweetheart. I already have.
Almost there, Ashley. Who would ever have guessed that you'd eventually make yourself useful?
VROOM ROOM ROOM

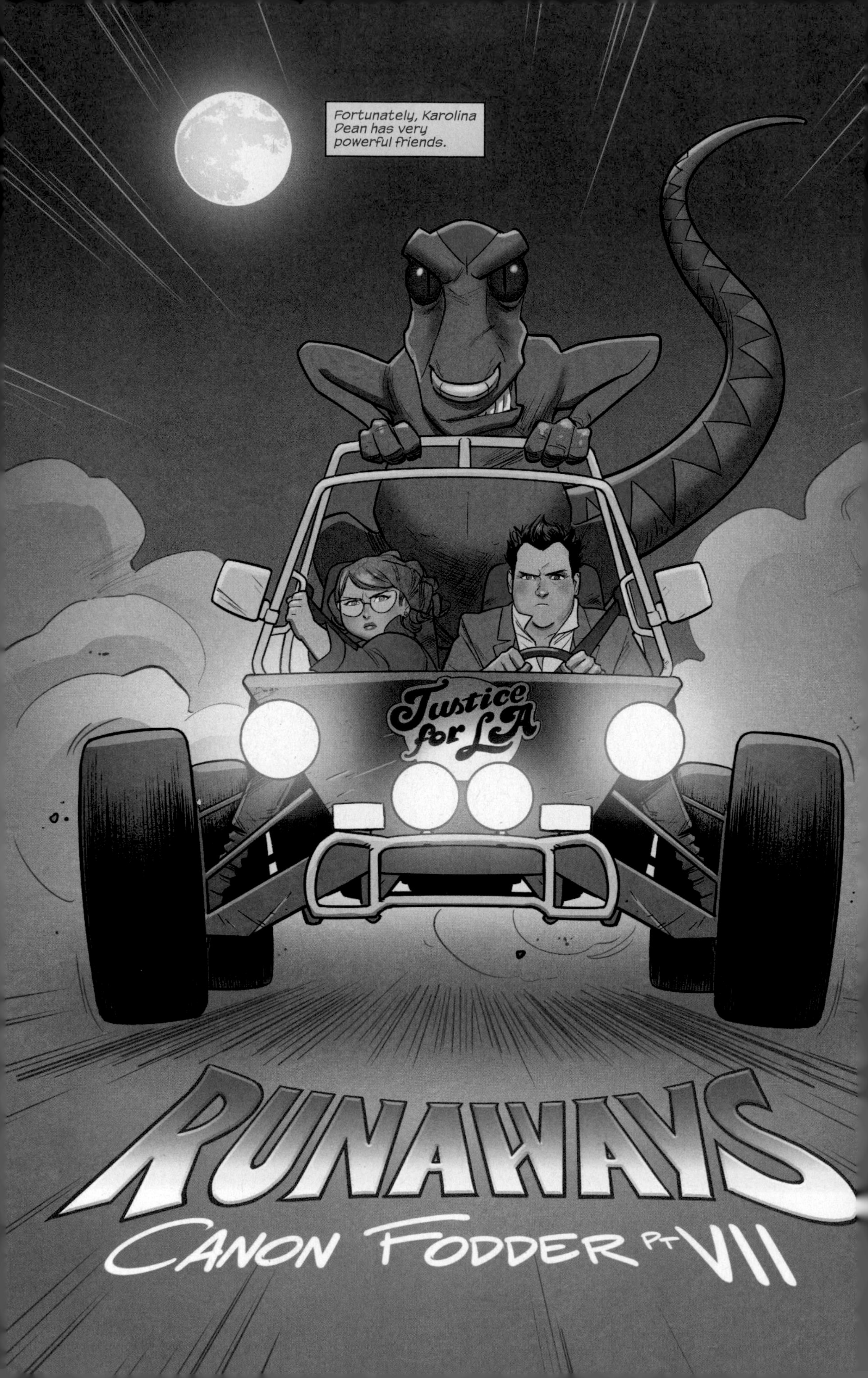
Fortunately, Karolina Dean has very powerful friends.
Justice for LA
RUNAWAYS
CANON FODDER PT VII

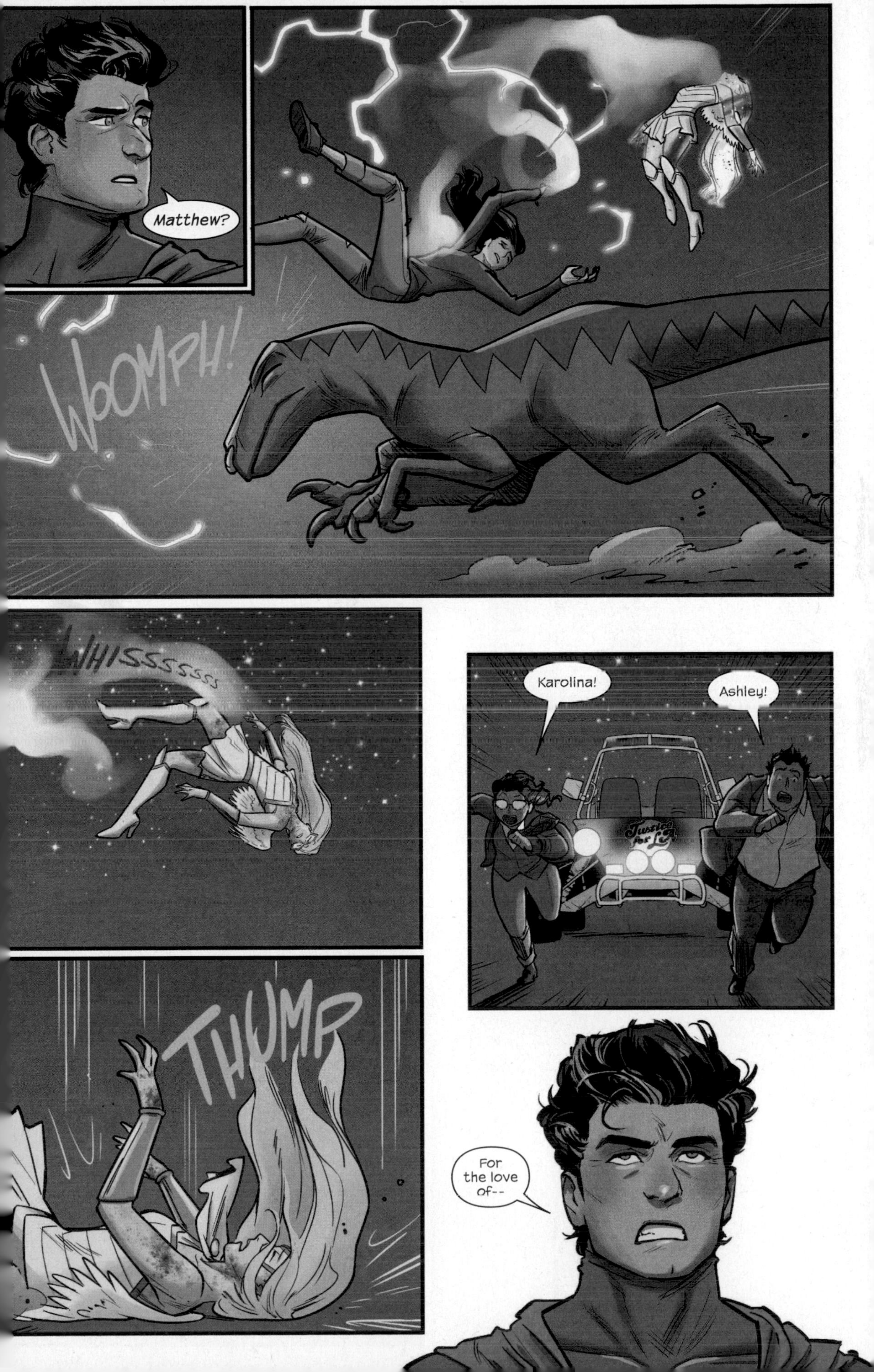
Matthew?
WOOMPH!
WHISSSSSSS
THUMP
Karolina!
Ashley!
For the love of--

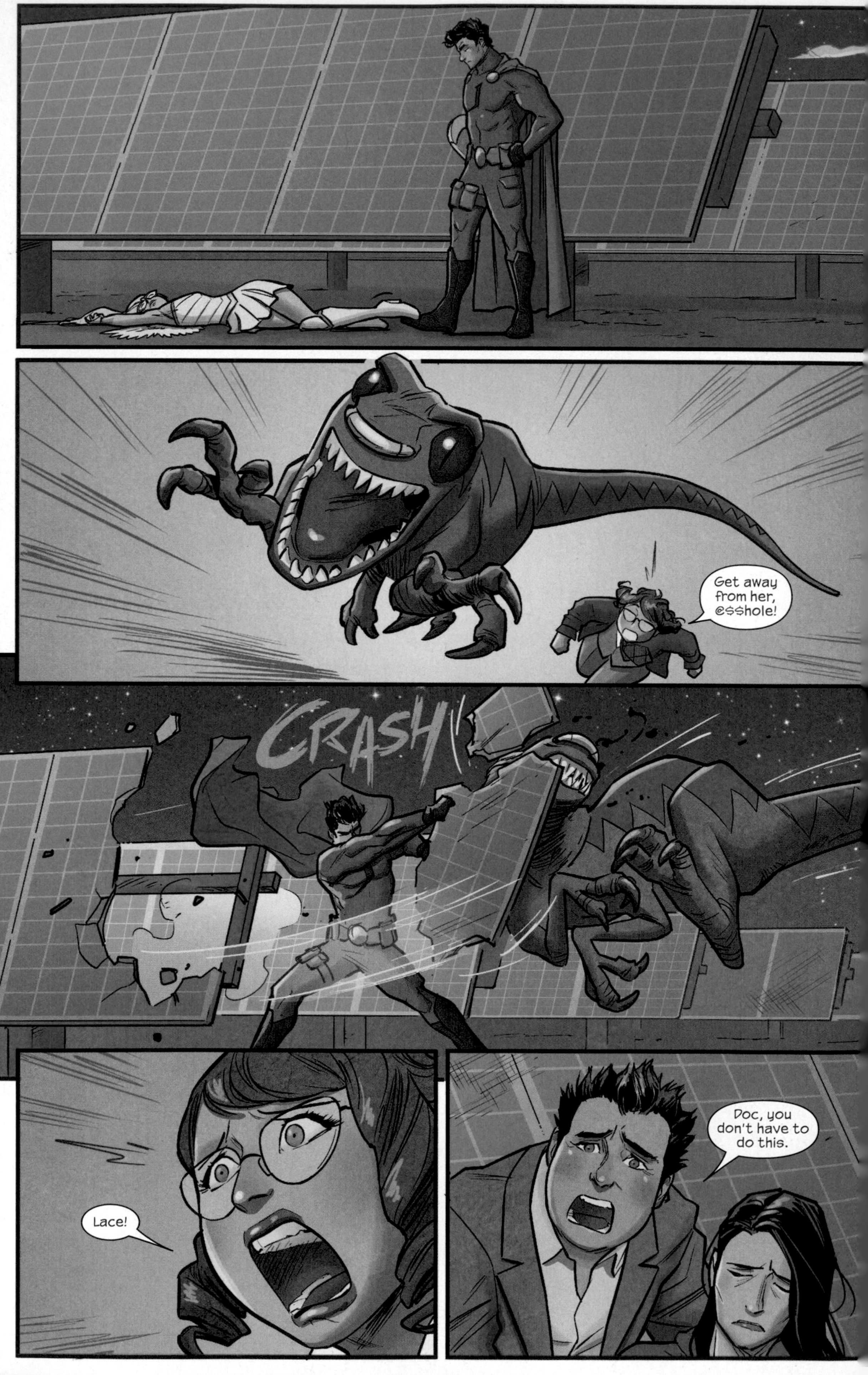

Get away from her, @$$hole!
CRASH
Lace!
Doc, you don't have to do this.

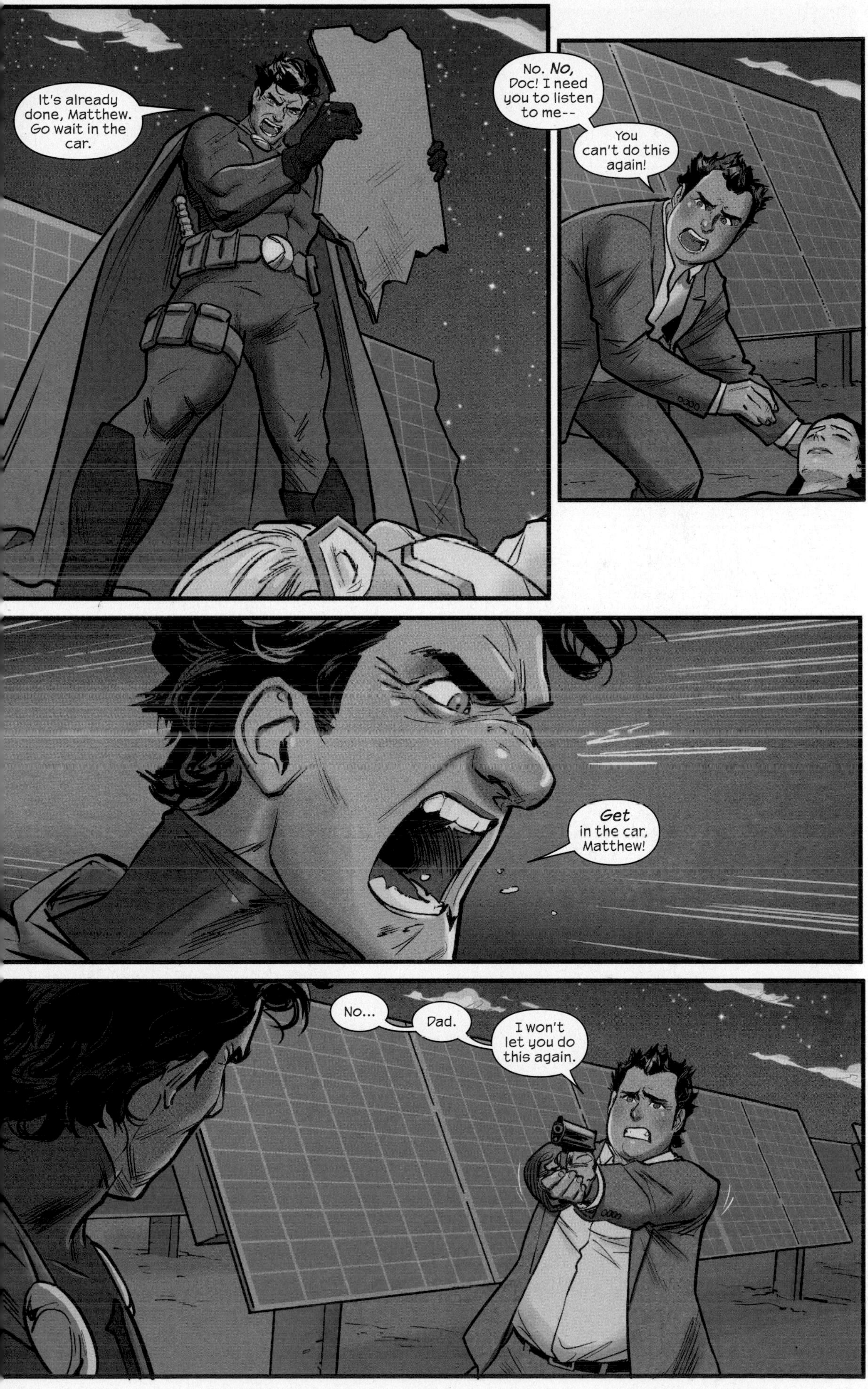
It's already done, Matthew. Go wait in the car.
No. *No,* Doc! I need you to listen to me--
You can't do this again!
Get in the car, Matthew!
No...
Dad.
I won't let you do this again.

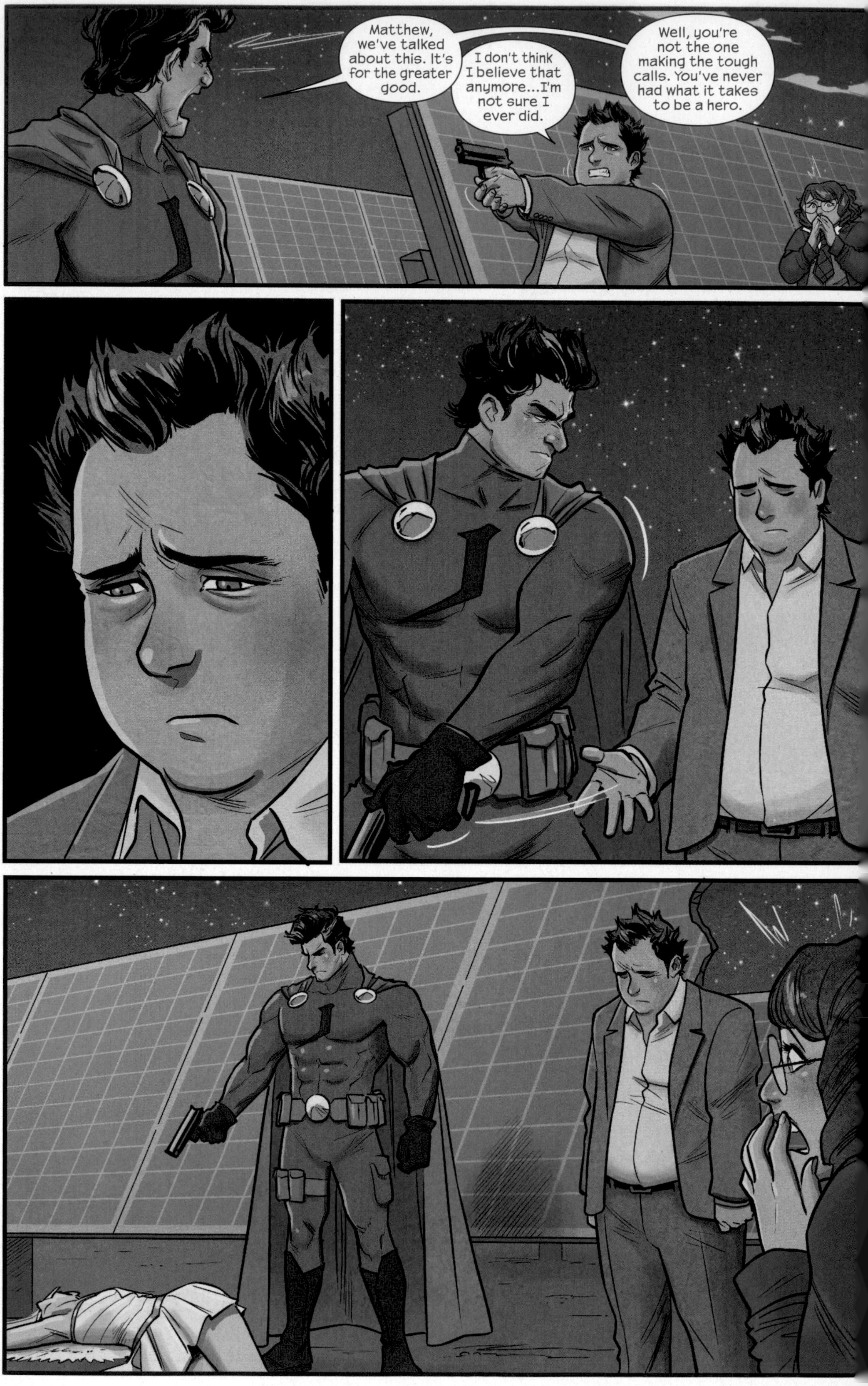
Matthew, we've talked about this. It's for the greater good.
I don't think I believe that anymore...I'm not sure I ever did.
Well, you're not the one making the tough calls. You've never had what it takes to be a hero.

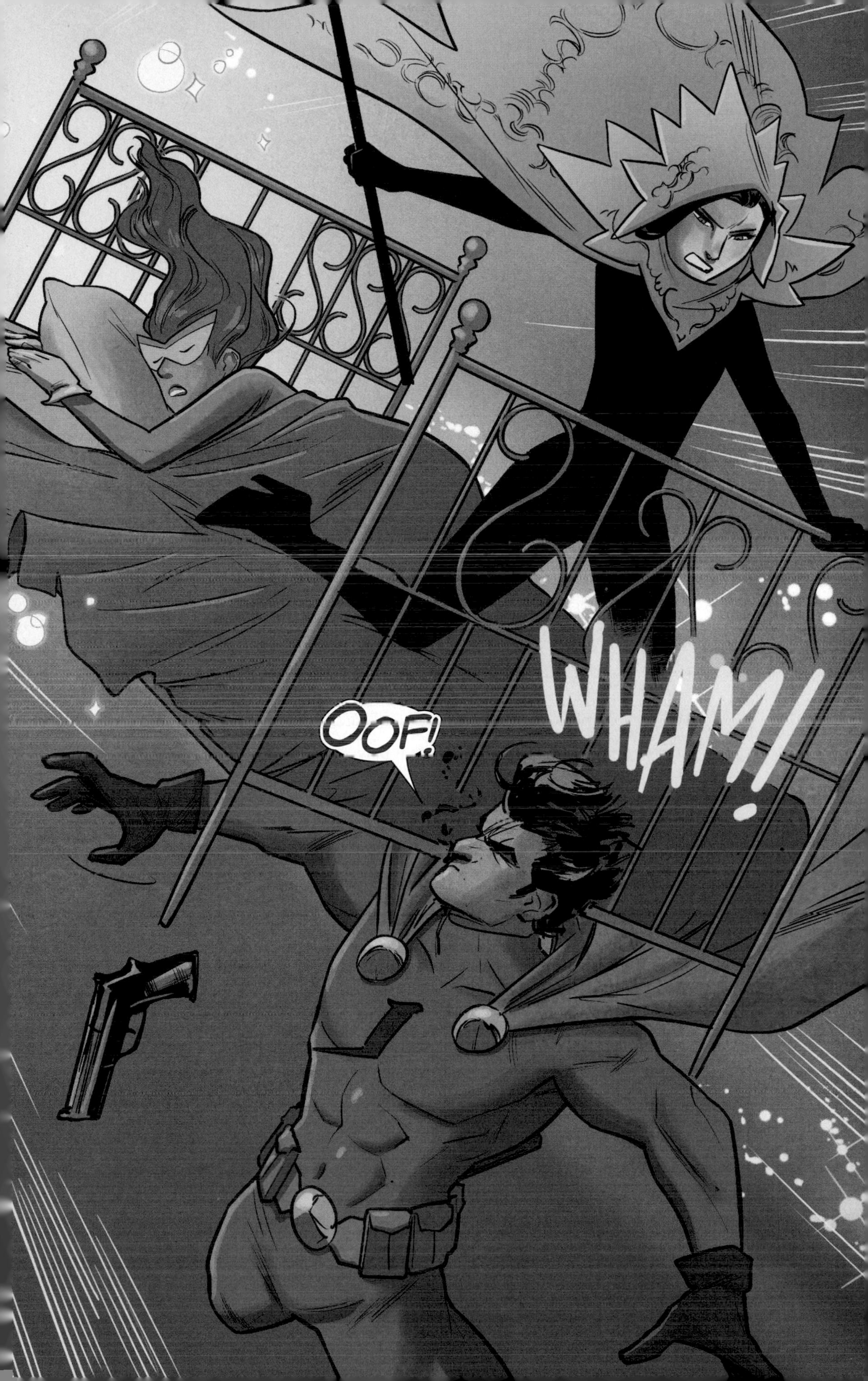
WHAM!
OOF!

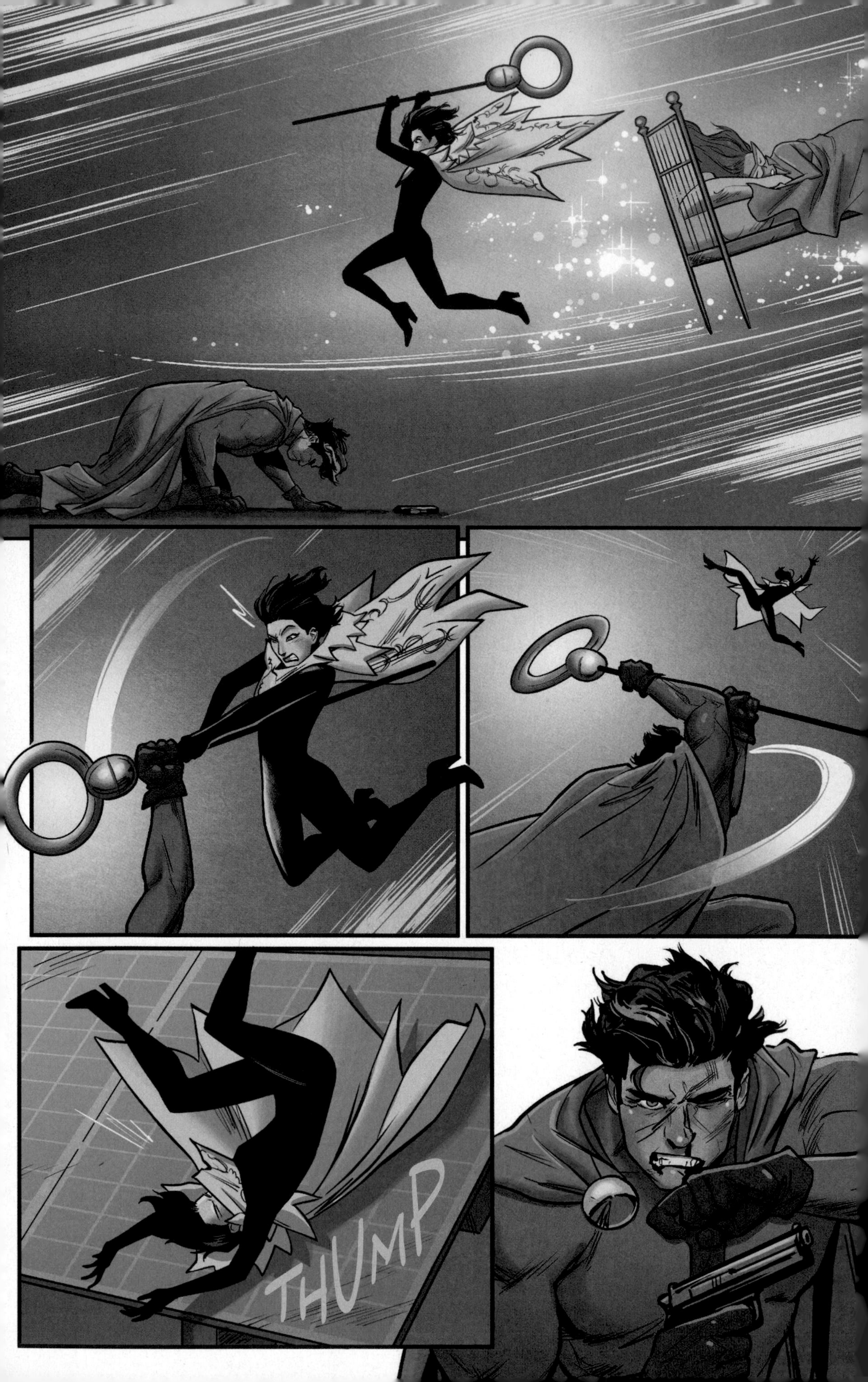
THUMP

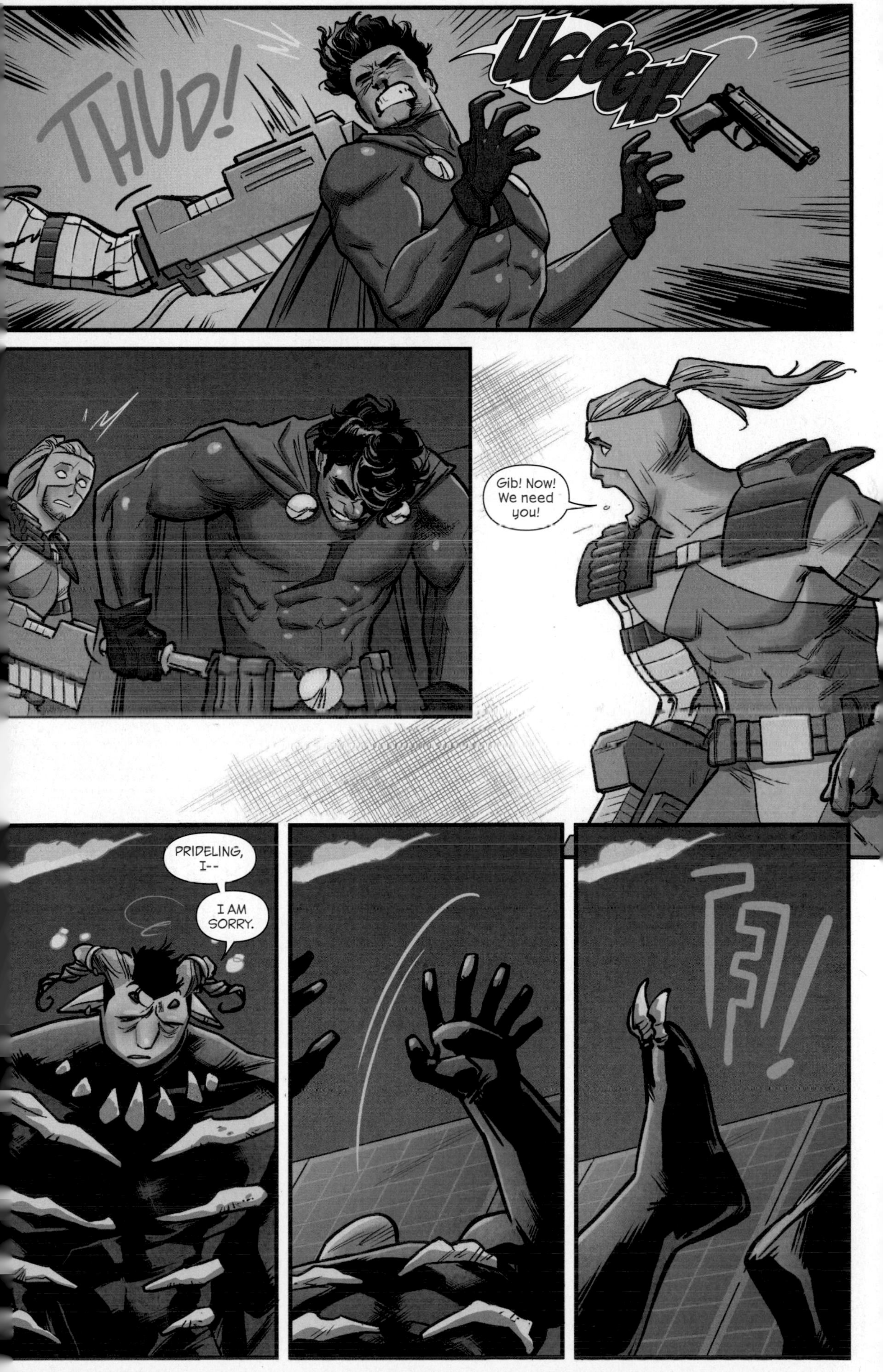
THUD!
UGGGH!
Gib! Now! We need you!
PRIDELING, I--
I AM SORRY.
?!

Shoot.

It didn't have to go like this, you know? You would have been fine.

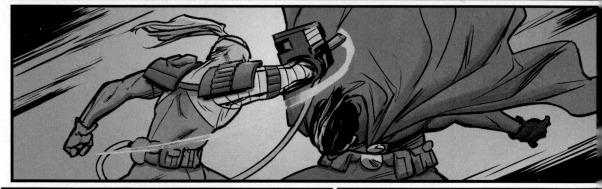

You would have had years of using that gun and that mask to pick up girls.

KRAK!

I was never going to kill you, Chase.

You know why?

PHUD!

Because no one would have cared!

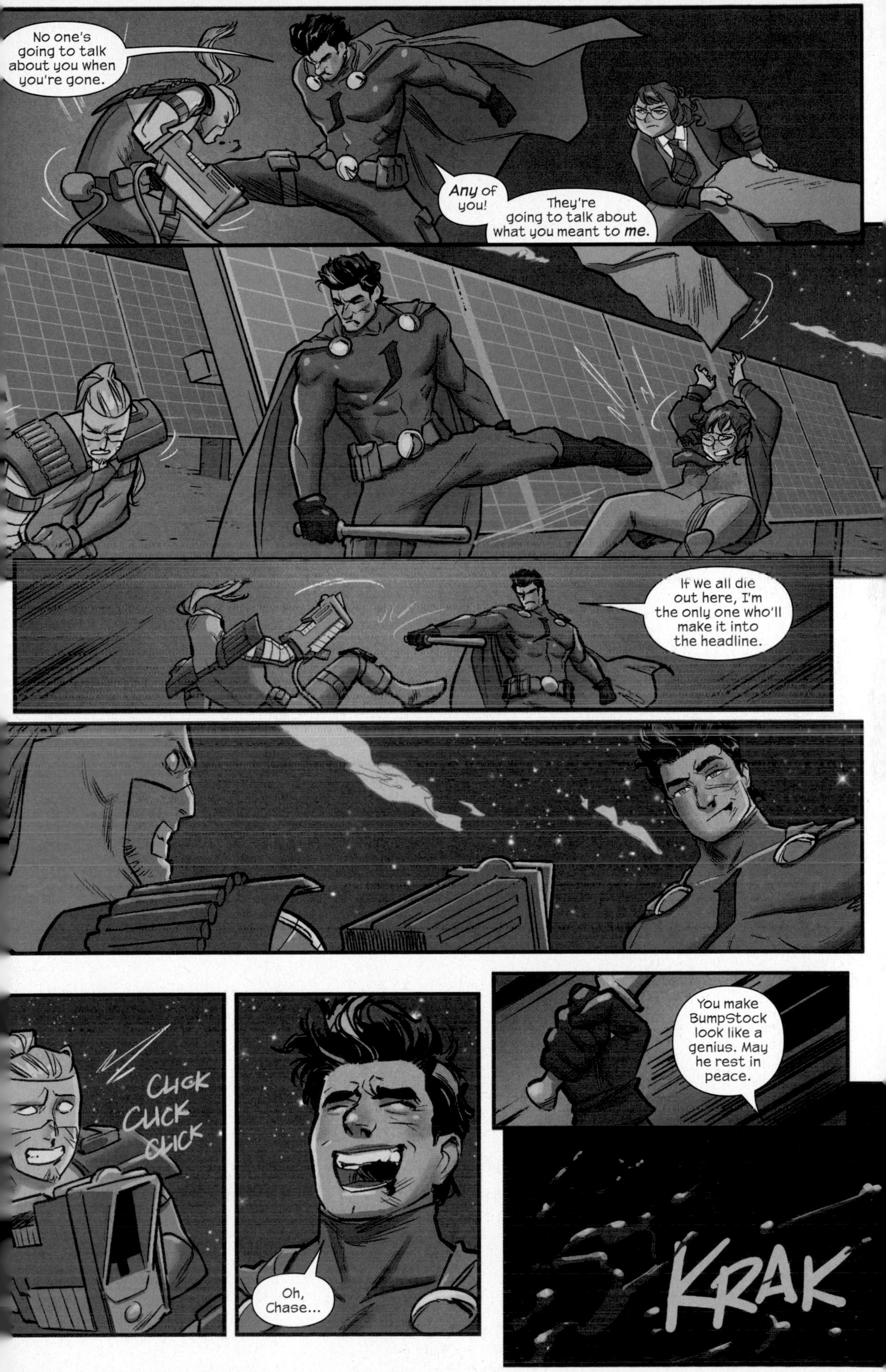
No one's going to talk about you when you're gone.
Any of you!
They're going to talk about what you meant to me.
If we all die out here, I'm the only one who'll make it into the headline.
CLICK CLICK CLICK
Oh, Chase...
You make BumpStock look like a genius. May he rest in peace.
KRAK

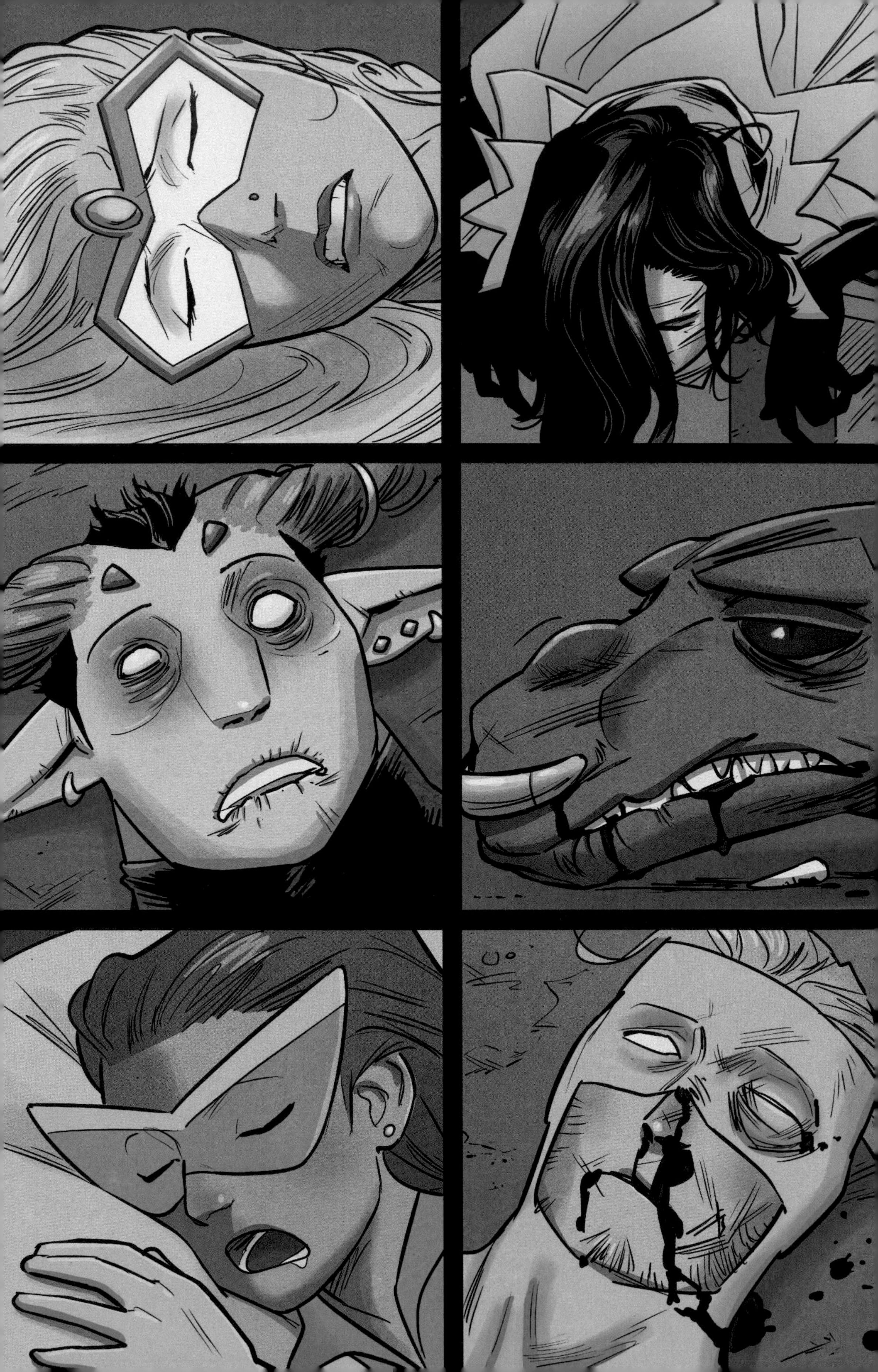

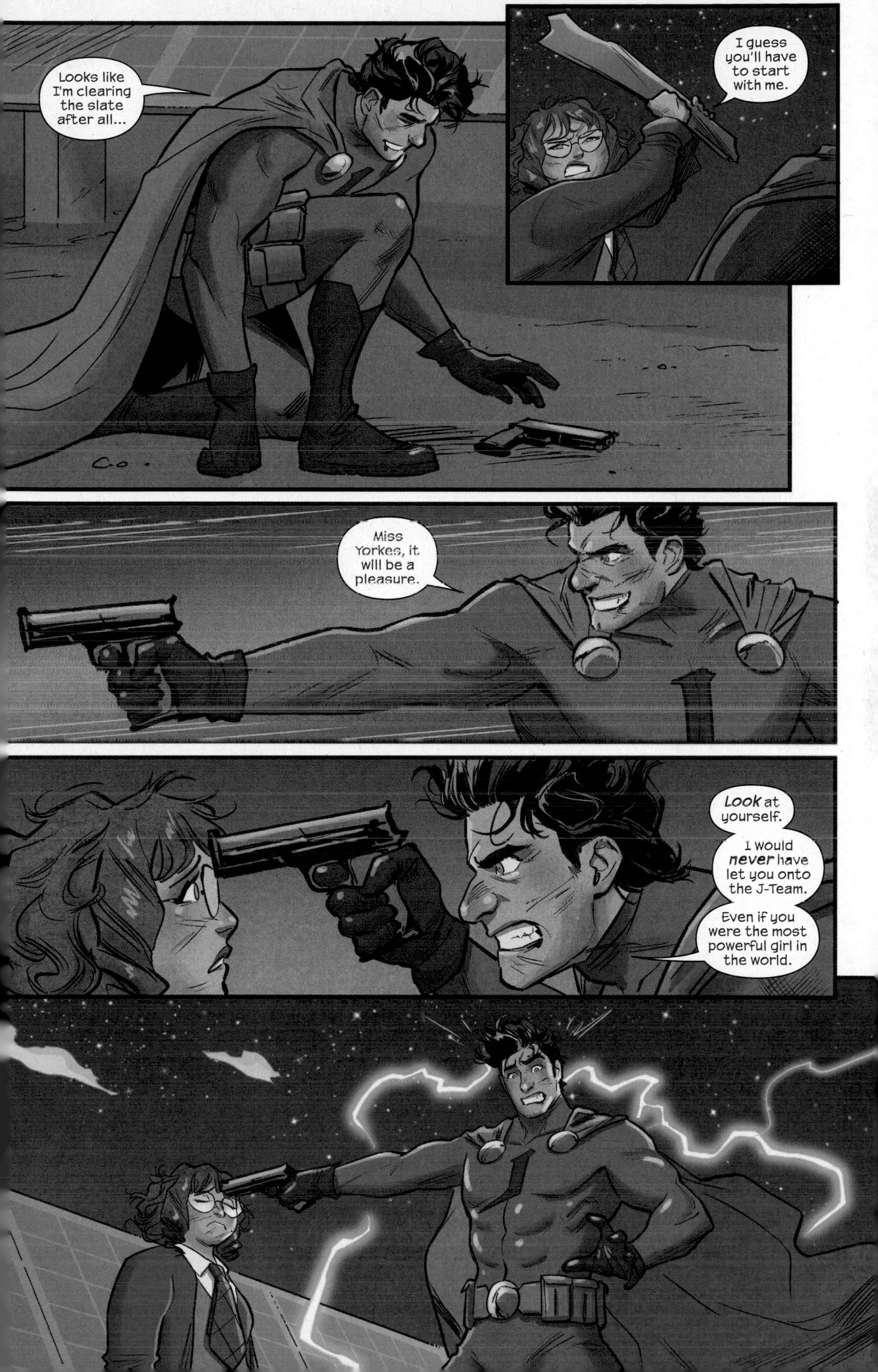
Looks like I'm clearing the slate after all...
I guess you'll have to start with me.
Miss Yorkes, it will be a pleasure.
Look at yourself.
I would ***never*** have let you onto the J-Team.
Even if you were the most powerful girl in the world.

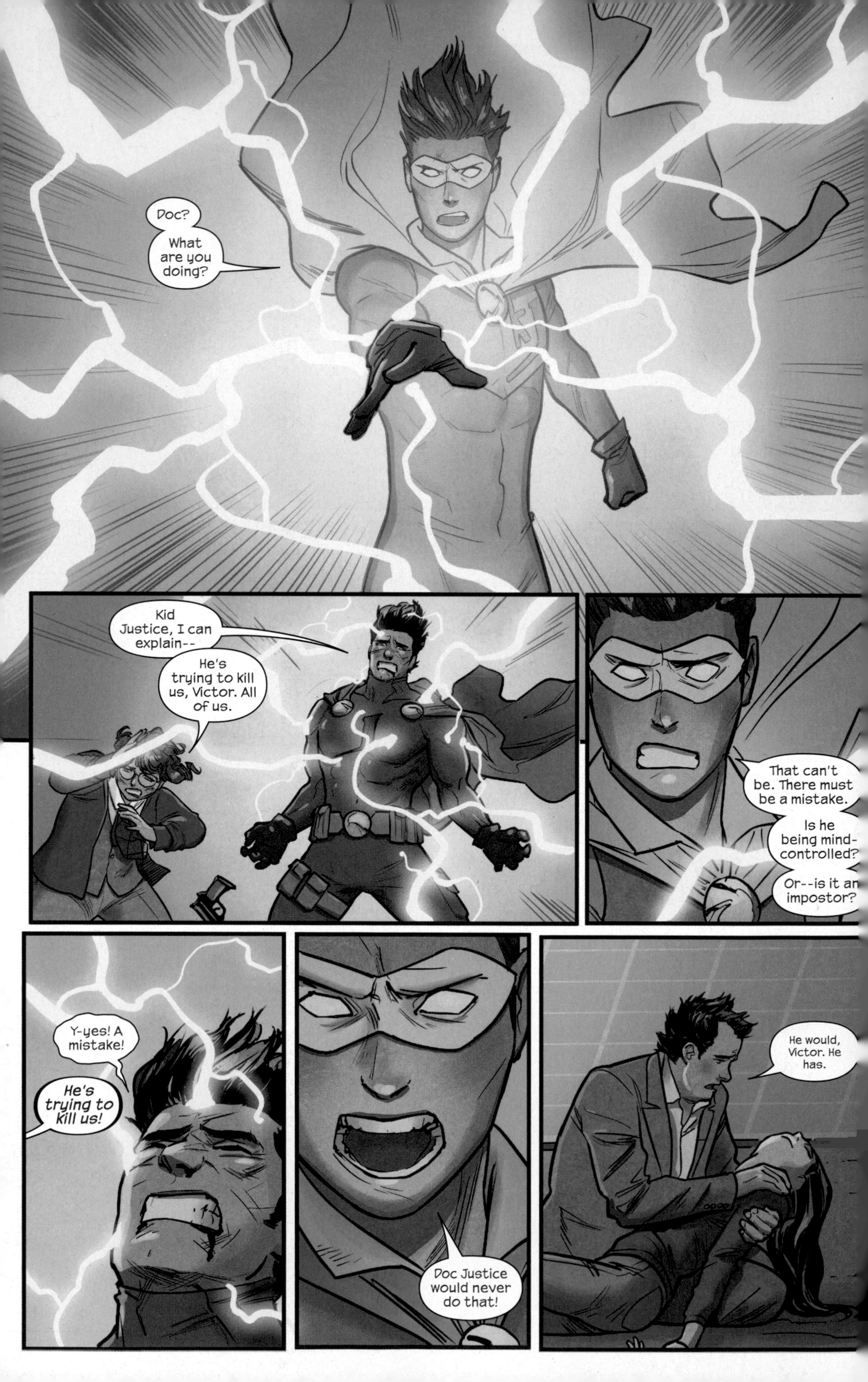
Doc?
What are you doing?
Kid Justice, I can explain--
He's trying to kill us, Victor. All of us.
That can't be. There must be a mistake.
Is he being mind-controlled?
Or--is it an impostor?
Y-yes! A mistake!
He's trying to kill us!
Doc Justice would never do that!
He would, Victor. He has.

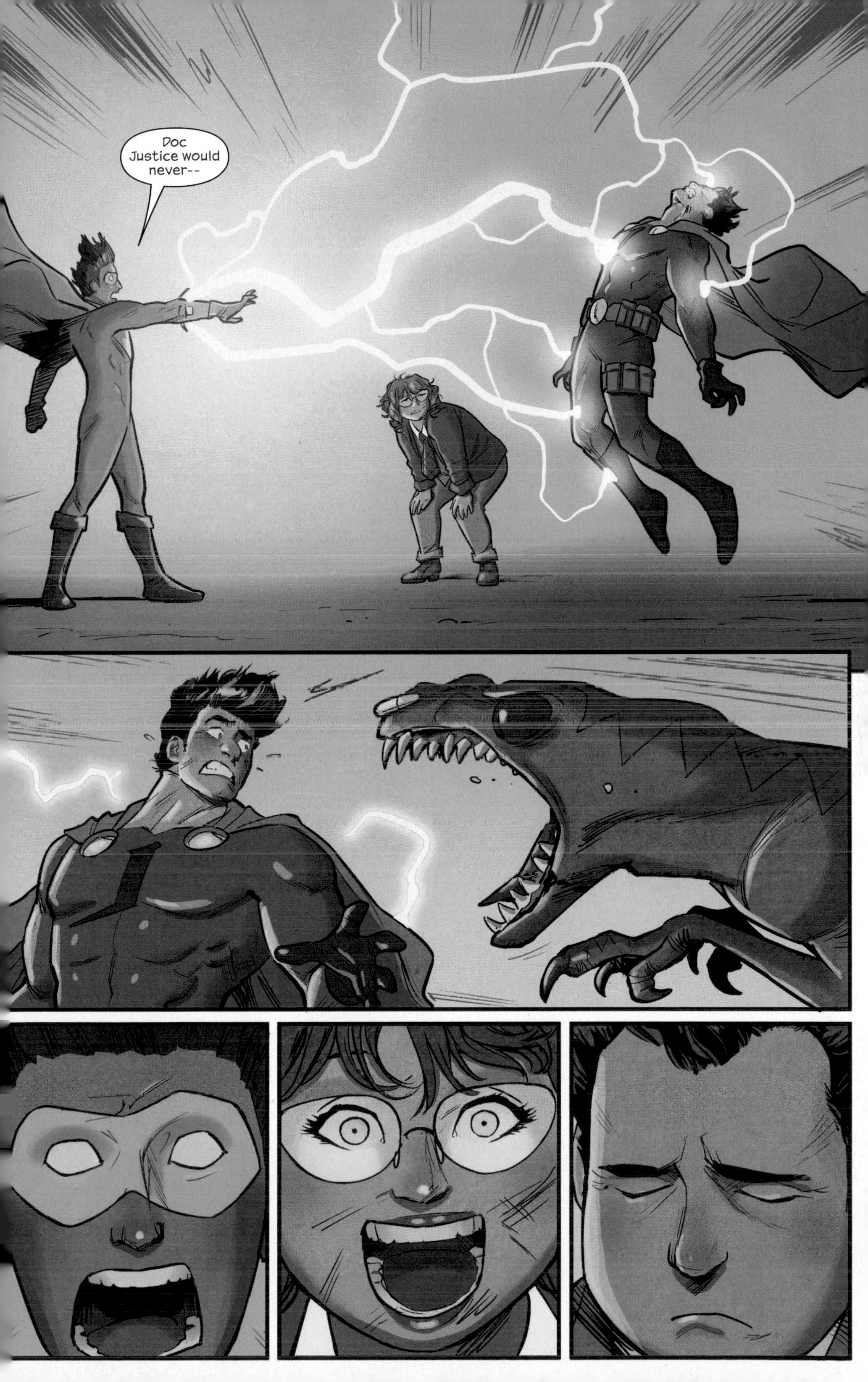
Doc Justice would never--

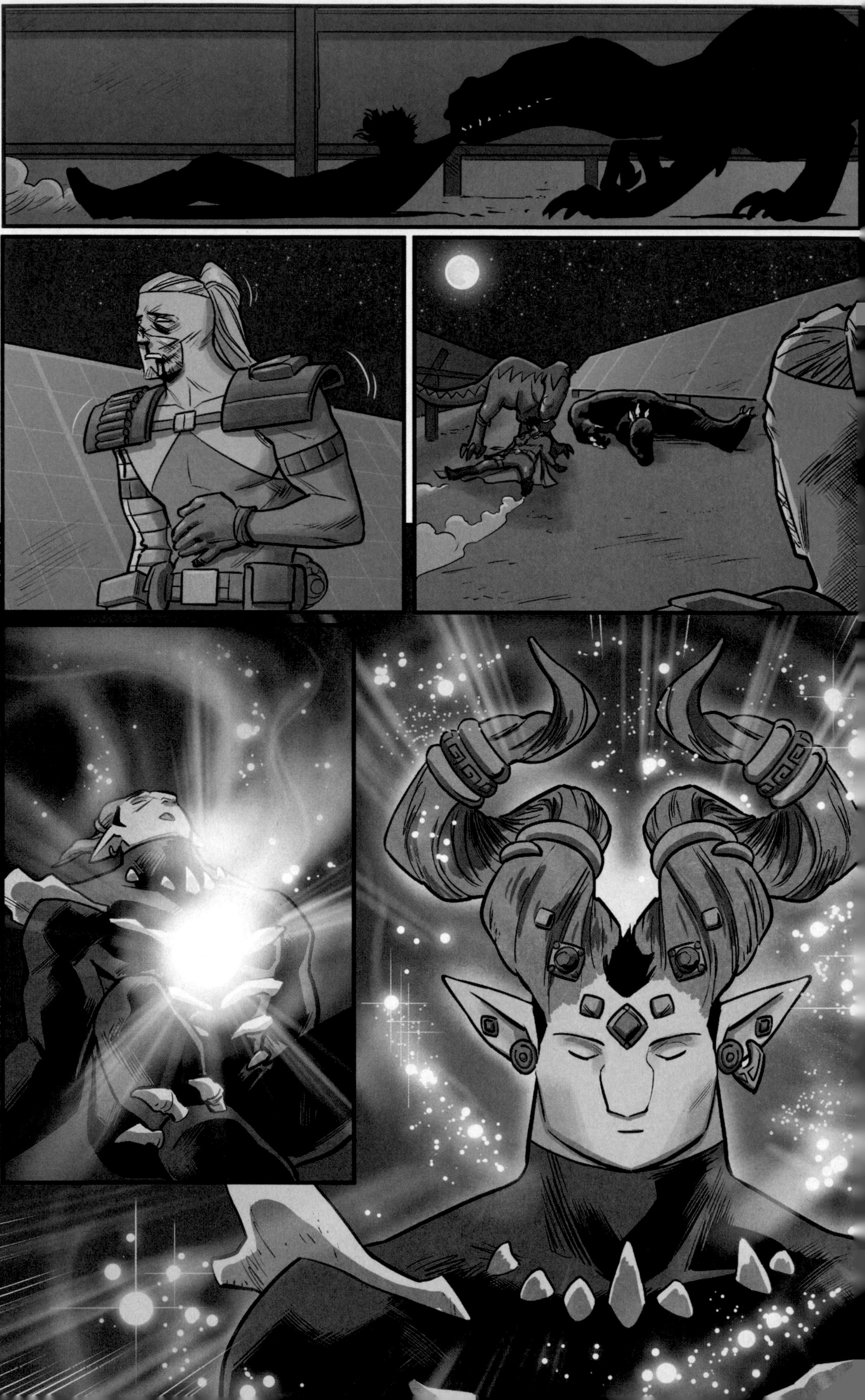

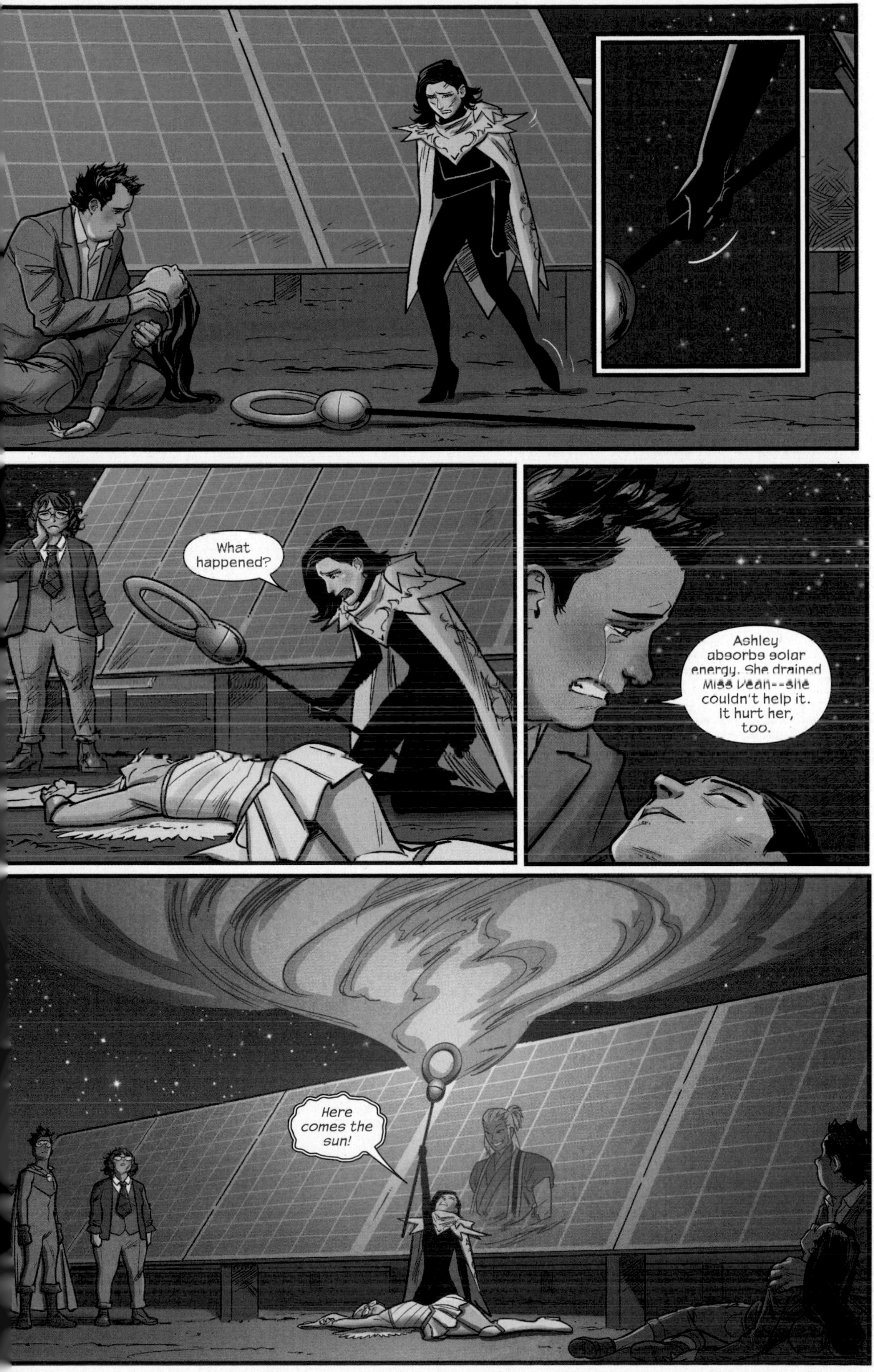
What happened?
Ashley absorbs solar energy. She drained Miss Vean--she couldn't help it. It hurt her, too.
Here comes the sun!

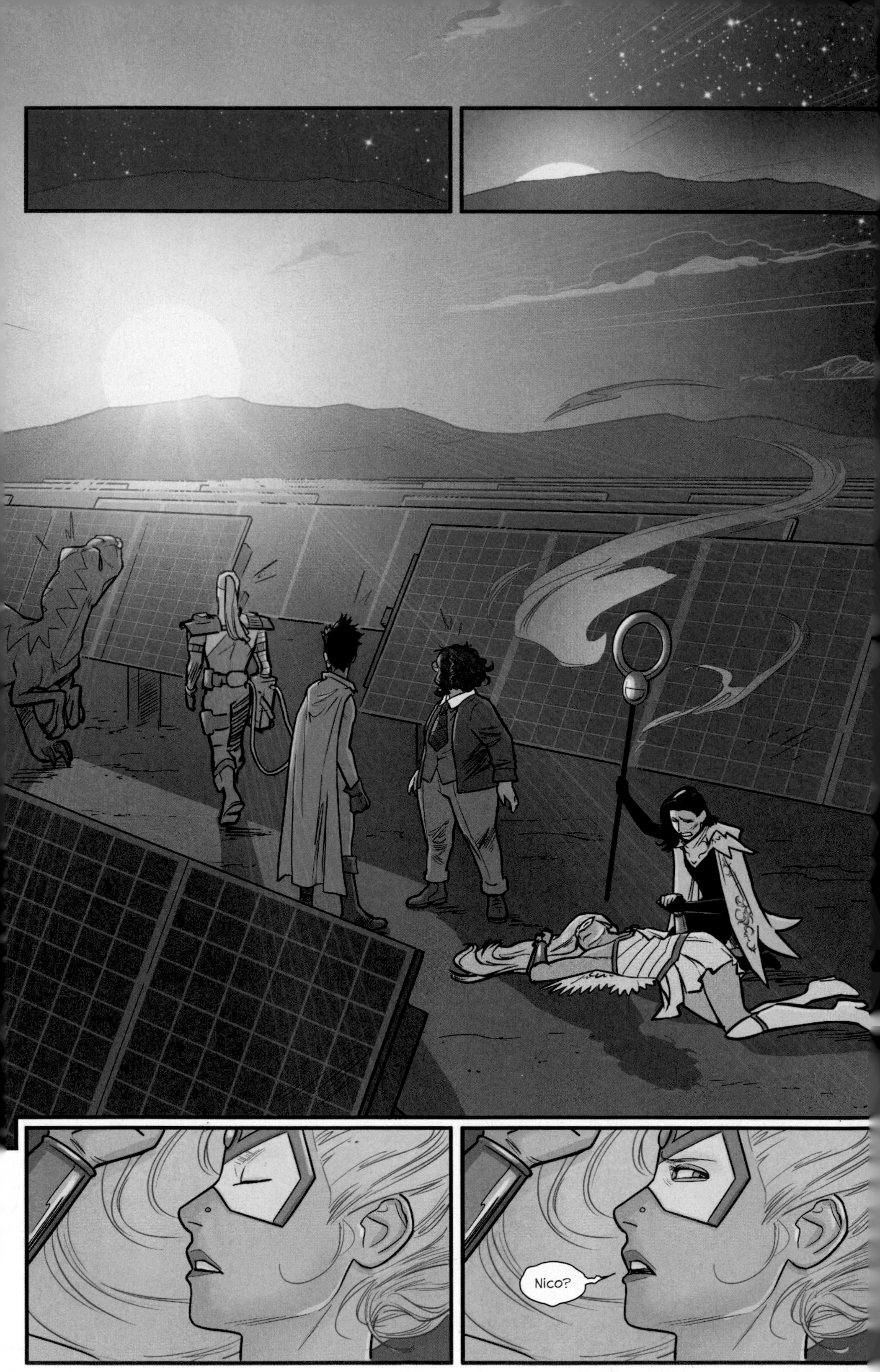
Nico?

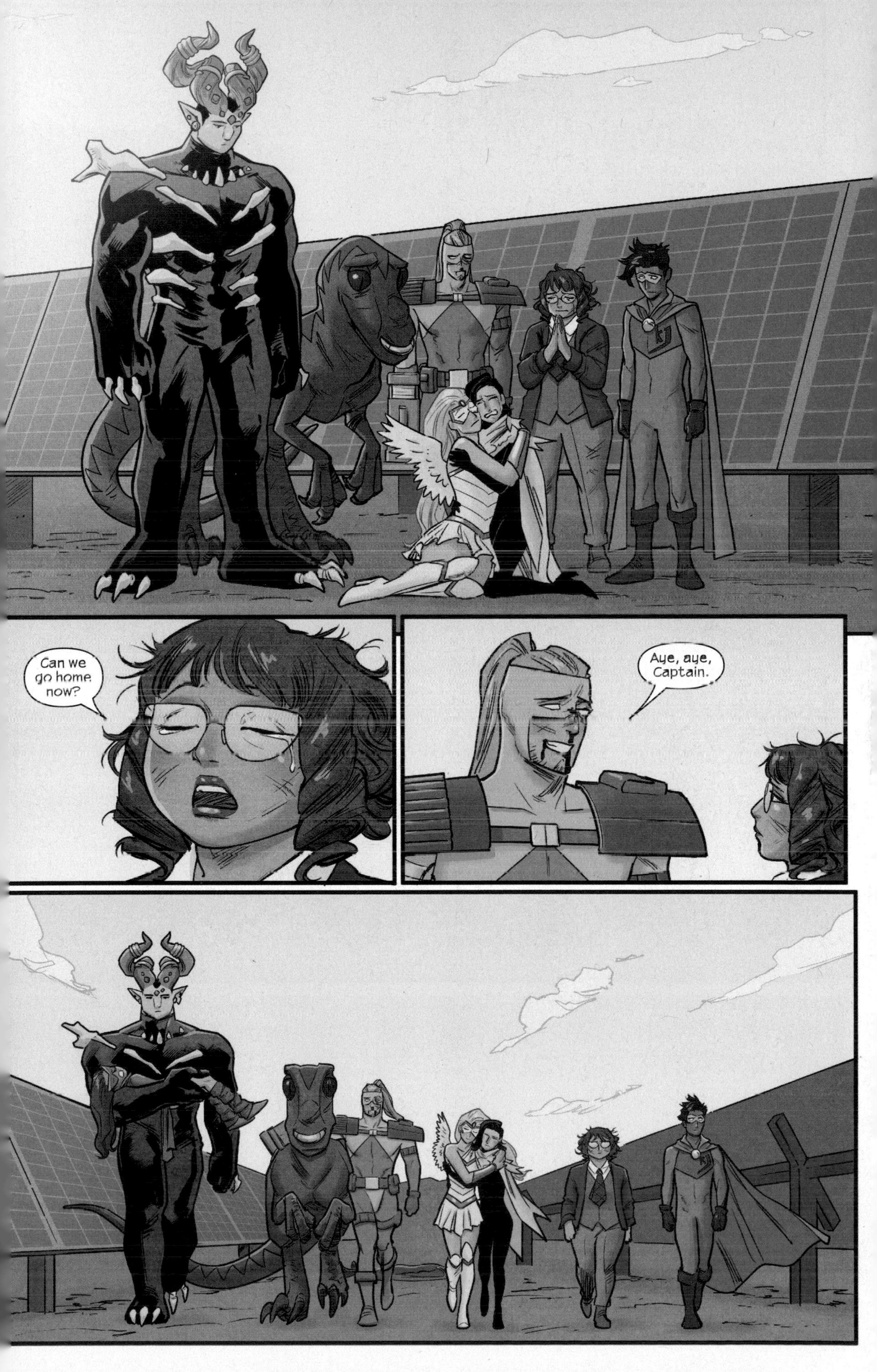
Can we go home now?
Aye, aye, Captain.

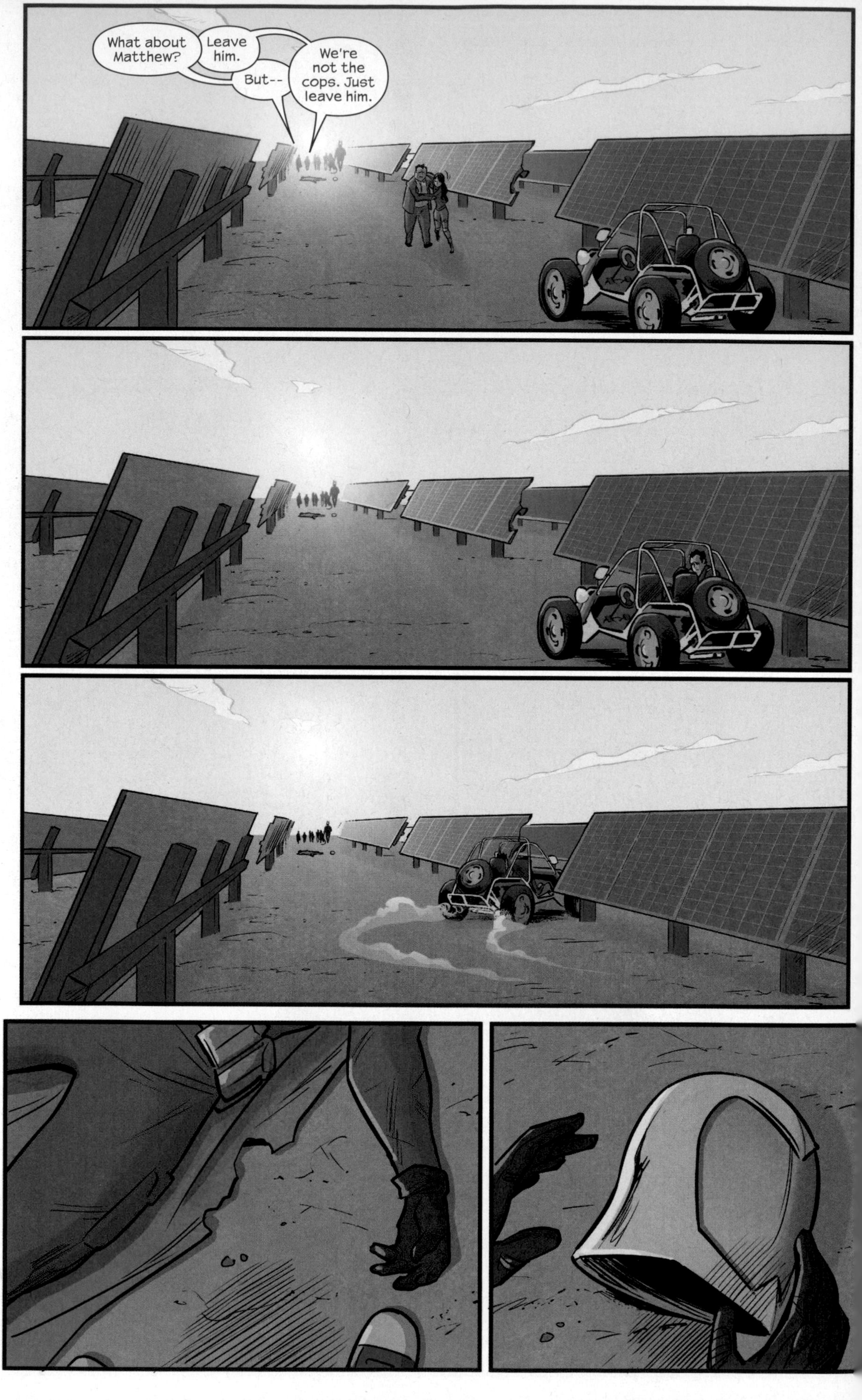
What about Matthew?
Leave him.
But--
We're not the cops. Just leave him.

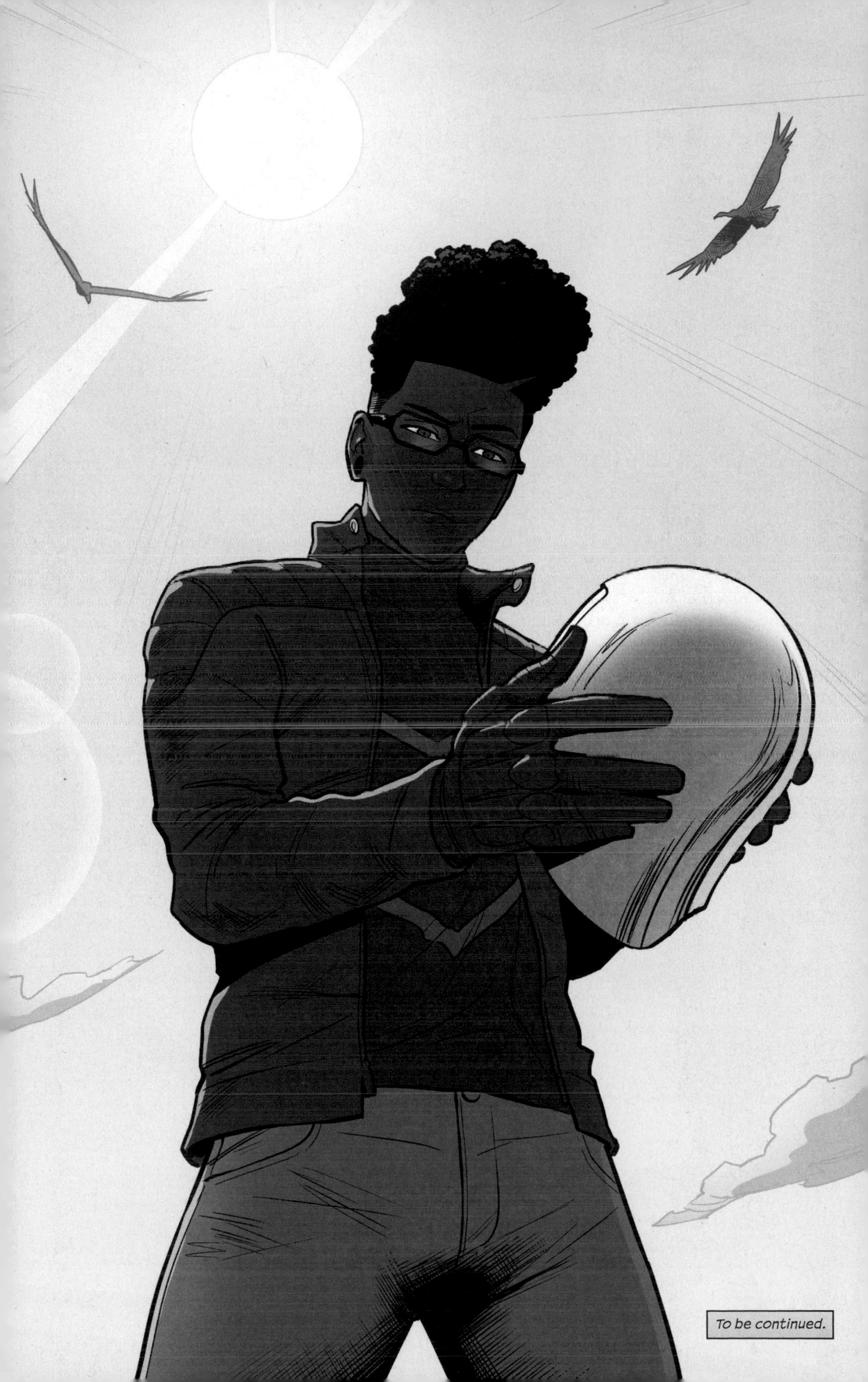
To be continued.

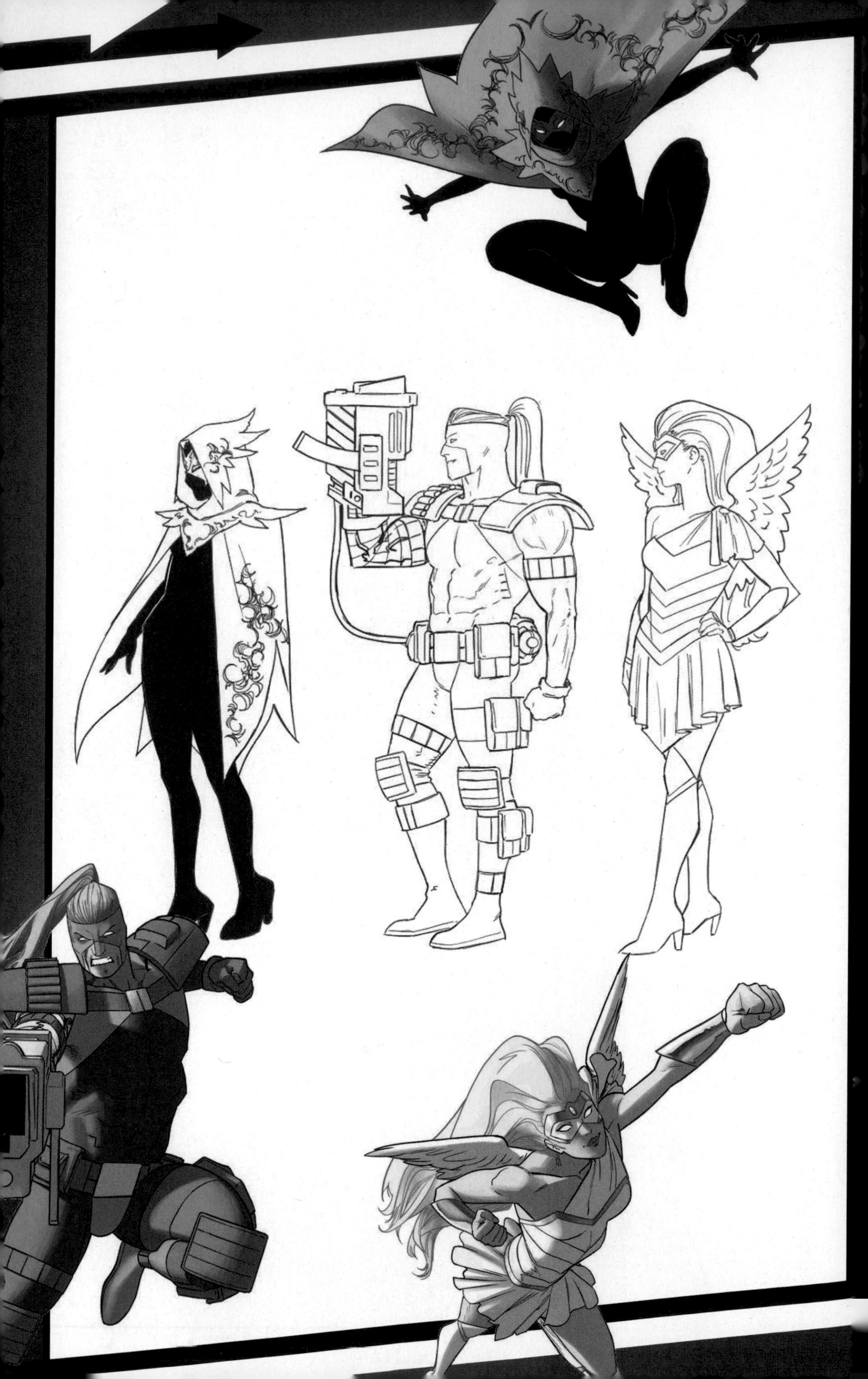

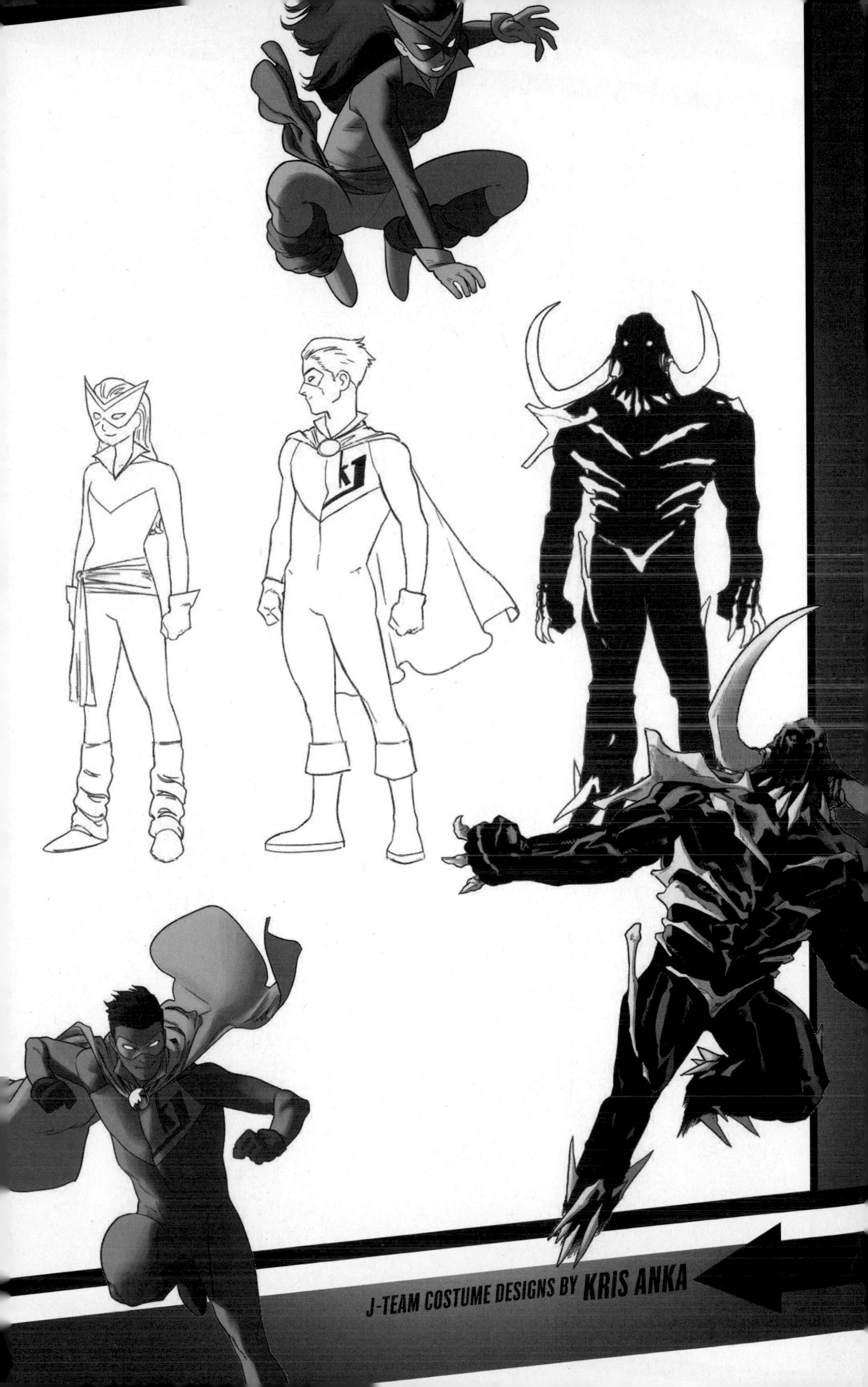

J-TEAM COSTUME DESIGNS BY **KRIS ANKA**

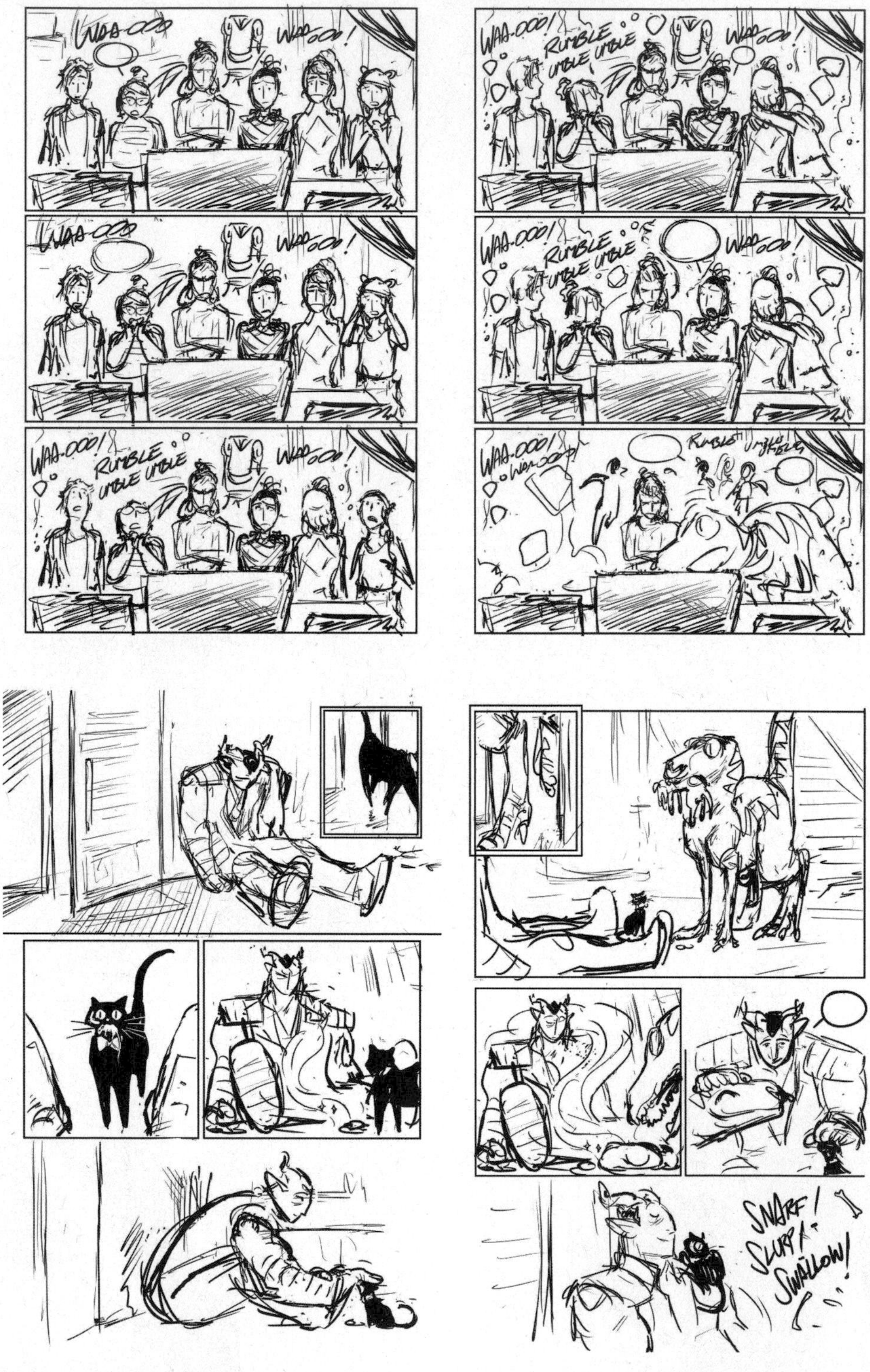
WAA-OOO
WAA-OOO!
WAA-OOO
WAA-OOO!
WAA-OOO!
RUMBLE UMBLE UMBLE
WAA-OOO!
WAA-OOO!
RUMBLE UMBLE UMBLE
WAA-OOO!
WAA-OOO!
RUMBLE UMBLE UMBLE
WAA-OOO!
SNARF!
SLURP!
SWALLOW!

LO ANGELES TODAY
A NEW WAVE OF JUTICE
NEW J-TEAM FIGHTS WILDFIRES!

#25, PAGES 17-18; #26, PAGES 19-20; #28, PAGE 5; #30, PAGES 3-4 LAYOUTS BY **ANDRÉS GENOLET**

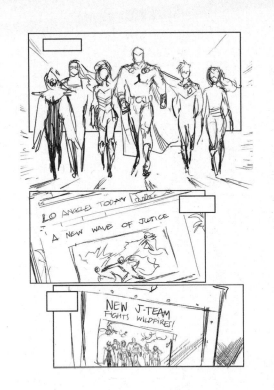

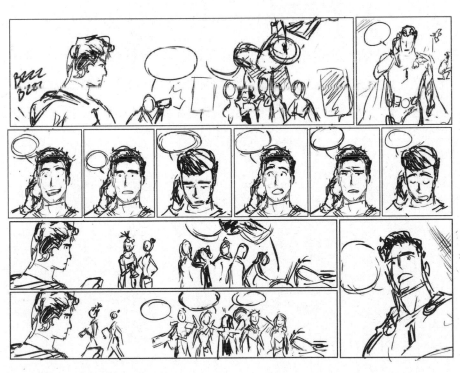

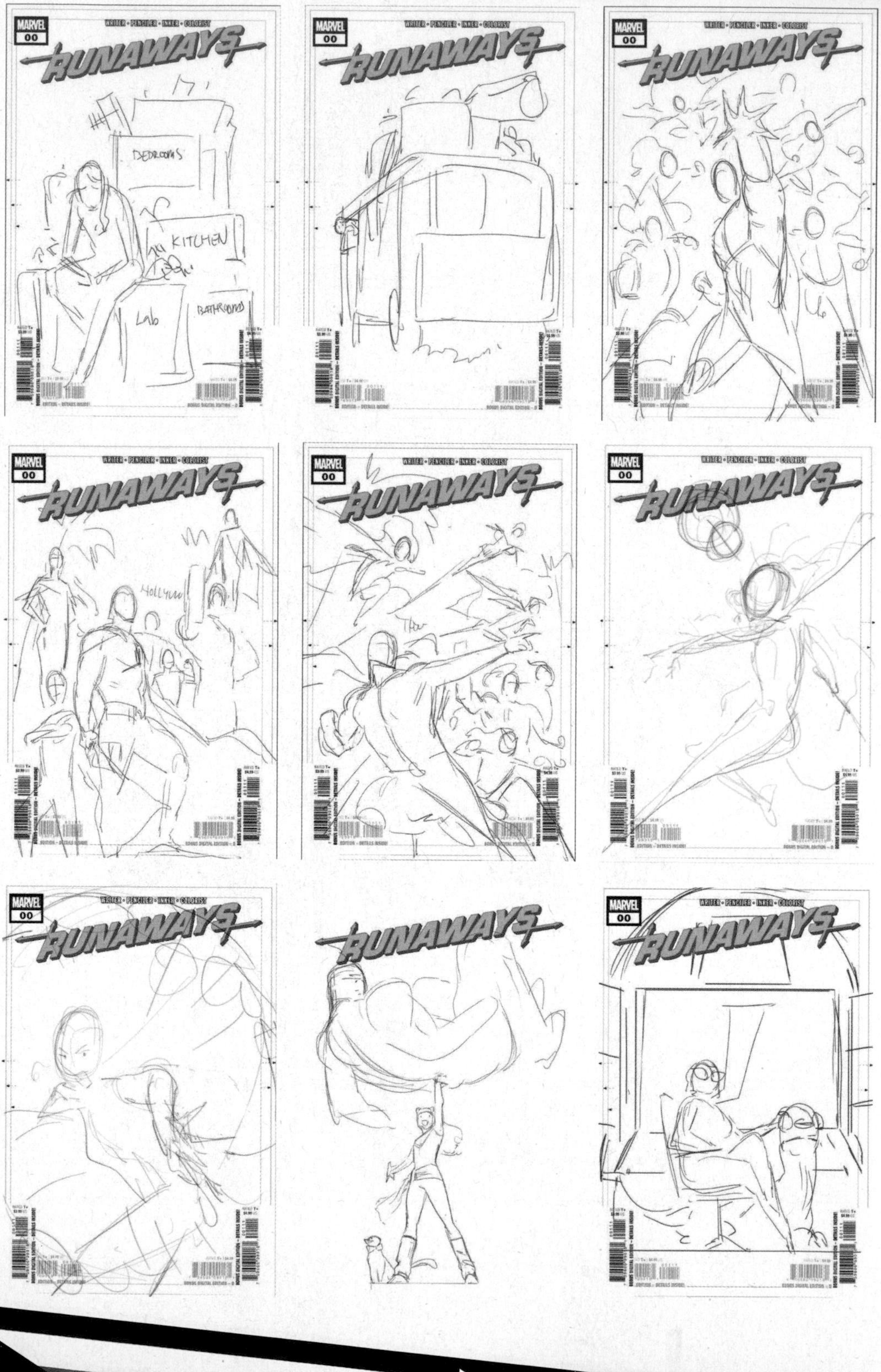
MARVEL
00
WRITER • PENCILER • INKER • COLORIST
RUNAWAYS
KITCHEN
Lab

COVER SKETCHES BY KRIS ANKA